Concur: Travel and Expense Management with SAP®

SAP PRESS is a joint initiative of SAP and Rheinwerk Publishing. The know-how offered by SAP specialists combined with the expertise of Rheinwerk Publishing offers the reader expert books in the field. SAP PRESS features first-hand information and expert advice, and provides useful skills for professional decision-making.

SAP PRESS offers a variety of books on technical and business-related topics for the SAP user. For further information, please visit our website: *www.sap-press.com*.

Baumgartl, Chaadaev, Choi, Dudgeon, Lahiri, Meijerink, Worsley-Tonks
SAP S/4HANA: An Introduction
2016, 449 pages, hardcover and e-book
www.sap-press.com/4153

Amy Grubb and Luke Marson
SuccessFactors with SAP ERP HCM: Business Processes and Use
(2nd edition)
2015, 644 pages, hardcover and e-book
www.sap-press.com/3702

Marson, Mazhavanchery, Murray
SAP SuccessFactors Employee Central: The Comprehensive Guide
2016, 590 pages, hardcover and e-book
www.sap-press.com/3834

Narayanan Veeriah
Configuring Financial Accounting in SAP (2nd edition)
2015, 907 pages, hardcover and e-book
www.sap-press.com/3665

Sven Ringling, Hannah Smith, Andy Wittmann

Concur: Travel and Expense Management with SAP®

Rheinwerk®
Publishing

Bonn • Boston

Editor Meagan White
Acquisitions Editor Emily Nicholls
Copyeditor Melinda Rankin
Cover Design Graham Geary
Photo Credit Shutterstock.com/415953211/© Tisha85
Layout Design Vera Brauner
Production Marissa Fritz
Typesetting SatzPro, Krefeld (Germany)
Printed and bound in the United States of America, on paper from sustainable sources

ISBN 978-1-4932-1456-3
© 2017 by Rheinwerk Publishing, Inc., Boston (MA)
1st edition 2017

Library of Congress Cataloging-in-Publication Data Control Number
2017002828

Contents at a Glance

1   Introducing Concur Travel and Expense   17

2   Employee and User Data   43

3   Concur Travel   59

4   Concur Expense   113

5   Concur Request   193

6   Concur Reporting   213

7   Integrating Concur with Third-Party Apps and Services   241

8   Integrating Concur with Other SAP Solutions   261

9   Making Concur Work for You: Tips for
    Implementation Projects   287

Dear Reader,

As I finished editing these pages, I found myself planning my travel for an upcoming SAP conference. I booked my flight through Expedia and my hotel through the conference website. When I return, I will gather up my (paper!) receipts, list them on a physical expense form, and submit them for approval and, eventually, reimbursement. With this book fresh in my mind, I have to say—we seem to be doing it wrong.

Whether you're also in the dark ages of T&E, using a third-party travel software, or somewhere in the middle (maybe you have an online booking platform, but still scan paper receipts every month), Concur will make your T&E processes easier. In this book, expert authors Sven Ringling, Hannah Smith, and Andy Wittmann have given you an A-to-Z look at Concur's most important features. From configuration to functionality to integration, they've shown you exactly what Concur can do for you!

As always, your comments and suggestions are the most useful tools to help us make our books the best they can be. Let us know what you thought about *Concur: Travel and Expense Management with SAP*! Please feel free to contact me and share any praise or criticism you may have.

Thank you for purchasing a book from SAP PRESS!

Meagan White
Editor, SAP PRESS

Rheinwerk Publishing
Boston, MA

meaganw@rheinwerk-publishing.com
www.sap-press.com

Contents

Preface 13

1 Introducing Concur Travel and Expense 17

1.1 Typical Issues and Constraints of T&E Processes 17
1.1.1 Efficiency Problems 18
1.1.2 Ineffective Management of T&E 19
1.1.3 Poor User Experience 20
1.2 A Vision for the T&E Process of the Future 21
1.2.1 Paper-Free 22
1.2.2 Mobile 24
1.2.3 Automated 24
1.2.4 Connected 25
1.2.5 Easy to Use 26
1.2.6 The Vision 26
1.3 Concur Travel & Expense at a Glance 27
1.3.1 Solution Overview 27
1.3.2 Travel 31
1.3.3 Expense 33
1.3.4 Request 34
1.3.5 Reporting 35
1.3.6 Configuring Concur 36
1.4 The Business Case for Concur 37
1.5 Summary 41

2 Employee and User Data 43

2.1 Employee Master Record Fields 44
2.1.1 System Settings 44
2.1.2 Personal Information 45
2.1.3 User Administration Data 48
2.2 Configuring Employee Forms 51
2.3 Permissions 53
2.4 Creating Employee Data 55
2.5 Summary 57

3   Concur Travel **59**

3.1   Business Principles 59
3.2   Using Concur Travel for Business Trips 62
      3.2.1   Concur Travel Profile 63
      3.2.2   Using the Travel Wizard and Result Pages 67
      3.2.3   The Booking Process 70
3.3   Concur TripLink Integration and Concur TripIt App 88
3.4   Basic Configuration for Concur Travel 90
      3.4.1   Rule Classes 91
      3.4.2   Travel Rules 92
      3.4.3   Custom Text 95
      3.4.4   Languages 96
      3.4.5   E-Receipts 97
      3.4.6   Travel Vendor Exclusions 98
      3.4.7   Regional Hotel Rates 98
      3.4.8   Travel Alternatives 99
      3.4.9   Ghost/BTA Cards 100
      3.4.10 Credit Card BIN Restrictions 101
      3.4.11 Reporting Requirements 101
      3.4.12 Your T&E Policy 103
      3.4.13 Managing Preferred Vendors in Concur 106
3.5   Advanced Configuration Options for Concur Travel 108
3.6   Summary 111

4   Concur Expense **113**

4.1   Business Principles 113
4.2   Using Concur Expense to Settle Expenses 115
4.3   Basic Configuration for Concur Expense 125
      4.3.1   Policy Group 126
      4.3.2   Expense Types 127
      4.3.3   Account Codes 128
      4.3.4   Forms 128
      4.3.5   Trip Mappings 130
      4.3.6   Taxation 130
      4.3.7   Approval Workflows 132
      4.3.8   Compliance Controls 134
      4.3.9   Company and Personal Mileage Rates for Cars 137
      4.3.10 Employee Reimbursement 139
      4.3.11 Company Cards 139

4.3.12 Reporting Configuration 141
4.4 Advanced Configuration for Concur Expense 141
    4.4.1 Policies 141
    4.4.2 Expense Types 145
    4.4.3 Group Configurations 146
    4.4.4 Audit Rules and Exceptions 148
    4.4.5 Expense Forms and Fields 151
    4.4.6 Feature Hierarchies 152
    4.4.7 Localization 153
    4.4.8 Currency Administration 155
    4.4.9 Mapping Concept Fields 155
    4.4.10 Receipt Handling 156
    4.4.11 Workflow 158
4.5 Concur Expense Pay Global 159
    4.5.1 Processes 159
    4.5.2 Configuration 161
    4.5.3 Maintenance of Concur Expense Pay Global 167
4.6 Market-Specific Requirements 169
    4.6.1 United States 169
    4.6.2 Canada 170
    4.6.3 United Kingdom 172
    4.6.4 Germany 177
    4.6.5 Australia and New Zealand 183
    4.6.6 Asia Pacific 190
4.7 Summary 191

5 Concur Request **193**

5.1 Business Principles 194
5.2 Getting and Giving Approvals with Concur Request 194
5.3 Concur Request Configuration 200
    5.3.1 Agency Proposals 201
    5.3.2 Booking Switch 203
    5.3.3 Budget Insight 205
    5.3.4 Country Groups 206
    5.3.5 Event Requests 206
    5.3.6 Risk Management 207
    5.3.7 Segment Types 207
5.4 Deploying Concur Request 208
5.5 Integration with Concur Travel and Concur Expense 210
5.6 Summary 212

Contents

6 Concur Reporting 213

6.1 T&E Analysis vs. Concur Intelligence Tools 214
    6.1.1 Concur Analysis and Concur Intelligence: Shared Tools ... 214
    6.1.2 Concur Intelligence-Only Tools 216
6.2 Using Existing Reports 217
    6.2.1 Set Reporting Preferences 217
    6.2.2 Running a Standard Report 220
6.3 Building and Editing Reports in Query Studio 224
    6.3.1 Creating a New Report 225
    6.3.2 Manipulating Data within Reports 227
6.4 Building and Editing Reports in Report Studio 228
    6.4.1 Report Types and Structures 230
    6.4.2 Creating a New Report 231
    6.4.3 Bursting Reports 234
6.5 Dashboards 238
6.6 Summary 239

7 Integrating Concur with Third-Party Apps and Services 241

7.1 The Value of Third-Party Integration 241
7.2 General Configuration of Third-Party Apps and Services 242
7.3 E-Receipt Integration 247
7.4 Further Selected Solutions 249
    7.4.1 Concur ExpenseIt 249
    7.4.2 Pivot Prime from Pivot Payables 252
    7.4.3 VAT IT Foreign VAT Reclamation 255
    7.4.4 Visage Mobile International Travel Roaming Alerts
          (ITRA) 258
7.5 Summary 259

8 Integrating Concur with Other SAP Solutions 261

8.1 Integrating with HR Master Data 263
    8.1.1 Integration with SAP ERP HCM 263
    8.1.2 Integration with SAP SuccessFactors 269
8.2 Integrating with SAP ERP Financials 270
    8.2.1 Financial Master Data Replication 271
    8.2.2 Financial Posting 274

	8.2.3	Feedback Loop	279
	8.2.4	Features for Financial Integration	280
8.3	Integrating with Payroll in SAP ERP HCM		282
	8.3.1	Import Data through Infotype 2010	283
	8.3.2	Import Data through SAP Travel Management Database	284
8.4	Integrating with Further SAP Solutions		285
8.5	Summary		286

9 Making Concur Work for You: Tips for Implementation Projects 287

9.1	Getting Your Scope Right		287
	9.1.1	Concur Solution Scope	289
	9.1.2	Project Scope	295
9.2	Project Planning and Methodology		297
	9.2.1	Concur Editions	297
	9.2.2	The Project Plan	299
	9.2.3	Tips for Project Management	302
9.3	Global Rollout		303
9.4	Change Management and Communication		306
9.5	Typical Pitfalls		308
9.6	Summary		309

Appendices

| A | Further Reading | 311 |
| B | The Authors | 313 |

| Index | 315 |

Preface

Welcome to the first book on Concur, SAP's bespoke solution for travel and expense (T&E) management. Acquired by SAP in December of 2014, Concur is a thoroughly modern T&E platform, allowing companies to go mostly, and sometimes entirely, paper-free. With a software-as-a-service (SaaS) model, it provides the opportunity for companies to rethink and reimagine their T&E policies to be faster, more transparent, and more cost-effective.

Target Audience

This book will be useful for business users, technical users, consultants, and decision-makers associated with T&E processes. Both current and prospective Concur customers will find information to help them evaluate the decision to move to Concur or to get more out of their current Concur implementation.

Different reader groups can reap different sets of benefits depending on their backgrounds. Since the text does not require any previous SAP or business process expertise, it is useful for a broad group of professionals. For business users, you'll find step-by-step instructions for key business processes including booking travel and submitting expense claims. For technical users, you'll find information on configuration and integration with third-party systems and SAP solutions.

Structure of This Book

This book is structured to best serve the various individuals who make use of T&E processes. While recommended, it is not necessary to read all chapters in order. The subject of each chapter is as follows:

▶ **Chapter 1**
  This chapter provides a broad introduction to Concur and T&E processes. It touches upon some typical issues found in older T&E systems and how Concur

manages T&E processes using Concur Travel, Concur Expense, and Concur Request.

▶ **Chapter 2**

This chapter discusses employee and user data. Before an employee can use any of the Concur modules, they must have either a user or employee record in Concur. This chapter covers the necessary settings to create these records.

▶ **Chapter 3**

This chapter covers Concur Travel. You'll learn how to book business trips using this module, get a brief introduction to the Concur TripIt app, and explore basic and advanced configuration options.

▶ **Chapter 4**

This chapter covers Concur Expense. You'll learn how to settle expenses using this module, walk through Concur Global Expense Pay, and explore basic and advanced configuration options. This chapter also details some market-specific requirements for the US, Canada, UK, Germany, and Australia and New Zealand, and how they are handled in Concur Expense.

▶ **Chapter 5**

This chapter covers Concur Request. You'll learn how to get and give approvals, explore basic configuration options, and see how Concur Request integrates with Concur Travel and Concur Request.

▶ **Chapter 6**

This chapter covers reporting with Concur. It includes information on both the standard Concur Analysis offering as well as Concur Intelligence, available for an additional fee. It also discusses the Report Studio and Query Studio.

▶ **Chapter 7**

This chapter discusses integrating Concur with third-party apps and services. It covers some general configuration for app integration, and provides detailed information on e-receipt integration.

▶ **Chapter 8**

This chapter discusses how to integrate Concur with SAP solutions. In particular, you will find information on integrating with SAP SucessFactors, SAP ERP Human Capital Management (SAP ERP HCM), and SAP ERP Financials. The chapter also covers integrating with Payroll in SAP ERP HCM.

▶ **Chapter 9**

This chapter contains information about your Concur implementation project. You'll learn how to set your project scope, plan your project, and avoid some typical pitfalls of implementing Concur.

Travel and expense are usually not considered core processes, but they still consume significant resources in time and money for most organizations. Traditional solutions are characterized by low levels of efficiency, effectiveness, and user satisfaction, so let's explore how Concur can serve modern organizations better.

1   Introducing Concur Travel and Expense

Before we get into the nitty gritty of processes and Concur configuration, we want to use this chapter to explore why implementing or optimizing Concur makes good business sense and to provide a high-level overview of Concur's travel & expense (T&E) processes. We'll start with the usually less than ideal current state in most organizations, then build a compelling vision for the future, provide a teaser of Concur's functionality, and eventually present a framework for building a business case for Concur.

1.1   Typical Issues and Constraints of T&E Processes

When was the last time you heard an employee in your organization say this? "I love doing my expenses. It's a quick and easy process." When was the last time your CFO or finance director was satisfied with the level of expenses and the efficiency of processing them? If the answer to either of these questions is "I can't remember," then this book is for you.

The bulk of businesses and public and charity sector organizations today are using last-generation T&E solutions (typically solutions designed for users in the accounting department, lacking a modern user experience [UX] and scope). Or they may use modern IT solutions like Concur without the processes designed to make use of their possibilities. In many cases, we find even more outdated solutions based on spreadsheets or paper. T&E processes in these organizations of all sizes and industries usually fall short of expectations in three main areas:

- ▶ Efficiency of the process

- ▶ Effectiveness of the process

- ▶ User experience

1.1.1 Efficiency Problems

Inefficient processes within the finance or procurement departments are problems usually acknowledged and tackled first when reevaluating T&E processes. The reason for this is easy to see: Whoever is responsible for the processing of expenses or procurement of travel can demonstrate a cost reduction in their own part of the organization if efficiency increases. The problems most likely to be high on the agenda are as follows:

- ▶ Filing of paper receipts

- ▶ High level of data-capturing work in accounting (most notably double capturing of data—cases in which the expense processing team keys in the same data that employees have already captured elsewhere)

- ▶ Lack of integration between the expense and finance systems

- ▶ Time-consuming reporting

Efficiency problems experienced by the organization's business travelers, line managers, or personal assistants who create or review expense claims on behalf of others are usually further down on the agenda, because the cost caused by these people is distributed across the whole organization. Line managers in the finance department, who can make decisions about the T&E process, are more likely to ignore these issues, because their own cost centers are barely affected.

The same holds true for ineffectiveness and poor UX in travel and expense processes, affecting both line managers across the organization and individual travelers. Again, decision makers in the finance department are not directly affected very much, unless they are pressured by internal customers such as the sales or customer service departments, in which we usually find a large number of frequent travelers.

Figure 1.1 illustrates this dilemma: Managers who make decisions about travel and expense processes are usually based in the finance department. Because this is not typically a department with lots of travel, these managers are affected primarily by inefficiencies in the back-office process. Therefore, it is not a coincidence that these processes are usually covered quite well in traditional expense management solutions.

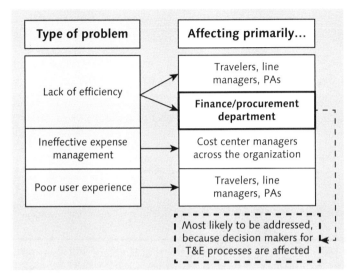

Figure 1.1 Groups Affected by Typical Issues of Traditional T&E Processes

1.1.2 Ineffective Management of T&E

Ineffective management of T&E leads to unnecessarily high expenses and makes it difficult for employees to travel when and where they need to.

Typical examples of ineffective management in the expense process include the following:

► Inaccurate data or receipts resulting in unrecoverable domestic value-added tax (VAT)

► No process at all for foreign VAT recovery

► Slow reimbursements leading to high demand for advance payments

► Inaccuracies leading to overpayment of mileage

► Lack of easy-to-use reporting for line managers to manage spending in their teams

► Lack of insightful analytics to improve expense strategy

► Weak fraud detection

Typical examples of ineffective management in the booking and travel process include the following:

▶ Higher ticket prices due to a slow booking and approval process

▶ Limited choice driving up travel cost and/or time

▶ Little guidance for travelers in making the best choices before and during the trip

▶ Agents making bookings without knowing the full context of the trip

▶ Poor management of discounts; affected by poor analytics and bookings from the main system

▶ Poor policy compliance, unless driven by the travel management company (TMC)

▶ Inadequate analytics to feed into individual choices and policies

Many organizations recognize some of these problems and address them through many manual checks, approvals, and reports. However, this makes the process even more inefficient, and when quick decisions are required to keep cost low, they can even be counterproductive. For a truly effective process, businesses require a highly integrated and automated system that provides information to empower users on all levels to make the right decisions at each stage of the process.

1.1.3   Poor User Experience

UX is about more than just a pretty and intuitive user interface (UI). A good UX results in users getting the best possible guidance to perform their tasks well and makes users feel good about using the system. Although traditional travel and expense systems often provide at least a decent experience for professional users who use the system daily, they rarely provide a good experience to travelers and approvers. For those users, booking travel, capturing expenses, and approving expenses are not elements of their core job but extra tasks, often considered a nuisance. Therefore, they require an intuitive, easy-to-use solution to capture expenses anywhere, at any time.

What users consider a good or bad experience when working with software does vary, but the visible impact of poor UX is similar across the board; some typical symptoms include the following:

- Employees don't capture and submit expenses in a timely manner but do so in bulk, often only after being reminded several times.

- Travelers and approvers try to have other people perform their T&E-related tasks for them, even if this is against policy.

- Data captured is of low quality.

- Line managers approve expenses without really checking them.

- Employees try to bypass the system, most notably in travel booking.

- For employees and line managers with many trips or approvals to handle, the travel and expense process is frustrating and contributes to job dissatisfaction.

- Travelers feel let down by their employer, because they don't get the support they expect when they're travelling for work.

1.2   A Vision for the T&E Process of the Future

The T&E process of the future needs to be paper-free, mobile, highly automated, easy to use, and connected. It must be integrated with all relevant vendors and supporting apps to make the process comprehensive, easy, and fast.

This can be a significant part of your digital transformation process, as it provides all employees with the information and guidance to make the right decisions and reduces manual work to a minimum. Therefore, a modern T&E process empowers employees and line managers to do their jobs better and to focus on the most important tasks. It also allows corporate T&E management teams to develop the best strategies and policies for expense management and travel based on comprehensive analytics.

In the past, employees usually felt that they serve the finance department by capturing expense data, collecting receipts, and adhering to policies they had to read up on every time they planned a trip. Under the new paradigm, illustrated in Figure 1.2, modern T&E software makes it as easy as possible for travelling employees to focus on the main job they're travelling for in the first place: serving customers or selling products and services. Corporate T&E management teams or TMCs support this. The T&E solution is no longer primarily designed to support 10 people in the finance department, but 5,000 people who travel to sell the organization's products and to serve their customers.

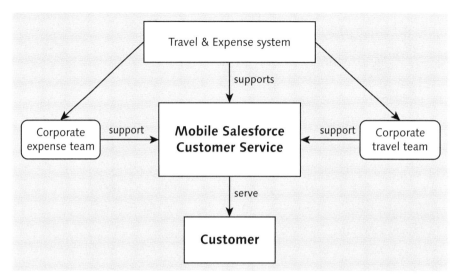

Figure 1.2 New Paradigm for T&E Systems

This doesn't mean that no improvements for corporate T&E teams are to be expected from a modern solution. To begin, better quality of data captured by all users is already a big improvement, but we'll see further advantages as we walk through the benefits of being paper-free, mobile, highly automated, easy to use, and connected in the following subsections.

1.2.1 Paper-Free

Handling paper receipts is frustrating and expensive. Employees need to carry and usually collate these receipts, and there's always a risk of losing them. Then, they need to be moved around the organization for checks and approvals. Finally, the accounts department needs to handle and store them.

The earlier in the process we can get rid of paper, the more convenient and efficient the process becomes. Figure 1.3 illustrates that there are several stages from paper-only receipt handling to the modern e-receipt process.

An *e-receipt*, as we understand it for the purposes of this book, is a receipt sent directly from the travel booking system or the vendor to the expense system without any action by the user. In the expense system, it can be reviewed and assigned to an expense report. However, even a modern expense system will use a mix of the top three methods from Figure 1.3, as not all vendors can provide receipts in the necessary format yet. Some vendors provide receipts as electronic documents via email or download, and users still need to send or upload these documents into the expense system.

Finally, there are still quite a few vendors who provide paper receipts only. The quickest way for travelers to handle these receipts is to take a photo with a smartphone app that automatically loads the receipts into the expense system.

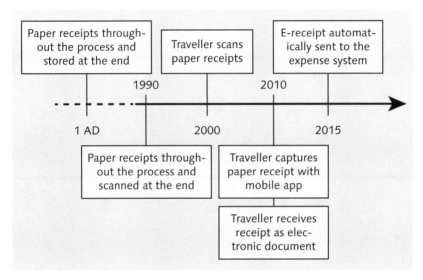

Figure 1.3 Evolution of Receipt Handling

In all three cases, we expect the system to prepopulate most of the data fields from the receipt, though there are always errors to be expected unless we have real e-receipts.

Are You Allowed to Use E-Receipts?

Not all countries are equally open to the use of e-receipts, and the requirements for them to be recognized by tax authorities may also vary between countries. We therefore recommend checking with your tax experts to find out how you can make use of a paper-free process. In some cases, your Concur or SAP account executive can also point you to the right experts, who know how to go paper-free in your country.

Please note that it's your responsibility to comply with regulations in all countries; nothing in this book should be interpreted as legal or tax advice.

1.2.2 Mobile

This is what we'd call a no-brainer. Expenses occur while travelling, and frequent travelers spend many hours on public transport, waiting in line, or in restaurants; they can fill otherwise worthless time with capturing their expenses. In the best of worlds, the expense report is ready to submit as soon as the traveler gets back to his office or home. This process has several benefits:

- It takes a frustrating burden of post-trip work off the employee.
- It improves quality, because expenses are captured when fresh in the user's memory.
- It allows for a fast turnaround of expense reports and therefore fewer requests for advance payments.
- It frees up time for the mobile workforce that can be used for value-adding activities.

Another big advantage of mobile solutions is the speed and convenience of approval; line managers can approve expenses and travel bookings anywhere. If your process requires pretrip approval before tickets can be booked, this will also reduce the average ticket price.

1.2.3 Automated

Automation is the classic objective of IT systems, and T&E processes are no exception. A cutting-edge process would automate the bulk of calculations, audit rules, and other checks, as well as provide reports and analytics at the push of a button.

A modern T&E solution also uses all the information available to reduce the number of manual steps and automatically guides the user in order to minimize the number of hotline calls or frequency with which the user needs to check the documentation.

Finally, we expect the flow of information and documents to be automated and fast. This refers to approval and information workflows, but also to information provided by other systems, apps, and vendors. In this respect, automation directly depends on integration or connectivity with third-party apps, as addressed in the next section.

1.2.4 Connected

Because the term *integration* is usually used for systems working closely together within one organization, we like to use the term *connected* to refer to T&E systems receiving information from a multitude of different systems, vendors, apps, and services.

The goal is to not only reduce manual activities by moving data from one system to another, but also to allow the T&E system and its ecosystem of connected apps and services to serve users more intelligently and proactively. We also include intelligent and predictive analytics in this section because such services usually connect data from different sources, even though this functionality is still in its infancy even in the most advanced T&E solutions at the time of writing.

Currently, the connections and integrations used by cutting-edge systems fall into the following categories:

▸ Integration with the HR system (including contingent workforce data) to automatically create and update user data in the T&E system

▸ Integration with the financial and payroll systems for automated posting and taxation, as well as financial planning

▸ Credit card data automatically transferred into the expense system

▸ Integration with TMCs to fulfill the bookings triggered in Concur Travel

▸ Booking data from the travel booking system automatically transferred to the expense system

▸ Connections with vendors outside the travel booking system to generate e-receipts in the expense system and create complete itineraries together with the tickets booked in the travel booking system

▸ Apps to automate expense capturing, such as mileage tracking apps to automatically add mileage to an expense claim

▸ Audit services (manual, semimanual, or automated) to detect errors and fraud

▸ Apps and services to help business travelers along their journey (e.g., tips or warnings about routes and destinations)

▸ Apps and services using expense data (e.g., foreign VAT recovery or expense billing)

We believe that improving connectivity and systems that use available information intelligently and proactively are going to be the most important value drivers in the T&E process of the future. This is at the core of digital transformation; today, we can only vaguely imagine the impact that Internet of Things (IoT), wearable technology, natural language understanding (NLU), big data, or predictive analytics will have on the future of travel when these technologies are connected.

1.2.5 Easy to Use

The four previous aspects all contribute to an easy-to-use solution, but apart from this we also need an intuitive and efficient UI for smartphones, tablets, and PCs.

In addition, we expect chatbots to be integrated into T&E systems to guide users through some processes and expect voice recognition availability.

1.2.6 The Vision

To sum up, the following box lays out the vision for the future, which you're welcome to copy and amend to guide your own T&E-related digital transformation.

A Vision for T&E in the Digital Age

Our T&E process must primarily serve those who travel locally or globally to sell our products and services and to serve our customers. Those colleagues need to focus on our customers and prospects. Therefore, the T&E process needs to make this as easy as possible for them. It also needs to ensure that expenses and processing costs are minimized and that we comply with all regulations.

To achieve this, we use cutting-edge technology and analytics to empower business travelers, approvers, and T&E specialists to make the right decisions for the organization. The solution must be mobile-enabled, paper-free, easy to use, highly automated, and highly connected with the ecosystem of related systems, apps, vendors, and services.

Once set up, we'll constantly innovate to keep the process as efficient, effective, and user-friendly as possible. We also consider T&E transformation a crucial part of our digital transformation, because it doesn't only transform a much-used internal process but also helps build the mindset and skills to apply digital principals to our customer-facing processes.

1.3   Concur Travel & Expense at a Glance

In this section, we'll take you briefly through Concur's main modules—Concur Travel, Concur Expense, Concur Request, and Concur's reporting capabilities—so you have the overall context before proceeding to the next chapters, which discuss individual modules in greater depth. We'll also provide an introduction into configuring Concur. However, we'll start with a solution overview, focusing on cross-module aspects.

1.3.1   Solution Overview

Concur is a solution for T&E management serving more than 30,000 organizations across all industries, from microbusinesses to global corporations.

The solution is provided in the software-as-a-service (SaaS) model, so it's cloud-based. Customers subscribe to use the solution and pay per transaction (the cost is driven by the number of expense report submissions). As per the nature of the SaaS model, customers don't require any infrastructure of their own, except for a PC with a current web browser.

> **Tip**
>
> Firefox works best in our experience, because of the reporting features in Concur, but other web browsers—like Internet Explorer, Edge, or Chrome—can be used as well.

The solution comes in three sizes, as follows:

- **Standard**
  This is a version with limited functionality and notably limited configurability, aimed at smaller organizations; it's currently only available in a few countries, including the United States, the United Kingdom, Canada, and Australia. It's designed for a very quick implementation (we've experienced implementations in less than two weeks with just four conference calls from kickoff to support handover).

- **Professional**
  This solution offers the full functional scope and all configuration options. It's available in a variety of countries and aimed at medium and large organizations.

It comes with an implementation service, which is aimed at lean implementations, with few resources provided by the implementation team and no on-site appointments.

▸ **Premium**

This solution comprises the same scope as the professional edition but comes with a more comprehensive (and therefore more expensive) implementation service, including on-site appointments. This service allows for more custom amendments than the professional implementation. Unlike the other editions, it also comes with a test instance included in the basic package.

How Can Users of Concur's Standard Edition Use This Book?

The features and configuration described in this book refer to the professional and premium solution, unless indicated otherwise. Therefore, users of the standard solution will find that they can't use everything described in the following chapters; most notably, the integration with SAP ERP discussed in Chapter 8 is not available for standard customers. However, users of the standard solution will still find a lot of valuable technical tips they can use, and most of the advice about process, project management, and change management is relevant for all editions.

Although Concur is not available for customers in all countries, it can be rolled out to subsidiaries in any country once it has been bought in one country. However, you need to check to what extent Concur includes regulations, common practice, and statutory reports for each country; additional configuration or workarounds may be required. The same holds true for translations; though Concur is available in most major languages, with the notable exception of Arabic, there are still many gaps, including several Eastern European languages. If in doubt, it's always worthwhile to ask a Concur sales executive to confirm in writing the scope for the country in question.

As indicated in Figure 1.4, Concur has four core modules. Concur Expense was Concur's first offering and is the heart of the solution. To cover the full T&E process, Concur acquired and developed further modules, most notably Concur Travel (an online booking platform) and Concur Request, which is used for pre-trip approval processes. Concur Intelligence for advanced analytics can draw on data from all other modules.

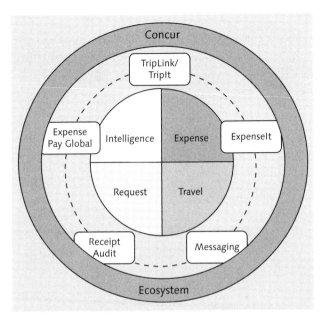

Figure 1.4 Concur Solution Overview

All modules are based on a common platform, which also manages interfaces. The preferred interface technology is web services, which are used for many standard integrations offered by Concur but need to be subscribed to separately if customers want to use them to build their own interfaces.

The core modules are complemented by further Concur offerings, most notably:

▶ **Concur ExpenseIt**
This is a mobile app that allows users to capture a photo of paper receipts and automatically have an expense created in Concur with the most important fields prepopulated via semiautomatic text recognition. It also offers a text recognition service for electronic documents emailed to *receipts@expenseit.com*.

▶ **Concur Messaging**

This service can warn travelers about any risk on their route or destination and help others locate and communicate with travelers in critical situations. However, it can also be used in a less serious context to provide guidance for travelers to find their way around an unknown city.

▶ **Concur Receipt Audit**

This service integrates with the expense solution and drives compliance for how expense data is captured and use of appropriate receipts. Although fraud detection is certainly one purpose, the service will primarily flag or correct mistakes such as typos or receipts missing proper VAT information.

▶ **Concur Expense Pay Global**

This service allows organizations to trigger reimbursements right out of Concur without needing to integrate with a finance system, download and upload payment lists, or make manual payments. It offers great value for organizations without full integration between Concur and their finance systems. However, it isn't available for all countries; most notably, it wasn't available anywhere in the European Union at the time of writing.

▶ **Concur TripIt**

This is a consumer-grade app that helps users track and plan their trips. It can come in a free or a professional version and can be used independently of Concur. However, when Concur TripIt professional is integrated with Concur, it shows its real value, as Concur and third-party bookings can be easily combined. Its features include an automatic itinerary and warning messages for delays or cancelations. Concur TripIt is included in Concur TripLink (see next item).

▶ **Concur TripLink**

This is one of Concur's latest big innovations. For vendors that are dedicated Concur TripLink partners, the service transfers booking data to Concur automatically if the booking is arranged directly with the vendor. This allows for more comprehensive reporting and compliance checks and includes these trips in the messaging service, so employers can still fulfill their duty of care even when travel is booked outside the normal process. For vendors that are not yet Concur TripLink partners, the employee or an admin can still transfer the itineraries into Concur via email.

Finally, as indicated by outer ring in Figure 1.4, there is the Concur ecosystem, which is made up of a large number of partner services and partner apps to help travelers or admins with their day-to-day jobs. Most ecosystem partners today are TMCs or vendors, which provide e-receipts for Concur Expense. However, there is an ever-larger variety of third-party apps for all types of services (see Section 1.2.4). Third-party apps can be activated and to some extent configured in the Concur App Center, accessible through the web browser. Figure 1.5 provides a taste of the Concur App Center, showing some app connections to be used by individual employees on the top and enterprise apps to be used by the back-office team on the bottom.

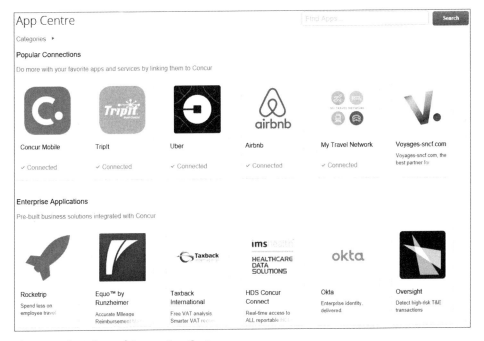

Figure 1.5 Start Page of Concur App Center

1.3.2 Travel

Concur Travel is sometimes also referred to as the online booking engine, although the module comprises features beyond mere booking transactions. It allows users to capture their travel preferences (see Chapter 2), search for and book transport or accommodation, track their itineraries, and get information and guidance, if configured accordingly.

Although not all bookings have to go through a TMC, Concur Travel always requires a TMC partner for implementation. When opening the travel module, you'll first see some notifications and (arguably the most important screen in the module) the search screen for transport and accommodation. Whether you only have options available from your TMC or options from further vendors depends on your configuration and third-party integration. The example in Figure 1.6 includes flight search (including Eurostar trains), rental cars, hotels, and trains and also offers a flight status check on the right-most tab.

Figure 1.6 Search Screen of Travel Module

One of the benefits of using Concur Travel is that booking data can automatically be turned into e-receipts in Concur Expense if the e-receipt provided contains the required information.

1.3.3   Expense

Concur Expense is the most widely used module. It comprises the capturing of expenses (manually or automatically), approval workflow, backend review and processing, and eventually transfer to the accounting system for posting and payment.

Concur Expense comes with preconfigured settings to comply with legal requirements in many countries, most notably VAT, and usually can be configured for those not covered out of the box. Watch out for any payments above the respective country's tax-free threshold, sometimes referred to as *benefits in kind* (BIK)—although that is, technically speaking, wrong, because they are not paid in kind but in cash. These payments often require extra configuration effort or work on the interfaces or payroll system to get right.

We highly encourage you to drive mobile usage for expenses, as this makes for a much more efficient process (see Figure 1.7 for an expense report overview in the Concur mobile app). The most efficient frequent travelers usually enter between 90 and 100 percent of their expenses on the mobile app only.

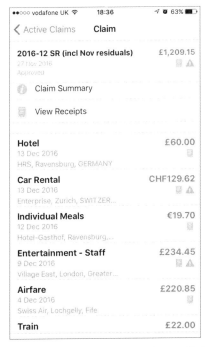

Figure 1.7 Expense Report in Concur Mobile App

Companies that use daily allowances instead of meal reimbursements by receipt may not have used the mobile app at all in the past, because automatic calculation for daily allowances wasn't implemented in the mobile app. However, this has changed in 2016, so nothing should stop users in countries such as Austria, Estonia, or Germany from reaching high mobile adoption rates.

1.3.4 Request

Concur Request serves two primary purposes:

1. Manages a pretrip approval workflow; employees gain approval for a trip from line managers based on some basic information and/or a cost estimate

2. Manages cash advance payments so that employees have the necessary liquidity to embark on their trips

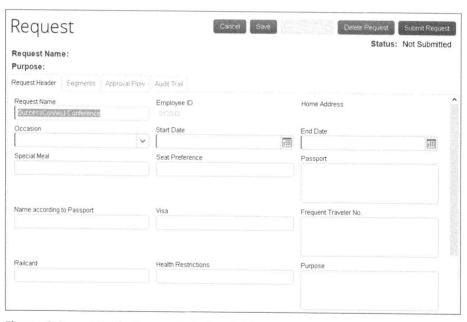

Figure 1.8 Request Header Screen with Custom Fields

Some customers who don't use Concur Travel use the Concur Request workflow to send booking requests to corporate travel teams or TMCs to make necessary bookings. However, this isn't what Concur Request is designed for; most customers find that the Concur Request workflow doesn't have all the information needed to make bookings. For this reason, the start screen for a request includes several custom fields, as seen in Figure 1.8. Also, note that travel-related user data (such as frequent traveler numbers or meal preferences) isn't available in the user profile without subscription to Concur Travel.

If your process requires pretrip approvals and/or cash advance payments, then Concur can support this with Concur Request. However, we always recommend making any advance payment an absolute exception, because such payments require an inefficient administrative process to handle. Formal pretrip approvals, unless statutorily required, can also be a sign of a culture in which disempowerment drives inefficiency, so whether such a process adds value should be reviewed.

1.3.5   Reporting

All three modules, Concur Travel, Concur Expense, and Concur Request, come with their own basic reporting capabilities in the Concur Analysis module, which is included in the subscription fee. For more advanced analytics and dashboards, Concur Intelligence can be added as a separate component. Both reporting solutions are based on Cognos technology, which some analytics specialists may be used to from other solutions.

Concur comes with several standard reports, covering all modules. Figure 1.9 shows an example from Concur Expense, listing the vendors with the highest spend. These reports don't focus on cost and statutory requirements only; they also allow users to monitor behavioral key performance indicators (KPIs) such as mobile adoption or approval times. With a bit of practice, customers can build their own reports, though we found that formal training exercises are usually more efficient than self-training after watching the standard video.

TOP SPEND BY VENDOR
Transaction Date: On or after Jul 6, 2015

Rank	Vendor	Expense Amount (rpt)
1	British Airways	15,381.06
2	SAP	4,012.67
3	Southern	3,226.90
4	Lufthansa	2,757.26
5	MK Hotel	1,891.14

Figure 1.9 Report Example: Top Vendors

The number of users for reporting activities—apart from one *BI-Manager*—that can be assigned to each user for decentralized reporting is limited, so further users may have to be purchased depending on your reporting strategy. Decentralized reporting by cost center or project is not yet supported.

1.3.6 Configuring Concur

By the nature of SaaS solutions, customers can't change any of Concur's coding; however, Concur is highly configurable. Configuration options include expense types, vendors, various calculations (including tax and allowances), workflows, data entry screens, and much more. Figure 1.10 shows just one example of a configuration screen in which customers can change the characteristics of and access to a particular field on a screen.

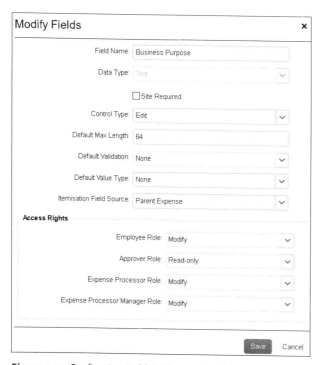

Figure 1.10 Configuring Field Settings and Field Access

However, customers' rights to access configuration are quite restricted. There can always be exceptions made in individual cases, but as a rule, the following restrictions apply:

- ▶ During the initial implementation, only Concur has access to the configuration until the customer has signed off on the solution for production readiness.

- ▶ After production readiness, the customer has access to a limited set of configuration settings considered easy to use. Many essential settings, such as those affecting data entry screens and fields, are not available for customers to change.

- ▶ To gain access to further configuration settings, the customer team needs to go through the advanced configuration training from Concur. As of the time of writing, this also applies if the customer doesn't want to access configuration settings but wants an official Concur partner that has worked through the training already to perform the configuration for them. As this is not at all in line with policies for other solutions within the SAP group, there is some expectation that this will change soon. After this training, the customer will have access to the majority of settings. A few are still accessible via Concur Support only, because they are considered critical.

1.4   The Business Case for Concur

Each organization's business case for Concur is different, because it needs to consider the current solution and the organization's business context and strategy. However, the types of benefits feeding into the business case are similar in each case.

As Figure 1.11 illustrates, we can divide the business benefits enjoyed from a solution like Concur into four major categories, two of which reduce cost and two of which create extra value:

1. Direct cost reductions occur when an organization simply pays less for services and goods related to T&E. This is often the category in which benefits from any kind of investment are easiest to prove, but in the case of Concur or T&E systems in general, some such benefits trigger controversial discussions.

2. Cash value represents an increase in revenue or other cash flow, such as a higher value of reclaimed VAT.

3. Process efficiency improvements are usually changes that save time due to easier processes or a higher level of automation.

4. The creation of intangible value refers to effects that we know improve the competitive situation of the organization but are difficult to measure directly. In many cases, they are the strongest part of the business case.

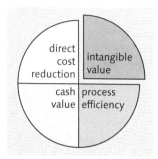

Figure 1.11 Among Business Benefits, Intangible Value Usually Stands Out

In some cases, reduction of IT costs (e.g., no infrastructure requirements, reduced maintenance effort) is also mentioned as a category, which is fine. In this book, we include these benefits in the direct cost reduction and process efficiency categories.

Table 1.1 provides examples in each of the four categories.

Category	Examples
Direct cost reduction	▶ TMCs charge much lower ticketing fees when booked through Concur rather than via email or phone.
	▶ Higher accuracy in mileage tracking reduces mileage cost.
	▶ Concur TripLink ensures company discounts are applied, even when booked directly.
	▶ The system enforces policy.
	▶ Analytics allow better policies and vendor agreements.
	▶ Quick reimbursement reduces the number of advance payments.
	▶ Travelers make better choices when they have all the information and can book themselves.
	▶ Lower ticket prices arise through faster approvals.
	▶ Infrastructure and maintenance costs for IT are dramatically reduced.

Table 1.1 Examples of Business Benefits

Category	Examples
Cash value	▸ Foreign VAT reimbursement is more effective and for some companies only becomes possible with the automation and third-party services in Concur.
	▸ A higher rate of domestic VAT can be recouped.
	▸ Automated rebilling of expenses avoids missing receipts in bills.
Process efficiencies	▸ Paper handling is eliminated.
	▸ Otherwise unproductive time becomes useful because of mobile enablement.
	▸ Integration with SAP and third-party apps and services increases the level of automation.
	▸ Fewer errors appear in expense claims.
	▸ Time-saving standard reports make an impact.
Intangible value	▸ The mobile workforce can better focus on sales and customer service.
	▸ Employers seem more attractive to employees and potential employees.
	▸ Concur can drive or support a culture of digital transformation.
	▸ Employees and line managers are empowered and therefore more engaged. Risk of non-compliance with regulations is reduced.

Table 1.1 Examples of Business Benefits (Cont.)

The benefits need to be compared with the following costs:

▸ Concur subscription fee (paid per expense report submission)

▸ Implementation cost (Concur, consulting partner, internal time)

▸ Maintenance and support

It's difficult to imagine a scenario in which the business case is not clearly positive when the old solution is a last-generation system such as SAP ERP Financials Travel Management (FI-TV), a feature-poor solution like Openbooks or Workday, or a system based on paper or spreadsheets. However, due to the packages used, some of the cost related to the old system doesn't go away immediately. For example, if you use SAP ERP FI-TV as a legacy system, switching to Concur may reduce the license fees for SAP ERP only marginally or not at all, and the infra-structure will still be needed for other processes in SAP ERP. In these cases, you may need to consider the benefits in all four categories thoroughly to make the right decision.

One of this book's authors was not only the main decision maker at but also involved in the implementation of Concur at his organization. The following box explains how his small business benefitted from Concur Expense and Travel, including Concur ExpenseIt and Concur TripIt.

Sample Business Case

Context

Our small IT consulting company expects around 500 trips (translating into around 90 expense reports in Concur, as claims are usually submitted monthly) per year. Travelling is a big part of most employees' working lives. Before implementing Concur in 2014, we used a much simpler cloud solution as part of our accounting system, which was not mobile-enabled and lacked many much-needed features. Because we still use the rest of the accounting system, we didn't save on any license fees.

Concur Implementation

We implemented the standard edition of Concur Expense in less than two weeks, requiring 12 hours of internal work from the contract stage to go-live. Concur Travel required two months and 24 hours of work.

Annual Cost

The subscription fee, implementation cost (written off over three years), and maintenance totaled £3,600 (internal time valued at £100/h).

Intangible Benefits

This always was to be the most important part for us. As an organization with a customer-facing digital transformation agenda, it's paramount that we drive the right culture, learn firsthand, and display the right image.

Even more important is employer attractiveness. As a small firm, we need to attract the brightest and most engaged talent. Frustrating employees with dull paperwork and annoying processes is not the way to achieve this. When one colleague said "Wow! Expenses are fun now!", we knew we'd done the right thing.

There wasn't even a need to look at tangible benefits, but next we'll show how they look in hindsight.

Tangible Benefits

▸ Foreign VAT recovery: £600.

▸ Flight cancellation warning: £1,500. This refers to one proven incident in which a notification from Concur TripIt professional allowed us to mitigate a cancelled flight and therefore avoid missing a client workshop. Concur TripIt professional makes business travel easier in many ways, but we only include a monetary value for this one incident in which we know that warnings from alternative sources, including the airline itself, would have been too late.

- ▸ Time saved on expense billing: £1,200.
- ▸ Time saved for approvers: £1,800.
- ▸ Time saved capturing expenses: £7,200.
- ▸ Loss of time for import into accounting system: -£600.

Results
- ▸ Net benefit of £8,100
- ▸ Important contribution to our digital transformation agenda
- ▸ Cultural fit between vision and internal reality
- ▸ Improved employee satisfaction

1.5 Summary

Traditional T&E solutions are usually ineffective, inefficient, and offer a poor UX. The vision for the future should be to change your T&E process from a nuisance to a value-adding service.

To achieve this, the system primarily needs to serve the high number of employees travelling to serve your customers and to sell your products and services and make this job easier and more enjoyable for them. The system also needs to help corporate T&E teams support your business travelers while minimizing cost and guaranteeing compliance with regulations. "The connected journey" and "the expense report that writes itself" are two marketing taglines used by Concur, but they illustrate the vision of a better T&E experience nicely.

The business benefits of Concur derive from direct cost reductions, process efficiencies, direct cash value, and intangible value. The intangible value, though often ignored by weak business leaders, can be the most important element for many organizations—most notably, if they have a digital transformation agenda or if attracting and retaining top talent is a high priority. *Intangible value* refers primarily to business culture, organizational learning, and brand image.

To summarize with a simple picture, a modern business doesn't want an employee to juggle paper receipts and spreadsheets or be involved in a cumbersome process assembling expense analytics on a Friday night when her grandmother pings her through WhatsApp to ask when she'll come for dinner.

Before your travelers can log into Concur to book travel or claim expenses, Concur needs to "know" them. This is what the user profile is for: It allows users to log in and holds all the information about each user that's required by the various Concur modules.

2   Employee and User Data

For any IT system, the minimum you need to log in is a user name and a password. In some systems, like SAP ERP Human Capital Management (SAP ERP HCM) and SAP Travel Management, the employee record and user account are two different things, so employee records can exist without those employees having user accounts to access the records themselves. This setup made sense for older systems, but modern systems like Concur are designed to let every traveler access the system to book/request trips and capture expenses for themselves. Therefore, there is only one record, which can be referred to as either the *user* or *employee* record in Concur.

The scope and purpose of the user profile depends on the Concur modules in use; some fields are only relevant for Concur Expense, whereas others are only required for Concur Travel. Across all solutions, the user data is primarily comprised of the following information:

▸ Roles and permissions a user holds in the process

▸ General data for identification (e.g., name) and reporting (e.g., organizational assignment data)

▸ Settings to define rules, screens, calculations, and workflows for a user

▸ Approvers and delegates

▸ Data required for parts of the process, such as credit card info, frequent traveler numbers, travel preferences, and personal or company car info

▸ Typical user preferences like language or time zone

In the following sections, we'll point out the most important fields of the user profile and explain how you can configure them. Then, we'll look at user permissions, which are an important aspect in all Concur modules. Finally, we'll discuss the various ways you can create employee data for new users.

2.1   Employee Master Record Fields

The employee data in Concur is divided into three parts, discussed in the following subsections. *System settings* are like personal settings in other software products; the user can choose his language and a variety of formatting choices. *Personal information* includes the bulk of employee data needed for the expense process and travel booking. The system settings and personal information sections are usually maintained by users themselves. The third section is for *administration data*, which can only be changed by an administrator, because it affects which features an employee can use in Concur.

2.1.1   System Settings

The system settings are usually maintained by users themselves via PROFILE • PROFILE SETTINGS • SYSTEM SETTINGS.

There are many settings to determine formatting, but the most important settings are as follows:

- ▶ LANGUAGE (options will include only the languages your system is set up to handle)

- ▶ The RUN IN CONCUR ACCESSIBILITY MODE checkbox (changes color settings and browser behavior to comply with US regulations for accessible user interfaces)

Also note the list of notification preferences (see Figure 2.1). The first two checkboxes (SEND AN EMAIL EVERY TIME SOMETHING IS PUT IN OR REMOVED FROM MY APPROVAL QUEUE and SEND A DAILY SUMMARY OF ITEMS IN MY QUEUE) are particularly important for approvers. It may seem more convenient to select only the second box and not the first to reduce the number of emails an approver receives. However, if approval includes travel booking rather than just expense reports, action may be required urgently to secure a flight on short notice.

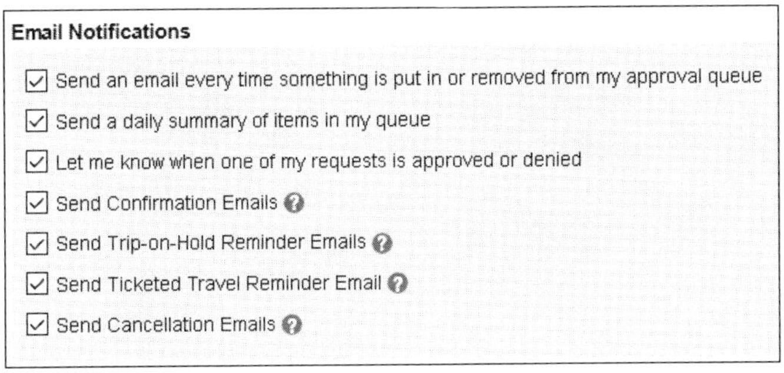

Email Notifications

☑ Send an email every time something is put in or removed from my approval queue

☑ Send a daily summary of items in my queue

☑ Let me know when one of my requests is approved or denied

☑ Send Confirmation Emails ❓

☑ Send Trip-on-Hold Reminder Emails ❓

☑ Send Ticketed Travel Reminder Email ❓

☑ Send Cancellation Emails ❓

Figure 2.1 User Notification Settings

2.1.2 Personal Information

The personal information section contains most user information and carries through all Concur modules. This information is accessible via PROFILE • PROFILE SETTINGS • PERSONAL INFORMATION.

The first task can be the most critical one, if you use the Concur Travel module: setting your full name (see Figure 2.2). It is important that the user's full name is captured here as shown on her passport or other travel documents, including her middle name. Any discrepancies can lead to a passenger not being allowed to board her plane, because her passport doesn't match her ticket. If you import this data from your human resources (HR) system, you should review it carefully; it's possible that this data could include a nickname rather than a full name.

Figure 2.2 Full Name, Including Middle Name, Is Crucial for Bookings

Note that some fields in the name and in the company information discussed ahead show a grey background, indicating they can't be changed by users themselves. These fields are considered critical for security and can only be changed by the administrator (see Section 2.1.3).

The COMPANY INFORMATION section (see Figure 2.3) always holds the EMPLOYEE ID—used as a unique identifier in communication with other systems—and the approving line manager. Additional fields—depending on your configuration—define an employee's organizational assignment. These fields can be important for reporting purposes, but most notably can be used to prepopulate fields in expense reports to determine the posting.

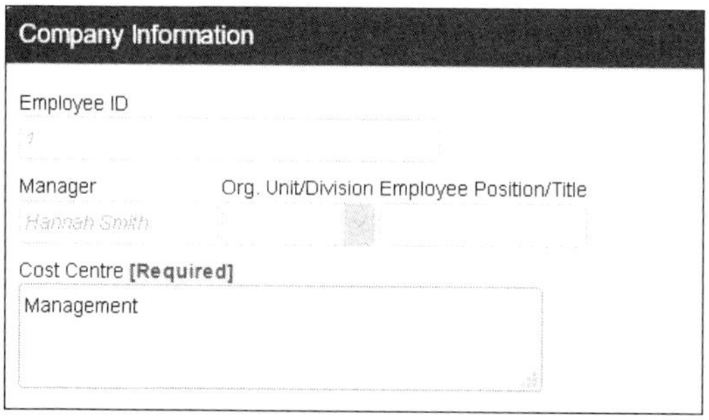

Figure 2.3 Company Information with Employee ID

Following the company information is a large section for addresses and contact data; note the following two points:

1. In some cases, phone numbers are preceded by a dropdown field for the country code. Although it seems counterintuitive to add the leading zero after the country code, this is exactly what the system requires. We recommend pointing this out to your employees, as they often remove the zero because they feel it looks wrong.

2. The email address is very important for communication with Concur. Not only is it used to send notifications to the user or link Concur to various third-party apps, but when users send data to Concur (e.g., receipts sent to *receipts@concur.com*) the sender email address also is used to identify the user. You may require more than one email address to be registered in Concur. The EMAIL ADDRESSES section in the personal profile guides users through the process of adding further email addresses. It's important that all email addresses are verified.

There are several fields for TRAVEL PREFERENCES, but they're self-explanatory. Users can simply indicate items such as food or seat preferences. However, you should educate users that some settings, such as TWIN ROOM for hotels or GPS for rental cars might go against company policy, because they're not the cheapest options. The TRAVEL PREFERENCES section also includes accessibility settings, so make sure any handicapped users know which options to pick here.

In TRAVEL PREFERENCES, employees also can capture their memberships in frequent traveler programs (see Figure 2.4). These programs constitute one of the little perks for employees who travel a lot, so making it easy for employees to collect points helps with workforce satisfaction.

Figure 2.4 Assigning Frequent Traveler Programs

As shown in Figure 2.5, Concur also alerts users on the home screen of the browser application if a card is about to expire or has expired already.

Figure 2.5 Alerts for Expiring Cards on Home Screen

Note that some company-level frequent traveler programs must be managed by the travel management company (TMC) and cannot be assigned through Concur. Examples include Lufthansa Partner Plus and British Airways onBusiness.

For a smooth automated booking process, travelers should also enter their passport and visa information in the INTERNATIONAL TRAVEL: PASSPORTS AND VISAS section. Unfortunately, there is only space for one passport, but you can add several visas of various types, including ESTA or Schengen Visa.

In the ASSISTANTS AND TRAVEL ARRANGERS section, each user can grant other users permission to perform tasks in Concur on their behalf or book travel for them in case of absences and emergencies.

If employees pay for booked travel with their personal credit cards, these cards need to be added to their personal profile in the CREDIT CARDS section as shown in Figure 2.6. An employee can add several cards; when adding one, he can decide whether it should be the default card used for booking flights, trains, cars, or hotels. In Figure 2.6, the second card is the default for all three vendor types, which are represented by the plane, car, and bed icon, respectively.

Figure 2.6 Credit Cards with Indicators for Default Cards and Expired Cards

This is also where one benefit of using Concur Travel becomes apparent for employees. When using Concur, they can book with almost all vendors using just one account: their Concur account. This is one of the quick wins for individual travelers, and we like to use this fact as an argument for the change management process. However, note that for a few vendors (e.g., Eurostar), the credit card data held in Concur can't be used for payment; the card needs to be held by the TMC in these cases.

CREDIT CARDS is the final standard section of the personal profile, but there are cases in which further data is required. One such example is shown in Figure 2.7, which shows a dynamic section of the screen that is active when integration with the German rail transport provider Deutsche Bahn (BIBE) is set up. In this case, users need an account at Deutsche Bahn and can capture their account details in this screen to allow booking through Concur.

Figure 2.7 Additional Fields for Partner Programs

2.1.3 User Administration Data

The data described in Section 2.1.2 is usually maintained by users themselves, unless it's fed through an interface from other systems. Administrators can access some areas (e.g., ADDRESSES), but not all (e.g., CREDIT CARDS). Now, let's look at user data that can only be accessed by administrators. These fields address the employee's organizational assignment, control what the user can or can't do in the system, and are crucial for proper functioning of the process; they're accessed via ADMINISTRATION • COMPANY • COMPANY ADMIN and then choosing EMPLOYEE MAINTENANCE or USER ADMINISTRATION.

Some of the most fundamental data is right at the beginning in the GENERAL SETTINGS section, as shown in Figure 2.8. The four checkboxes shown at the top determine basic rights and menu options available for the user, as follows:

1. TRAVEL WIZARD: Is Concur Travel available?

2. EXPENSE USER: Is Concur Expense available?

3. EXPENSE APPROVER: Can the user approve expense reports?

4. AUTHORIZED SUPPORT CONTACT: Can the user raise support tickets with Concur?

Figure 2.8 Basic User Data for Administrator

Under GENERAL SETTINGS, the user name (CTE LOGIN NAME) (must be the company domain as agreed upon with Concur) and PASSWORD can be captured, as well as the user's full name, including fields that can't be changed by the users themselves.

The ACCOUNT TERMINATION DATE field allows the administrator to set a user as inactive, which usually happens when an employee leaves the organization, because users can't be deleted in a live system (users created during the implementation project can be deleted by Concur before go-live with a so-called purge). The EMPLOYEE ID is a unique identifier, and the primary EMAIL ADDRESS is also maintained in this section.

The TRAVEL SETTINGS section holds various fields for organizational assignment and information purposes, but the most important field to consider in your fundamental system design is RULE CLASS. The content of this field determines which travel policy rules apply for the employee. For example, you might have one rule class for frequently traveling sales reps and customer service teams, who don't need preapproval for trips within Europe, and another rule class for all other employees, who need preapproval for all bookings.

Other important fields in this section are as follows:

▸ Checkbox to enable e-receipts from Concur Travel for Concur Expense (ENABLE E-RECEIPTS)

▸ Approving manager for travel booking (MANAGER NAME)

The PAR/LEVEL 2 STAR and XML PROFILE SYNCH ID technical fields should only be changed by interface programs or when advised by Concur.

The following sections on the screen hold straightforward contact data that would usually be updated by the users themselves; these fields don't require any further explanation here. So, we jump right to next section shown in in Figure 2.9, EXPENSE AND INVOICE SETTINGS, which contains the settings for Concur Expense and Concur Invoice. Because Concur Invoice is outside the purview of this book, we will focus on Concur Expense.

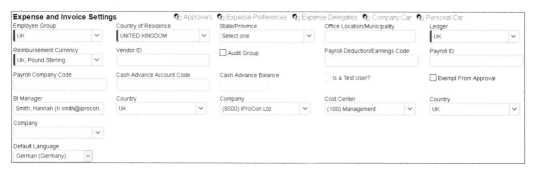

Figure 2.9 Expense and Invoice Settings

The links at the top of Figure 2.9 (APPROVERS, EXPENSE PREFERENCES, EXPENSE DEL-EGATES, COMPANY CAR, and PERSONAL CAR) lead to detailed data, usually maintained by the users themselves. The following list describes some of the most important fields in the main screen:

▸ EMPLOYEE GROUP determines assignment to a policy, audit rules, expense forms, and more (see Chapter 4 for more information).

▸ COUNTRY OF RESIDENCE and in some cases STATE/PROVINCE trigger statutory rules.

▸ When selected, the AUDIT GROUP checkbox adds an employee to the group going through an audit, if that process is in place.

▸ Various payroll-related fields can be used in interfaces with payroll systems. Which of these fields will be used in a future standard interface with Payroll in SAP ERP HCM is not yet known as of February 2017.

▸ If the cash advance process is used (something we recommend you avoid), the CASH ADVANCE ACCOUNT CODE field can be used to refer to the respective ledger account and the CASH ADVANCE BALANCE field will show the current advance amount.

▸ The IS A TEST USER? checkbox can be selected only when a new user is created and can't be changed again. Test users allow for some testing in live Concur instances, as their data is not used in real reports, payments, or postings.

▸ The EXEMPT FROM APPROVAL checkbox often is selected for members of the executive board or other users who don't require approval for their expenses.

▸ The BI MANAGER field determines who will see this user's data in line manager reports.

Other fields for organizational assignment often include custom fields and are used for information, reporting, and posting.

2.2 Configuring Employee Forms

The configuration for employee forms is the basically same as for expense forms, which will be covered in Chapter 4. As this is part of the advanced configuration and therefore not accessible for most customers, we will only give a brief indication of what's possible with a simple example here. Please note that this configuration affects only the employee form fields relevant for Concur Expense, not those for Concur Travel.

Go to ADMINISTRATION • EXPENSE • FORMS AND FIELDS and select EMPLOYEE as the FORM TYPE. You'll see the DEFAULT EMPLOYEE INFORMATION form in the list of forms along with various tabs to allow changes in the form.

The most common and simple changes made change the properties of a field, such as making it mandatory or hiding it in the employee or administrator view. To achieve this, chose the FORM FIELDS tab and select a field, such as PAYROLL ID. Then, click MODIFY FORM FIELDS to open the window shown in Figure 2.10.

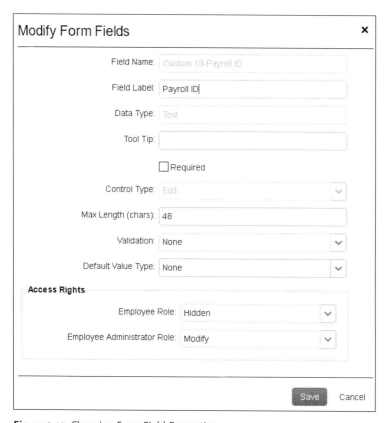

Figure 2.10 Changing Form Field Properties

As you can see in the ACCESS RIGHTS box at the bottom, the field is hidden for the employee but can be changed by the administrator. If we don't need this field for integration with a payroll system, we can hide it for the administrator as well. Other typical changes include the following:

- Making a field a required field
- Changing the label displayed on the form to match the corporate jargon
- Changing the label displayed if the field will used for a different purpose than the standard label indicates, such as using the standard CUSTOM2 field to capture the division.

Other activities you can perform for a form include the following:

- Creating a new form via copy
- Adding or removing fields
- Adding dropdown lists to fields
- Adding validation rules to fields
- Adding fields that are only available under certain conditions (a general feature of fields and forms, but not used for employee forms)

We highly recommend that you keep employee forms as clean as possible, as users are confused easily by unnecessary fields; because filling in their user profile in the employee form is one of the first activities for users, it can be detrimental for system adoption if the forms are unnecessarily long. Also, make sure that labels are self-explanatory and fields needed for reporting or posting are flagged as required. In your initial implementation, this setup must be performed by your Concur implementation manager. Make sure you make your requirements clear, and don't forget to test the employee data screens before you sign off on the system.

2.3 Permissions

To change permissions, go to ADMINISTRATION • COMPANY • COMPANY ADMIN • USER PERMISSIONS.

The permissions concept in Concur is managed separately for each module, but in each one is a list of roles you can assign to users in one of two ways:

1. Start with a role, then assign this role to one or several users.
2. Start with a user, then assign one or several roles to this user.

Figure 2.11 shows how to select a user to assign expense roles. In the lower right of the screen, you'll see the two roles the user already holds. In the lower left, you'll see further roles available.

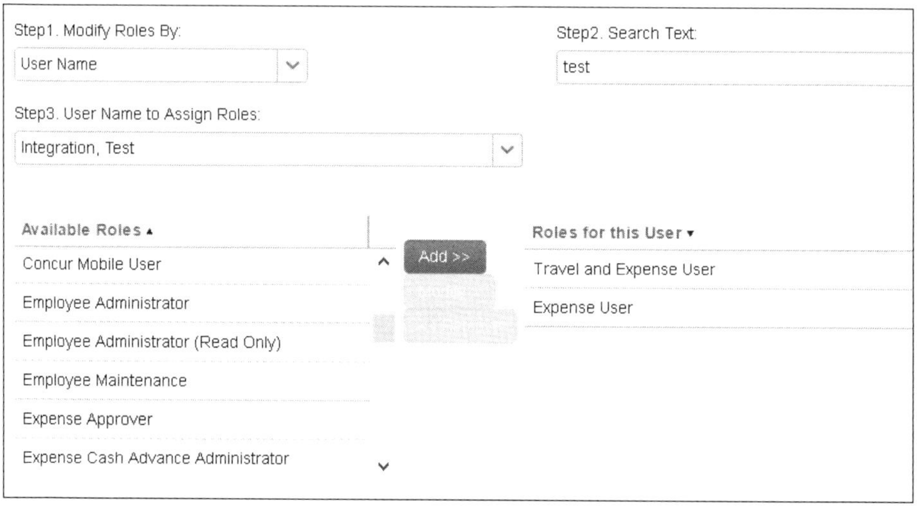

Figure 2.11 Assigning Role to User

Some of the roles are valid without a *target group* (the users for whom a certain activity can be performed). Other roles can be restricted to a group of users. For example, the EXPENSE APPROVER role doesn't require a target group here, because approvers can always approve for those people they are assigned to as an approver (including via forwarding, if that feature is used). However, if we select a role that requires a target group, such as the EMPLOYEE MAINTENANCE role, then we have to define which groups the user should have access to for employee maintenance tasks, as illustrated in Figure 2.12.

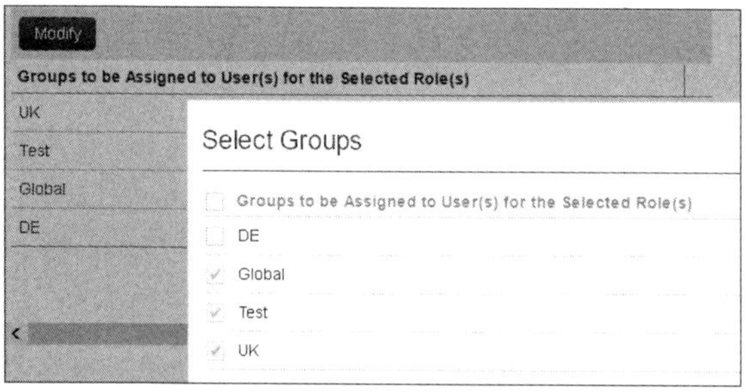

Figure 2.12 Restricting Groups for Role

Employee groups are the only way to restrict the target group in permissions. If you have additional requirements, you may need to consider additional workarounds or process changes.

> **Tip**
>
> In Concur, you don't really build roles; you pick from a set of predefined roles. As a customer, you can receive a document listing all available roles with a brief explanation from your Concur implementation manager during implementation. If you are live and you don't have it yet, ask your account manager. The document title at the time of writing is "CS Expense Training—User Roles and Permissions."

Note the following additional tips:

▸ In Concur Travel, you can assign permissions to a rule class so that you don't always have to assign them to many individual users.

▸ Usually, the ALL group is set up automatically, and all users are assigned to it. Therefore, users inherit whatever is assigned to ALL. The Travel Wizard permission is assigned to ALL, but there is no need to remove it for users not allowed to book travel, as you wouldn't flag them as travel users in their user profiles (see Section 2.1.3); therefore, they wouldn't have access to Concur Travel.

▸ Use the filter options in Concur Expense permissions view to assign a role to a large group of users in one go.

▸ The number of users you're allowed to assign the COGNOS PROFESSIONAL AUTHOR role in reporting permissions to is determined by your Contract. Check with your Concur implementation manager or account manager to confirm this number.

2.4 Creating Employee Data

Employee records can be created by an administrator manually or imported through a file upload or an interface (see Chapter 8, Section 8.1.1 for the interface with SAP ERP HCM). Once created, users can amend their own records by going to PROFILE • PROFILE SETTINGS. Administrators can create or change user records by going to ADMINISTRATION • COMPANY • COMPANY ADMIN and then choosing EMPLOYEE MAINTENANCE or USER ADMINISTRATION.

Customers can also set their systems up to allow users to self-register. If you don't intend to import user data from other systems and have more than about 10 users, we recommend this approach. However, you need to contact Concur Support for a registration code to set it up.

Once you have the registration code, go to ADMINISTRATION • COMPANY • COMPANY ADMIN • SELF-REGISTRATION SETUP. On the right-hand side of the screen, you'll see a preview of the self-registration page for users. This page guides users through capturing their data and creating their accounts in one step. You can change the logo and the texts on this page to provide bespoke guidance to your users.

On the left-hand side of the screen, you'll find the settings to control the process and fields to be filled in (see Figure 2.13).

Figure 2.13 Settings for Self-Registration Page

We recommend you switch the approval step on (check REGISTRATION REQUIRES APPROVAL) so that your administrator can check and then approve or reject self-registrations via ADMINISTRATION • COMPANY • COMPANY ADMIN • SELF-REGISTRATION APPROVAL. You can then add a section on self-registration for Concur to your organization's onboarding guide for new employees so that they know where to find T&E functionality on day one.

The best way to create users in Concur is to import them from a file, provided you can get this information from another system, such as your HR system. There are two ways to do so:

1. From your PC, go to ADMINISTRATION • COMPANY • COMPANY ADMIN • USER ADMINISTRATION and then choose IMPORT USERS. There is some guidance available on that screen and links to the templates you need to use for the import. Concur doesn't allow changes to these templates, so make sure the files you eventually import using the BROWSE and UPLOAD YOUR DATA buttons further down match the templates exactly.

2. Use the automated file transfer features in Concur, which can be set up as background jobs. This is something you should discuss with your Concur technical consultant in the implementation project. Make sure you plan enough time for this as well as other automated file transfers during the project, as you may incur extra costs if you do it at a later time. For this discussion, you should have the right experts available from your organization to cover IT security, including encryption, data privacy, and a good technical understanding of the data sources (e.g., HR systems) available.

2.5   Summary

You've now learned that user data is the foundation for all processes in Concur. There are a lot of data fields available, and you need to understand what's really required for your bespoke T&E processes. The choices you make here, especially in the groupings and organizational data, are crucial for further setup, so they should be driven not by your legacy system employee data structure but by your requirements in Concur.

Permissions in Concur are easy to understand but restricted in their options if you're used to large ERP systems, so try to keep it simple.

For larger numbers of employees, user import and update is best performed through an automated process—ideally through the new standard integration if you're using SAP ERP HCM or SAP SuccessFactors (see Chapter 8). However, there are other options available, and self-registration can also be a good choice.

Once user records are in the system, the foundation is laid to start using the core Concur Travel and Concur Expense modules described in the next two chapters.

The first step of any business trip is planning the trip, which makes Concur Travel our first focus. Its objective is to simplify and accelerate the booking process and to ensure compliance with organization policies. This chapter shows how the travel process should be: what steps a user takes and how it looks in the system.

3   Concur Travel

Concur Travel is an online booking platform for business travel that connects your employees with available flights, hotels, car rentals, trains, and ground transportation options. All options are provided on the same platform your employees use to create or approve expenses and add or process invoices, offering an all-in-one solution.

In this chapter, we'll look at the business principles and concept of Concur Travel, see how the process of booking travel is reflected, touch on Concur TripLink and Concur TripIt, and go over both the basic and advanced configuration options in Concur Travel.

3.1   Business Principles

A booking platform for business needs to be highly configurable based on a company's T&E policy. Deploying a company-wide travel booking platform also ensures that employees don't waste their work time browsing through multiple websites or searching other booking options to try to find the best possible flight, hotel, or rental car.

Companies that spend considerable amounts on specific hotels, hotel chains, airlines, or car rental agencies often have contracts in place that guarantee better prices during booking, additional services for free, or kickbacks at the end of the year based on the volume spent. Ensuring that vendors (and the company itself) can recognize and account for all bookings isn't fully possible without configuring and using a platform like Concur.

Employers also have a duty of care; they need to know where their employees are during business travels, to be able to reach them should an emergency occur in a city/region/country an employee is traveling to or within. An online booking platform such as Concur Travel allows companies to meet that need.

In the case of Concur Travel, the platform is configured by Concur and a client's TMC for (and on behalf) of the client. They ensure that a client's T&E policy is correctly reflected in the system and that every time an employee uses the system it shows all the available travel/booking options at the best prices—and that every booking/reservation request is forwarded to the TMC's backend system and from there to the final vendor.

For most airline tickets, the TMC is also still the responsible party to make changes—either communicated by the traveler through the Internet (web browser or mobile app) or by phone. This ensures that the TMC is always up-to-date on an employee's travel plans and can provide these details to the employer in case of an emergency.

In addition, TMCs mostly have umbrella contracts with airlines, hotel chains, and car rental agencies that grant them specific discounts on available travel options. Those discounts are accessible to any of the TMC's clients, resulting in reduced cost for business travel.

To be able to use Concur Travel, you need a contract with a TMC that supports Concur Travel. The TMC will provide employees with booking options (for flights, hotel rooms, cars, trains, etc.) and prices based on your employee's searches. The data is pulled from a *global distribution system* (GDS), a databank containing the flights, rooms, cars, and airlines/hotels/car rental info for all agencies that publish their offerings in the GDS.

TMCs will work with different GDSs depending on the country of operation. In the United States, most TMCs operate with Sabre or Apollo, and in Europe they work mostly with Amadeus (some TMCs in some countries use Galileo or Sabre).

Concur Travel shows the users all data provided by the TMC, applies the configured rules based on your T&E policy, and presents it differently based on what's within policy and what isn't—and allows employees to book/purchase (or not, depending on policy). Once an employee has chosen the elements of a trip, Concur Travel submits the ticketing/reservation requests to the TMC for execution.

The TMC will ask for the travel policy, for your vendor contracts, and for your spending over the last year. Concur will ask you whether you want Concur Travel to work through Concur (direct) or through a TMC (indirect). The TMC might have sold you Concur Travel if you've been in a long-standing relationship, in which case you're working indirectly. The differences are as follows:

▶ **Indirect**
The TMC has full control over your site. That may not be a bad thing, but it means that if you want to change the TMC down the line, you'll have to start from scratch. TMCs usually offer Concur for free—but of course they'll charge a certain amount per booking for giving your company an online booking tool to use and for maintaining it.

The TMC will also control the system, be it during the configuration, afterwards, or for additional services offered in Concur Travel. For example, services that would potentially reduce the TMC's profit will most likely never come up during meetings/discussions—or will be fought (or declined as options the TMC doesn't offer).

The charge from the TMC is per booking, but it's a reduced rate when booked online through Concur compared to how much a company has to pay for booking through an agent (on the phone).

Multiple TMCs can't be contracted (be it within the same country or region or globally) to be used through Concur Travel if it was purchased through a TMC; in that case, the direct approach is needed.

▶ **Direct**
You own your Concur Travel site/configurations. Should the need arise, you can switch the TMC but keep the current site; all changes related to the TMC take place in the backend/the configuration itself and are handled by Concur and the new TMC.

You're free to use additional services as long as the TMC supports them; even if the TMC doesn't, some services function without the TMC (e.g., Concur TripLink), so you can use them independently of the TMC and add them to your Concur Travel site.

Concur will add a certain amount to the cost per expense report submitted, not by trip booked—which in turn means that if an employee travels eight times during a month but you ask them to submit only one expense report per month, the additional charge by Concur for the use of Concur Travel only applies once. This excludes bookings through Travelfusion, which are charged per booking.

The TMC will still charge per booking, but online bookings should be comparatively cheap. We usually see a cost of around $5 per booking through Concur if the TMC supports electronic end-to-end processing. If the TMC requires every booking to be "touched" by an agent, the cost will be higher. This is not usually the case in the United States or Europe, but something we see often with TMCs operating in other countries, especially for smaller companies or affiliates of bigger TMCs, such as Amex Global Business Travel (Amex GBT), Carlson Wagonlit Travel (CWT), BCD Travel, or Hogg Robinson Group (HRG). Offline bookings (bookings made on the phone with an agent) cost much more because an actual person is involved.

The direct option allows for multiple TMCs to be used with Concur Travel. Especially with clients planning to utilize Concur Travel globally, the need for multiple TMCs can arise; no TMC we're aware of can fulfill their services in every country.

3.2   Using Concur Travel for Business Trips

This section will explain how an employee can search for trip segments in Concur, how to apply filters to results, and generally how to navigate the result pages and the actual booking process.

> **Note**
>
> Unlike most online booking tools, Concur shows the actual availability and the full price from start; others often initially show a seat count and price (for flights) based on how many seats were available at a certain price (e.g., one day ago), then, once a customer selects a specific flight, the online booking tools connect with the airline to get the actual availability and price. Both pieces of information will most likely change, so the price a customer eventually is charged differs from the original listing.
>
> For hotel rooms, most online booking tools show the prepaid rate, whereas Concur shows all rates. Business travel is generally subject to change, and companies don't want employees to book prepaid rates or rates requiring a deposit.

3.2.1 Concur Travel Profile

The first step for any business traveler should be to complete the Concur Travel profile. Most importantly, the name fields must be correct—not only the first and last name, but also (if applicable) the middle name. The company information also must be verified (it should be prepopulated based on your employee information), as well as your work address (see Figure 3.1).

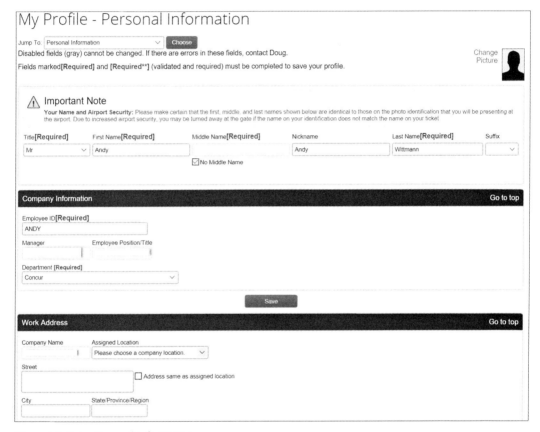

Figure 3.1 Enter Personal Information

The second step is to make sure that your personal address and contact information, as well as email address(es), are entered (see Figure 3.2). A verified email address can also be used to send receipts to Concur.

Figure 3.2 Add Required Contact Information

Third, your emergency contact's details must be provided (see Figure 3.3).

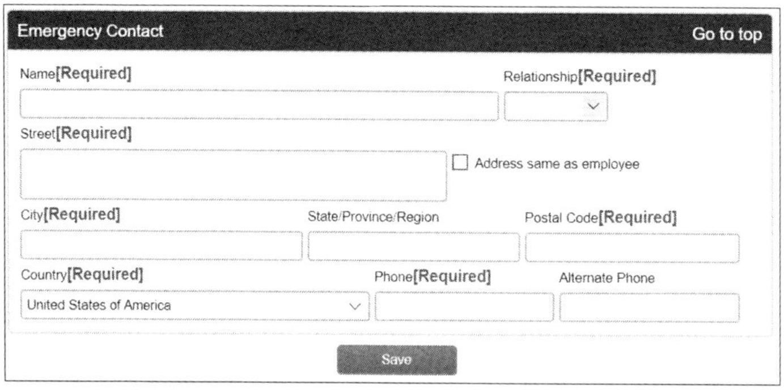

Figure 3.3 Add Emergency Contact Information

Next, define all your travel preferences (see Figure 3.4).

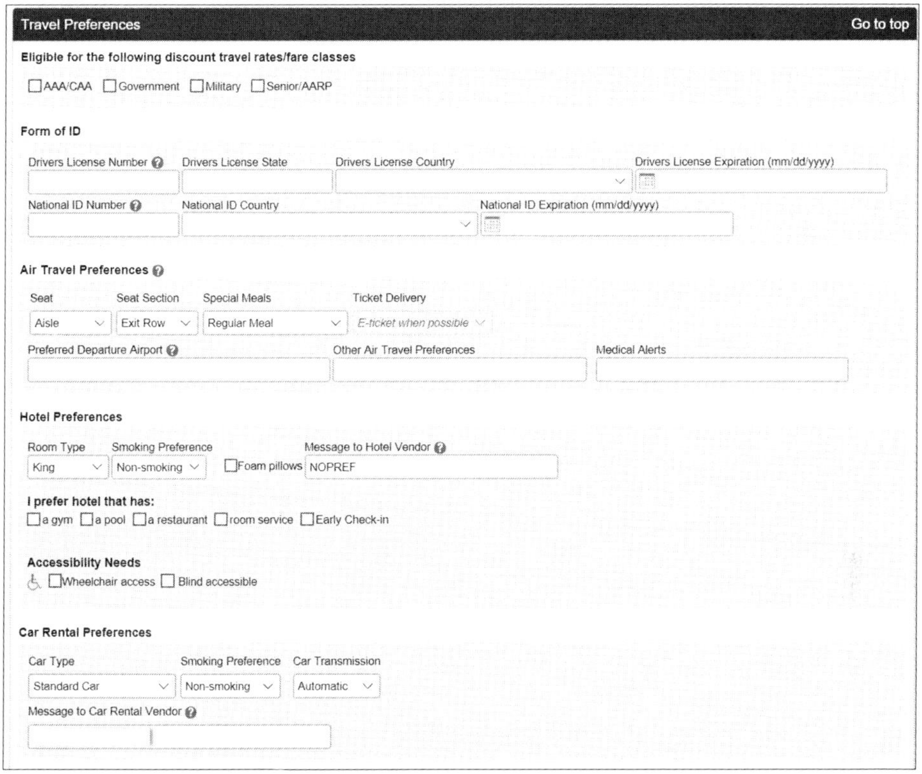

Figure 3.4 Add Travel Preference Information

Now, add your frequent traveler program info—and potentially discount cards (e.g., for European rail programs such as SNCF)—which can be entered in the ADVANTAGE PROGRAMS section (see Figure 3.5).

Next, enter your personal details, such as gender, date of birth, and DHS or TSA number. For international travel, also enter your passport information. You can also designate an assistant who can book travel on your behalf (see Figure 3.6).

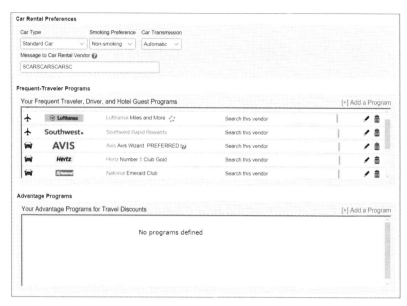

Figure 3.5 Add Frequent Traveler Information

Figure 3.6 Add Passport, Gender, Date of Birth, TSA Information, and Personal Assistant Information

Finally, a form of payment (see Figure 3.7) has to be added if your company doesn't offer a BTA/ghost card program, discussed in greater detail in Section 3.4.9.

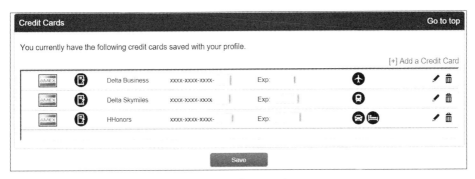

Figure 3.7 Add Form of Payment for Concur to Allow Bookings

Although any given card can be added by default, be it a personal credit card or a company-issued credit card, employers can limit the option to cards within the range provided by the company's card-issuing bank (via TRAVEL ADMIN • CREDIT CARD BIN RESTRICTIONS).

3.2.2 Using the Travel Wizard and Result Pages

The Travel Wizard is located on the left side of the Concur start page and is used to enter trip details for flights, trains, hotels, or rental cars (see Figure 3.8). Other booking tools and websites let employees define everything at this stage and therefore limit the search results to only a select few, but Concur's principle is different: An employee enters the basic information, and Concur finds all results within the search parameters entered (taking into account any additional settings defined by the company). At that time, Concur applies all T&E policy-related rules to the search results (and categorizes them into allowed, allowed with comment, and not allowed). Only then are employees allowed to narrow down/filter the search results. This ensures that employees do not cheat the system by limiting their searches to such a degree that their desired option (perhaps one not within policy) appears within policy.

Figure 3.8 Travel Wizard for Flight/Train Bookings

The Travel Wizard also shows business travel-specific options for hotel searches. An employee can search for hotels within a certain distance of an airport, near a specific address, or close to the company's office locations (which usually are loaded into Concur by the TMC or can be manually maintained by the client under Travel Admin • Company Locations; see Figure 3.9).

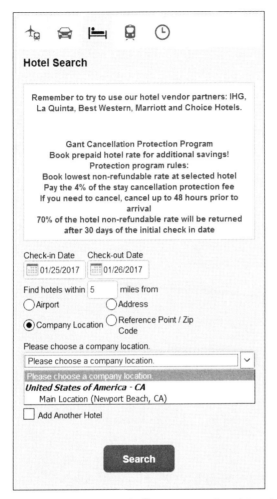

Figure 3.9 Travel Wizard Offers Option to Search Hotels Near Company Locations

The Concur search results screens shows filter options to the left, including options for flights, trains, hotels, and car rentals. The flight/train search results screen shows a matrix on top that allows employees to reduce the results to specific airlines, number of stops, or a combination of both. The hotel search results screen shows a map with a red dot near where an employee looked for a hotel and the hotels nearby marked. For more details, see Section 3.2.3.

Train bookings are only available in countries in which train companies allow bookings through a distribution system (similar to how airlines offer flights). The most common countries in which train bookings (in most cases and with most TMCs) can be implemented in Concur are as follows:

- ▶ United States (Amtrak)
- ▶ Canada (Rail Canada)
- ▶ France (SNCF, Thalys, and Eurostar)
- ▶ United Kingdom (Trainline Europe, Evolvi, and Eurostar)
- ▶ Germany (Deutsche Bahn)
- ▶ Spain (Renfe, coming in 2017)
- ▶ Sweden (Swedish Rail, coming in 2017)

Which trains specifically can be set up in a country depends on the chosen TMC, since the TMC must offer the connection to the train services via the available connectors. Concur is constantly in discussions with additional railways and doesn't stop extending its features and offerings, so you can expect more partnerships to be announced regularly.

3.2.3 The Booking Process

The following subsections look at how to book flights, hotels, and car rentals and discuss options for canceling or changing existing trips.

Flights

Once the trip details have been entered in the Travel Wizard on the start page and the search started, Concur will present an employee with all available flights based on the search parameters. On the left-hand side of the screen (see Figure 3.10 and Figure 3.11), the traveler can refine the search and reduce the results shown to the right.

The options shown in Figure 3.10 define the departure/arrival time slots for both the outgoing and return flight, as well as the price, whereas the options shown in Figure 3.11 allows for the selection of fare type, plane type, and departure/arrival airports as well as connecting airports.

Figure 3.10 Filter Options for Flight Results: Part 1

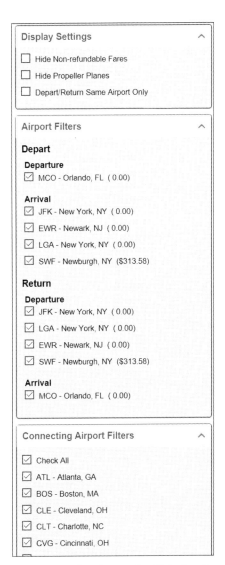

Figure 3.11 Filter Options for Flight Results: Part 2

On the top of the screen, the matrix can be used to limit the results to a certain number of stops or specific airlines (or a mix of both; see Figure 3.12).

ORLANDO, FL TO NEW YORK, NY
TUE, JAN 31 - WED, FEB 1

Show as USD ∨

Hide matrix   Print

	American Airlines	Delta	spirit Spirit Airlines	United	Multiple
All 319 results					
	Preferred				
Nonstop 3 results	—	316.38 3 results	—	—	—
1 stop 301 results	186.10 200 results	347.99 96 results	326.58 2 results	942.60 1 results	726.98 2 results
2 stops 15 results	—	359.51 13 results	—	498.69 2 results	—

Figure 3.12 Filter Flight Results by Airline, Number of Stops, or Both

The results themselves appear sorted either by fares or by schedule (see Section 3.5 for more information). Sorting by fares shows return flights; sorting by schedule allows the selection of outgoing and return flights separately.

Each result can be opened to SHOW ALL DETAILS (see Figure 3.13) and, if allowed, you can select a different fare/booking class.

jetBlue JetBlue	06:24a MCO → 08:57a EWR	Nonstop	2h 33m	**$128.40**
	06:46p EWR → 09:46p MCO	Nonstop	3h 00m	View Fares
Least Cost Logical Fare				Show all details ∨

Figure 3.13 Example of Flight Results

If a result with a yellow triangle is selected, this means that it's out of policy, and a pop-up window will prompt for a reason to be selected and an explanation to be entered (see Figure 3.14). See Table 3.1 for examples of reasons that can be selected.

Figure 3.14 Travel Policy Violations Require Reason and Explanation

Once the requested information has been provided, the booking process can continue. The next page (see Figure 3.15) shows a summary of the flights, some personal information for the traveler, and asks for the frequent traveler program and the payment method. Seats on the flight can be selected at this point.

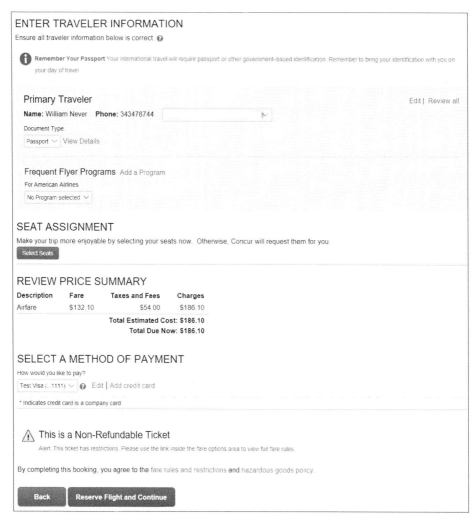

Figure 3.15 First Summary Page for Flight Bookings

After all the information has been provided and the traveler has clicked on RESERVE FLIGHT AND CONTINUE, the flight will be reserved and the final summary (including price and disclaimer) shown (see Figure 3.16). To continue, the employee clicks on NEXT.

The next page (see Figure 3.17) allows the traveler to enter a TRIP NAME and TRIP DESCRIPTION, add an additional email address for notifications, and—if required by the company—select the PURPOSE OF TRIP.

Figure 3.16 Second Summary Page for Flight Bookings

Trip Booking Information

Trip Name
This will appear in your upcoming trip list

Trip from Orlando to New York

Trip Description (optional)
Used to identify the trip purpose

Send a copy of the confirmation to: ❓

Send my email confirmation as
◉ HTML ○ Plain-text

Purpose of Trip [Required]

- Internal Meeting
- External Meeting(Customer/Bottler/Supplier)
- Company Sponsored Event/Trade Show
- External Conference/Convention/Trade Show
- Relocation/Recruiting/Short Term Assignment

...ervation until: 01/20/2017 03:00 pm **Eastern**

Please enter information about this trip then press Next to finalize your reservation. If you close at this point your reservation may be cancelled.
Note: Any part of the trip that is instant purchase or has deposit required will not be cancelled.

[Display Trip] [Hold Trip] [<< Previous] [Next >>] [Cancel Trip]

Figure 3.17 Third Summary Page for Flight Bookings

After clicking on Next for the last time, another summary is shown. This is the final summary; up to this point, the flight reservation isn't final yet. When the employee clicks on Purchase Ticket, the purchase request will be submitted to the travel agent.

Hotels

Once the trip details have been entered in the Travel Wizard on the start page and the search started, Concur will present the employee with all available hotels based on the search parameters. On the left-hand side of the screen (see Figure 3.18), the traveler can refine the search and reduce the results shown to the right.

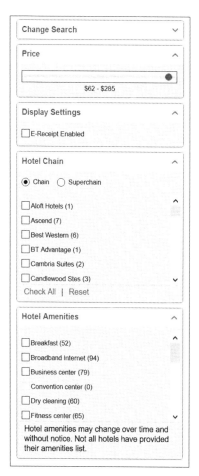

Figure 3.18 Filter Options for Hotel Search Results

On the top of the screen, a map of the area to which the employee is traveling will be shown, and each hotel will be marked (see Figure 3.19). This is helpful if the traveler wants to search for hotels in a certain vicinity, near a landmark or a company office location.

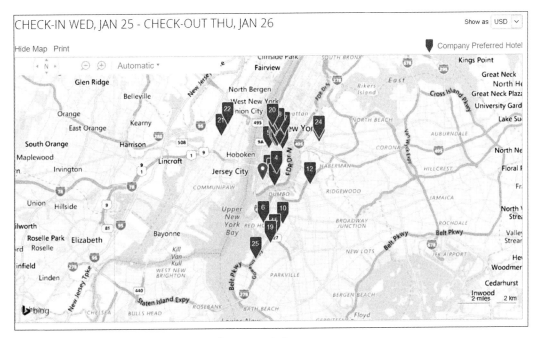

Figure 3.19 Map Showing Hotels Near Employee Search Area

The search results usually show the price of a room for the first 10 to 20 hotels, after which the employee has to click on GET RATES for Concur to show the price. Clicking on HOTEL DETAILS opens a pop-up with all available hotel details. To see the prices for other rooms at the hotel as well, click on the VIEW ROOMS button (see Figure 3.20).

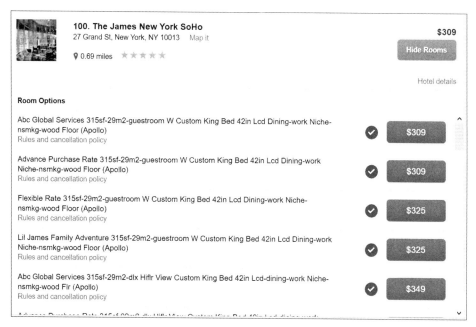

Figure 3.20 Available Rooms at Selected Hotel

If a result with a yellow triangle is selected—that is, a result that's out of policy—a pop-up window will ask for a reason to be selected and an explanation to be entered. Once that information has been provided, the booking process can continue.

The next page (see Figure 3.21) shows a summary of the hotel room, some personal information of the traveler, and asks for the frequent traveler program and the payment method. At the bottom of the page, the traveler must agree to the hotel's rates, restrictions, and cancellation policy.

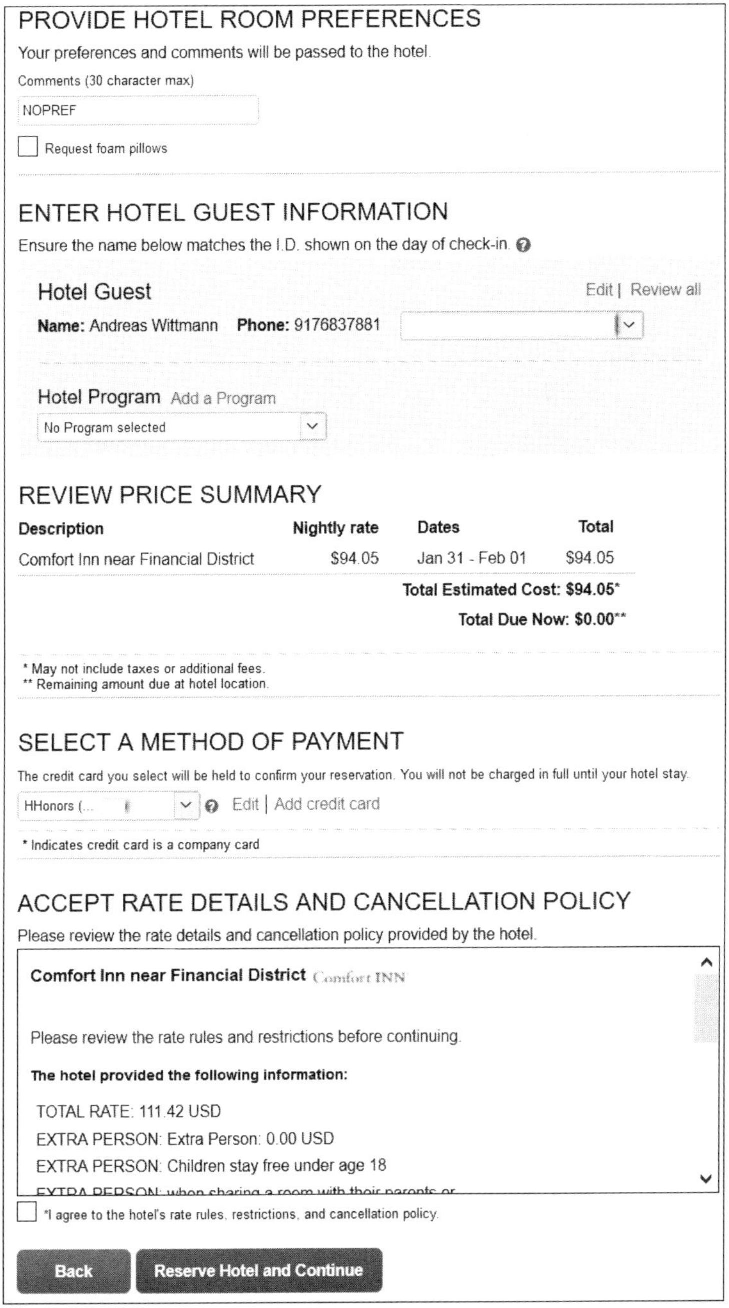

PROVIDE HOTEL ROOM PREFERENCES

Your preferences and comments will be passed to the hotel.

Comments (30 character max)

NOPREF

☐ Request foam pillows

ENTER HOTEL GUEST INFORMATION

Ensure the name below matches the I.D. shown on the day of check-in. ❓

Hotel Guest   Edit | Review all

Name: Andreas Wittmann   **Phone:** 9176837881   [_____ ⌄]

Hotel Program Add a Program

[No Program selected   ⌄]

REVIEW PRICE SUMMARY

Description	Nightly rate	Dates	Total
Comfort Inn near Financial District	$94.05	Jan 31 - Feb 01	$94.05

Total Estimated Cost: $94.05*

Total Due Now: $0.00**

* May not include taxes or additional fees.
** Remaining amount due at hotel location.

SELECT A METHOD OF PAYMENT

The credit card you select will be held to confirm your reservation. You will not be charged in full until your hotel stay.

[HHonors (...   ‖   ⌄] ❓ Edit | Add credit card

* Indicates credit card is a company card

ACCEPT RATE DETAILS AND CANCELLATION POLICY

Please review the rate details and cancellation policy provided by the hotel.

> **Comfort Inn near Financial District** Comfort INN
>
> Please review the rate rules and restrictions before continuing.
>
> **The hotel provided the following information:**
>
> TOTAL RATE: 111.42 USD
> EXTRA PERSON: Extra Person: 0.00 USD
> EXTRA PERSON: Children stay free under age 18
> EXTRA PERSON: when sharing a room with their parents or

☐ *I agree to the hotel's rate rules, restrictions, and cancellation policy.

[Back]   [Reserve Hotel and Continue]

Figure 3.21 First Confirmation Page for Hotel Bookings

After all the information has been provided and the traveler has clicked on RESERVE HOTEL AND CONTINUE, the room will be reserved and the final summary shown (see Figure 3.22). To continue, the employee must click on NEXT.

Figure 3.22 Second Confirmation Page for Hotel Bookings

The next page (see Figure 3.23) allows the traveler to enter a Trip Name, add an additional email address for notifications, and—if required by the company—enter a Trip Purpose.

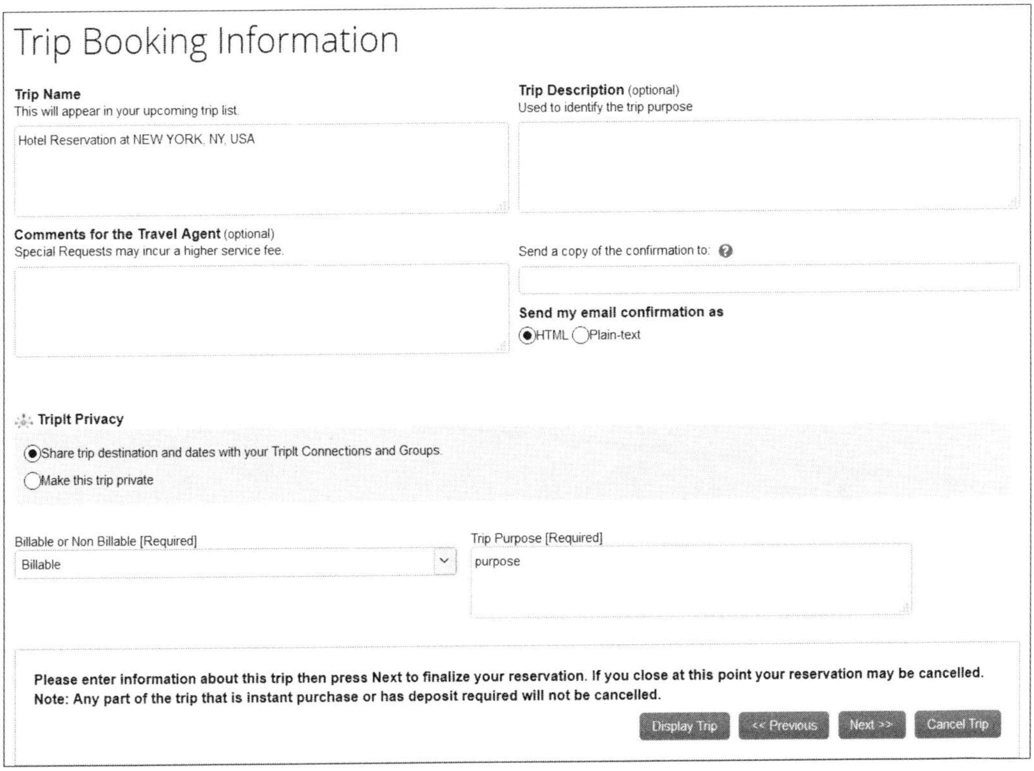

Figure 3.23 Third Confirmation Page for Hotel Bookings

After clicking on Next for the last time, another summary is shown. This is the final summary; up to this point, the hotel reservation isn't final yet. When the employee clicks on Confirm Booking, the purchase request is submitted to the travel agent.

Car Rental

Once the trip details have been entered in the Travel Wizard on the start page and the search started, Concur will present the employee with all available rental cars based on the search parameters. To the left of the screen, the traveler can refine the search and reduce the results shown to the right (see Figure 3.24).

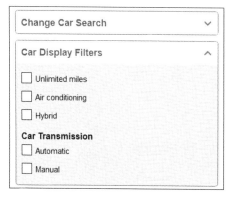

Figure 3.24 Filter Options for Car Rental Search

On the top of the screen, a matrix shows all available car rental agencies and car classes (depending on the configuration and on which car rental agencies and which car classes are allowed; see Figure 3.25).

PICK UP: (LGA) ON THU, JAN 26 12:00 PM
RETURN: FRI, JAN 27 12:00 PM
Show as USD

Hide matrix   Print

All 50 results	Economy Car	Compact Car	Intermediate Car	Standard Car	Full-size Car	Premium Car	Luxury Car	Mini Van	Compact SUV	Intermedia
AVIS Most Preferred	66.50	66.50	67.50	68.50	70.50	79.50	152.00	89.50	--	112.0
enterprise Preferred	65.09	67.00	67.96	69.88	74.66	99.16	76.66	62.88	51.03	53.7
Budget Preferred	62.50	62.50	63.50	65.50	67.50	79.50	174.00	88.50	--	102.0
National Preferred	66.20	67.10	68.00	71.63	72.56	95.19	98.72	95.50	--	72.2

Figure 3.25 Matrix to Filter by Car Type or Rental Agency

The search results show the most important information about a car and the total cost. Clicking on LOCATION DETAILS opens a pop-up with all available details about the rental location.

If a result with a yellow triangle is selected—a result that's out of policy—a pop-up window will open asking for a reason to be selected and an explanation to be entered. Once that information has been provided, the booking process can continue.

The next page shows a summary of the car, some personal information of the traveler, and asks for the frequent traveler program and the payment method (see Figure 3.26).

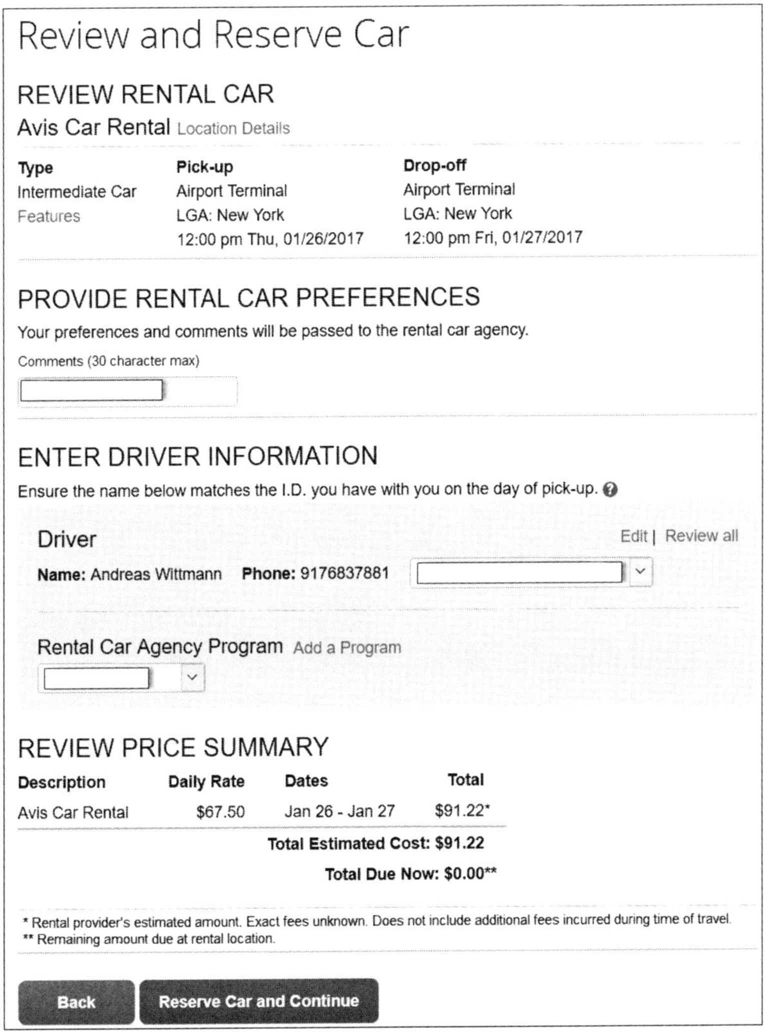

Review and Reserve Car

REVIEW RENTAL CAR
Avis Car Rental Location Details

Type	Pick-up	Drop-off
Intermediate Car	Airport Terminal	Airport Terminal
Features	LGA: New York	LGA: New York
	12:00 pm Thu, 01/26/2017	12:00 pm Fri, 01/27/2017

PROVIDE RENTAL CAR PREFERENCES
Your preferences and comments will be passed to the rental car agency.

Comments (30 character max)

ENTER DRIVER INFORMATION
Ensure the name below matches the I.D. you have with you on the day of pick-up. ❓

Driver   Edit | Review all

Name: Andreas Wittmann   **Phone:** 9176837881

Rental Car Agency Program   Add a Program

REVIEW PRICE SUMMARY

Description	Daily Rate	Dates	Total
Avis Car Rental	$67.50	Jan 26 - Jan 27	$91.22*

Total Estimated Cost: $91.22
Total Due Now: $0.00**

* Rental provider's estimated amount. Exact fees unknown. Does not include additional fees incurred during time of travel.
** Remaining amount due at rental location.

Back | Reserve Car and Continue

Figure 3.26 First Summary Page for Car Rental Search

After all the information has been provided and the traveler has clicked on NEXT, the car will be reserved and the final summary shown (see Figure 3.27).

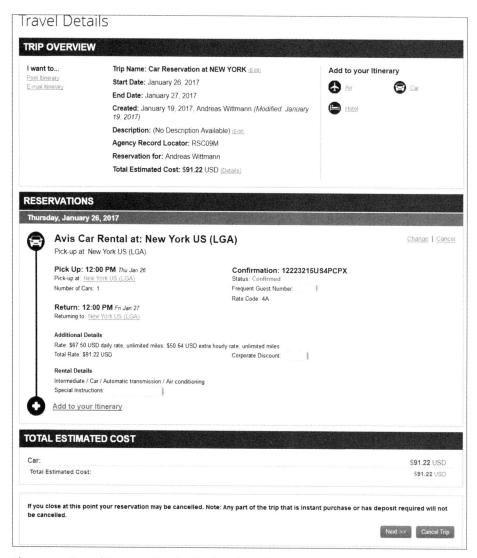

Figure 3.27 Second Summary Page for Car Rental Search

To continue, the employee must click NEXT.

The resulting page allows the traveler to enter a name for the trip, add an additional email address for notifications, and—if required by the company—select a trip purpose (see Figure 3.29).

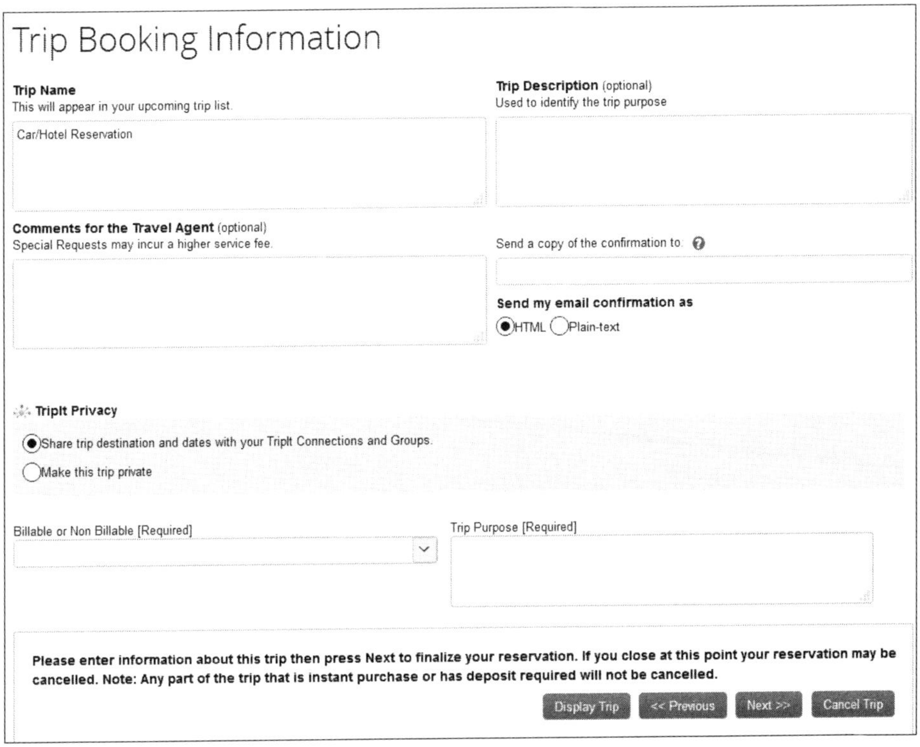

Figure 3.28 Booking Information for a Car Rental Segment

On the following page, the traveler sees the trip confirmation summary. The employee must click on CONFIRM BOOKING (Figure 3.29).

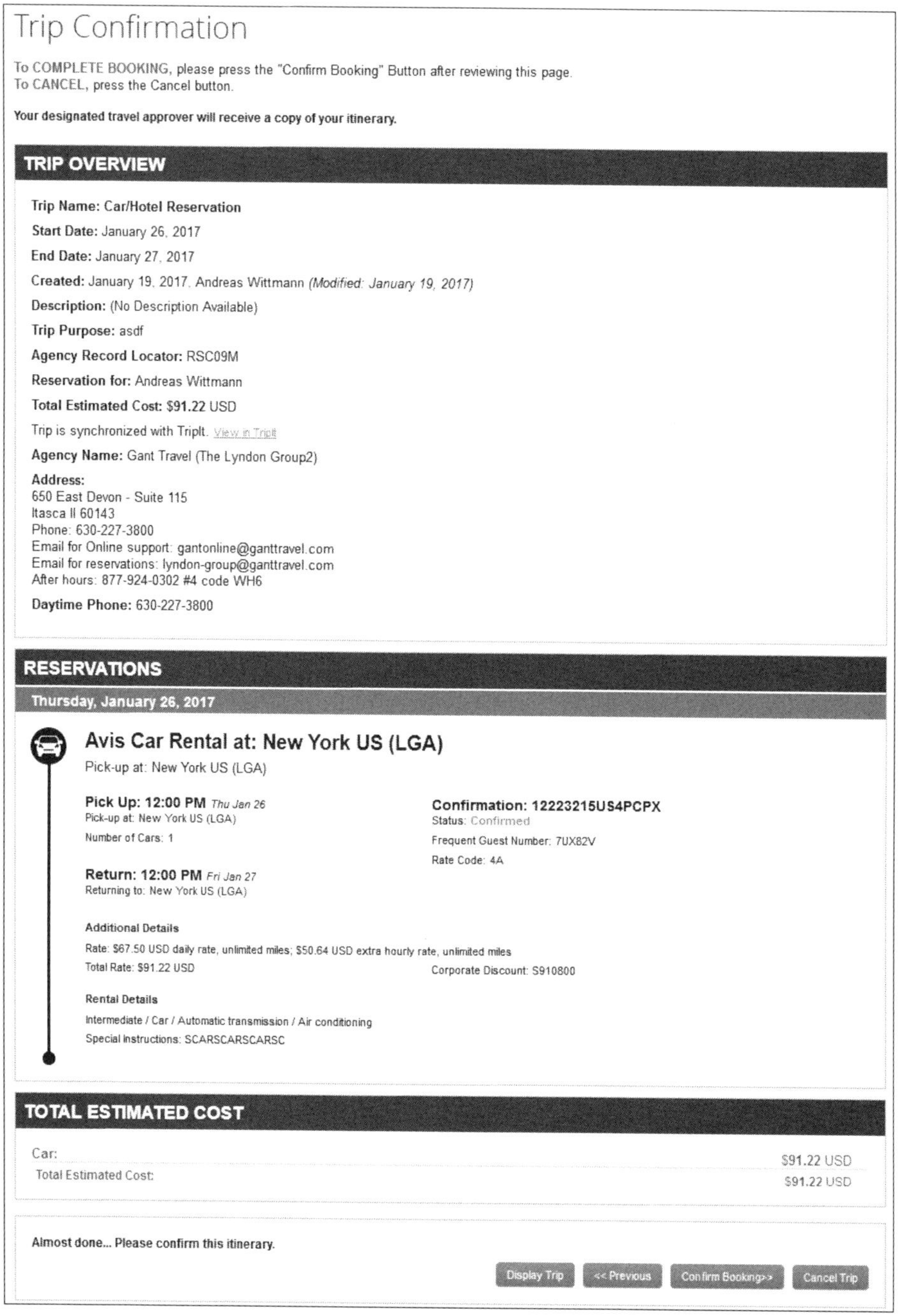

Trip Confirmation

To COMPLETE BOOKING, please press the "Confirm Booking" Button after reviewing this page.
To CANCEL, press the Cancel button.

Your designated travel approver will receive a copy of your itinerary.

TRIP OVERVIEW

Trip Name: Car/Hotel Reservation

Start Date: January 26, 2017

End Date: January 27, 2017

Created: January 19, 2017, Andreas Wittmann *(Modified: January 19, 2017)*

Description: (No Description Available)

Trip Purpose: asdf

Agency Record Locator: RSC09M

Reservation for: Andreas Wittmann

Total Estimated Cost: $91.22 USD

Trip is synchronized with TripIt. View in TripIt

Agency Name: Gant Travel (The Lyndon Group2)

Address:
650 East Devon - Suite 115
Itasca Il 60143
Phone: 630-227-3800
Email for Online support: gantonline@ganttravel.com
Email for reservations: lyndon-group@ganttravel.com
After hours: 877-924-0302 #4 code WH6

Daytime Phone: 630-227-3800

RESERVATIONS

Thursday, January 26, 2017

Avis Car Rental at: New York US (LGA)

Pick-up at: New York US (LGA)

Pick Up: 12:00 PM *Thu Jan 26*
Pick-up at: New York US (LGA)
Number of Cars: 1

Confirmation: 12223215US4PCPX
Status: Confirmed
Frequent Guest Number: 7UX82V
Rate Code: 4A

Return: 12:00 PM *Fri Jan 27*
Returning to: New York US (LGA)

Additional Details
Rate: $67.50 USD daily rate, unlimited miles; $50.64 USD extra hourly rate, unlimited miles
Total Rate: $91.22 USD   Corporate Discount: S910800

Rental Details
Intermediate / Car / Automatic transmission / Air conditioning
Special Instructions: SCARSCARSCARSC

TOTAL ESTIMATED COST

Car:	$91.22 USD
Total Estimated Cost:	$91.22 USD

Almost done... Please confirm this itinerary.

[Display Trip] [<< Previous] [Confirm Booking>>] [Cancel Trip]

Figure 3.29 Third Summary Page for Car Rental Search

After clicking on Next for the last time, another summary is shown. This is the final summary; up to this point, the car reservation isn't final yet. When the employee clicks on Confirm Booking, the purchase request is submitted to the travel agent.

Upcoming Trips: Cancel and Change

In Concur Travel, on the Upcoming Trips tab, an employee will see all booked trips yet to take place and trips from the past that have not been expensed yet. This list also offers a quick way to cancel trips by clicking on Cancel Trip next to the trip that needs to be canceled (see Figure 3.30).

Company Notes	**Upcoming Trips**	Trips Awaiting Approval	Remove Trips	
Trip Name/Description		**Status**	**Start Date**	**End Date**	**Action**
Trip from Orlando to New York (ZRW3CM) *User Group New York*		Ticketed	11/15/2016	11/16/2016	Expense
Car/Hotel Reservation (RSC09M)		Confirmed	01/26/2017	01/27/2017	Cancel Trip
Trip from Orlando to Atlanta for Coca-Cola (JTBTNQ)		Ticketed	02/06/2017	02/10/2017	Cancel Trip	Expense

Figure 3.30 All Upcoming Trips and Trips Not Yet Expensed

Clicking on the trip name shows the details of the trip and allows additional actions to be taken (see Figure 3.31).

Figure 3.31 Options in Trip Details

Although it's simple to cancel or change hotel and rental car bookings, it's usually not possible to do so for flights. Most TMCs require that travelers call an agent to change or cancel flights, even when they're booked in Concur.

3.3 Concur TripLink Integration and Concur TripIt App

Even though travel managers put huge effort into developing the best possible travel program and the best possible vendor discounts for their company, employees can stray away. Travelers also don't always book with preferred suppliers. These actions cause gaps in the data and reporting that travel managers need for their CFOs and reduce negotiating power when trying to get vendors to offer more benefits or higher discounts. Those outside bookings are referred to as *leakage*, and they represent an ever-increasing challenge for today's managed travel programs.

Leakage can have a big impact not one on the success of a corporate travel program but on the bottom line of a company's financials due to the following issues:

- Less tracking of planned to actual spending
- Managing travel budgets becomes more difficult
- Supplier discounts not maximized
- Less negotiating leverage for future agreements
- Duty of care regulations can't be fulfilled

This is where Concur TripLink comes into play. It captures data from flights, hotels, and ground transportation, no matter where travel is booked. It leverages direct supplier connections and email forwarding to enable companies to capture reservations that have been made outside of Concur Travel (or on the phone with a TMC agent). With all those itineraries in Concur, policies can be enforced, reports will show spending, and audit requirements can be fulfilled.

Also, because every itinerary will be in Concur Travel, employees are safe during their business trips; the company is always aware of the employee's location and can use tools such as Concur Messaging to reach out to employees when support is needed. All that is required is for Concur to be provided with your travel program partners/vendors and their company codes.

Employees have multiple options for how to connect a Concur account with Concur TripLink suppliers:

1. They can use My Travel Network, a service offered by Concur and accessible through the Concur App Center or the Concur profile once Concur TripLink is activated by Concur and the employee has agreed to join (in the FREQUENT-TRAVELER PROGRAMS section; see Figure 3.32). This service will automatically connect an employee's Concur account with all suppliers for which the employee entered frequent traveler reward numbers (so long as the suppliers support Concur TripLink).

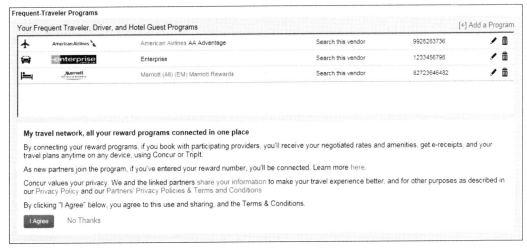

Figure 3.32 *My Travel Network Option in Frequent-Traveler Programs Section of Concur Profile*

2. They can connect to each supplier individually through the Concur App Center (which is also used to connect with suppliers that do not offer reward numbers or used if an employee doesn't want to join the My Travel Network program).

If an employee doesn't want to connect suppliers with Concur but still wants their trips booked outside of Concur to appear in Concur, they can use Concur TripIt, a trip management service by Concur that functions with or without a Concur account. It can be used to organize trips (e.g., leisure trips in which airfare, hotel, and car are booked separately but a traveler wants them summarized in one place) or to stay updated on delays or receive general trip reminders. Any booking from any place can be added to Concur TripIt by forwarding the booking confirmation or reservation confirmation to the email address *plans@tripit.com*. Bookings will be assigned to the Concur TripIt account associated with the email address from which you send the email to Concur TripIt.

If you connect your Concur TripIt account with your Concur account, trips will automatically (or selectively, if you use your Concur TripIt account for leisure trips as well) flow into Concur.

The global Concur TripLink partner list is growing constantly but differs per region (some partners are mainly available in Europe, others in North America, and others in Asia). The up-to-date list can be found at *https://www.concur.com/en-us/triplink-supplier-connections* (scroll to the bottom of the page).

3.4 Basic Configuration for Concur Travel

In the following subsections, we'll look at the basic configuration of Concur Travel. Your TMC and Concur will guide you through the various configuration options, ensuring your setup is tailored to your business needs—but the information presented here will give you additional insight into what's possible.

All configuration items discussed in this section are accessible in Concur through ADMINISTRATION • TRAVEL ADMIN and are either listed on the left side of the screen or found under the various tabs at the top (see Figure 3.33). To access this part of the Concur configuration, you'll need travel administrator permission granted by your TMC or Concur.

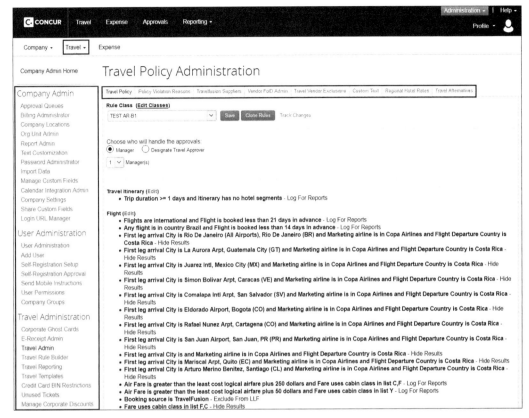

Figure 3.33 Travel Policy Administration Options

3.4.1   Rule Classes

The first step is to set up different rule classes. *Rule classes* are different sets of configurations/rules based on an employee's level (grade) within the company or based on the business unit an employee belongs to.

Common RULE CLASS options include GENERAL POPULATION (or DEFAULT) and EXECUTIVES (or VIP); we often see these two rule classes set up once per country in which Concur Travel is used. Figure 3.34 shows two classes being set up for a client in Canada, using Merit Travel as the TMC; one class (MERIT DEFAULT CLASS) is the class for the general population, while the other (VIP) is used for executives.

Figure 3.34 Example of Two Travel Rule Classes for Client in Canada

Other examples for when to use multiple rule classes include the following:

► A company acquires another company, and the latter needs to be integrated with its existing policy—for example, during a transition period before the new employees become a full part of the new company.

► A merging of different configurations or Concur Travel sites is eventually be followed by a full-blown integration into one rule class.

► Multiple TMCs are merged into one.

► Different rules are used for administrative personnel and other business units, such as the sales department.

► Different rules apply for corporate (nonbillable) travel and travel billable to clients.

► Different rule classes are used for general population, directors, executives, or different employee grades (e.g., A–F/1–15).

Rule classes are usually set up separately for each country, due to the following:

► Different rule sets per country (based on differing local T&E policies)

► Different currencies in which travel is to be booked

► Different TMCs

► Different GDSs (Galileo, Sabre, Amadeus, etc.)

3.4.2   Travel Rules

Each rule class contains multiple sections in which rules are set up (see Figure 3.35), as follows:

▶ Travel Itineraries

▶ Flight

▶ Flight—Class of Service

▶ Flight—Flex Fare Bucket

▶ Ticket Change

▶ Train

▶ Car

▶ Hotel

▶ Web Air

▶ Concur TripLink

▶ Messages (for all search criteria and results)

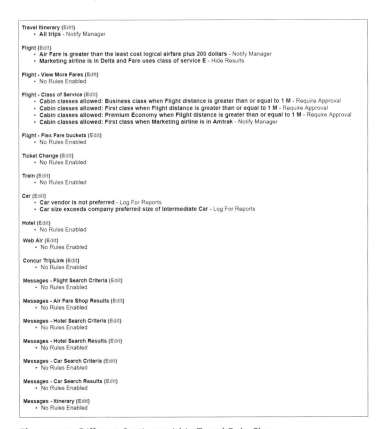

Figure 3.35 Different Sections within Travel Rule Class

Concur Travel comes with predefined rules that cover most customers' require-ments. Each section contains various rules that can be activated/modified/deacti-vated as needed (see Figure 3.36).

Figure 3.36 Examples of Travel Rules in Flight Section

Whenever a rule is triggered (e.g., an employee is searching for a business flight, but an established rule doesn't allow business flights), the search results will appear with a yellow triangle highlighting the fact that an explanation is required or a manager will be notified.

Rules can also be set up to automatically hide results, which is often used to hide hotel rooms that require prepayment or a deposit.

Should the rules provided not be sufficient, Concur or the TMC can configure specific, custom rules via the Travel Rule Builder, in which existing rules can be changed or new rules created. It works much like audit rules on the Concur Expense side (see Figure 3.37).

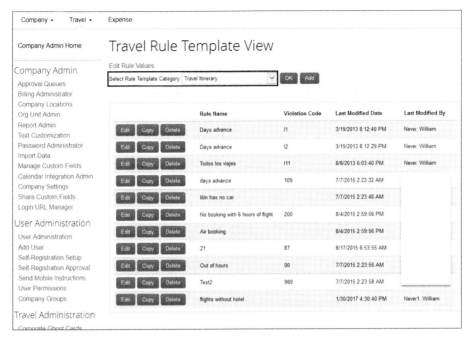

Figure 3.37 Travel Rule Builder in Concur Travel

3.4.3 Custom Text

The Concur start page can be designed to show any information you decide your employees should have at hand once they log into Concur. It usually shows the contact details of the travel agency, links to company internal documents such as the T&E policy of preferred airlines/hotels/rental car agencies, and potentially links to other T&E-related intranet pages (see Figure 3.38). The start page can contain different information for each country and language.

Every custom text within Concur Travel can be customized to show exactly the verbiage a company needs employees to see. The most common places we see clients adding custom texts are as follows:

- ITINERARY TEXT
- ITINERARY CONFIRMATION
- AIR SCHEDULE
- AIR FARES
- CAR SEARCH

- ▶ C Λ R R ESULTS
- ▶ H OTEL S EARCH
- ▶ H OTEL R ESULTS
- ▶ T RAIN S EARCH
- ▶ T RAIN S CHEDULE

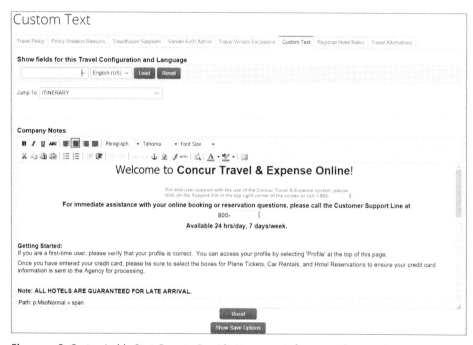

Figure 3.38 Customizable Start Page to Provide Necessary Information for Travelers

3.4.4 Languages

Concur Travel (and Concur Expense) are available out of the box in 12 different languages. All out-of-the-box fields and verbiage are automatically translated into the supported languages by Concur. As soon as an employee changes to one of the supported languages (on the Concur login page or in the system settings within his or her profile), all standard fields and verbiage will appear accordingly.

For custom verbiage to appear in a selected language as well, a client must translate it. Custom verbiage includes everything that was created or renamed based on a client's requirements.

3.4.5   E-Receipts

Concur offers clients the possibility of using e-receipts to automatically collect electronic receipts and folio data from vendors that support it. This functionality automatically prepopulates employees' expenses with the associated travel/trip data provided by Concur Travel, as well as data from airlines, hotel chains, and car rental agencies.

This functionality can be turned on via TRAVEL ADMIN • E-RECEIPT ADMIN, by configuration or country (depending on your setup). You can also choose whether air tickets booked in Concur Travel should appear as e-receipts in an employee's expense inbox (see Figure 3.39).

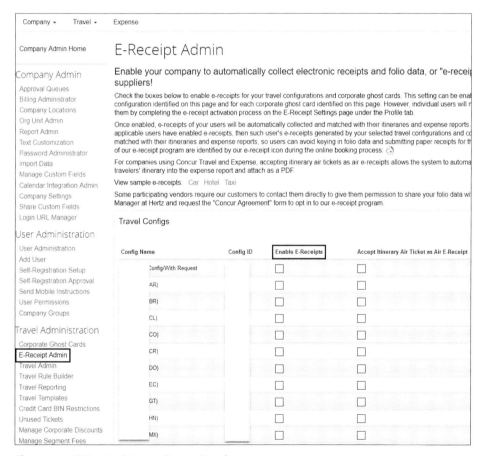

Figure 3.39 E-Receipt Setup in Concur Travel

3.4.6 Travel Vendor Exclusions

Like with everything else, there are both good travel vendors—and those that have a bad track record as far as safety, service, or value goes. Concur allows you to define which air carriers, hotel chains, and car vendors you want to exclude from ever appearing in the search results (see Figure 3.40). This is as simple as going to the TRAVEL VENDOR EXCLUSIONS tab, selecting the ones you don't want, and clicking on SAVE. This setting can also be defined separately for each configuration.

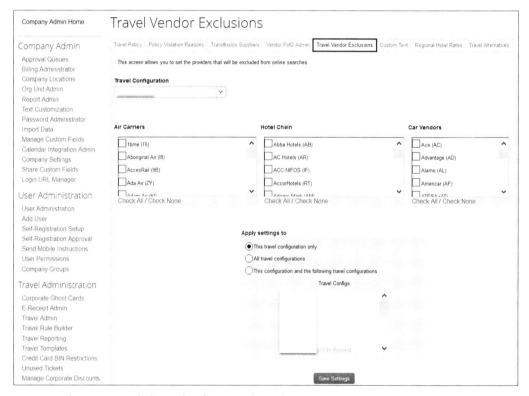

Figure 3.40 Exclude Vendors from Search Results in Concur

3.4.7 Regional Hotel Rates

Concur offers the option to define limits on hotel rates by region. Regions can be defined as a certain radius from an address (e.g., a two-mile radius from Times Square in New York), a state or province (e.g., Florida), a country, or global (see Figure 3.41).

Figure 3.41 Regional Hotel Rates in Concur

3.4.8 Travel Alternatives

In our modern age, some business trips can be replaced by tele- or videoconferences. In Concur, when an employee is looking to book a one-day trip, a pop-up can open to ask for information about the meeting the trip is for. Based on what the employee enters (e.g., how long the actual meeting with the client will take), the system can show the cost to use a tele- or videoconference instead (see Figure 3.42).

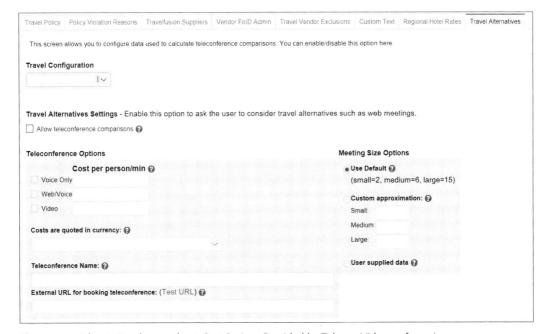

Figure 3.42 Educate Employees about Cost Savings Provided by Tele- or Videoconferencing

3.4.9 Ghost/BTA Cards

Instead of having employees charge their travel bookings to their individual corporate credit cards (or personal credit cards), companies can set up a *business travel account* (BTA) *card*, also called a *ghost card* (cards that in the financial world are commonly known as purchasing cards, or *P-cards*). These cards can be assigned to all employees, specific business units within the company, or specific, custom groups of employees. It is also possible to have multiple BTA/ghost cards within a company.

The use of said cards can be mandatory (all bookings must go through those cards) or selective (employees can choose to book using one of those cards or to use one of the cards in their Concur Travel profiles). You can also define for what type of bookings the card will be used and whether it will be the mandated form of payment or optional (see Figure 3.43).

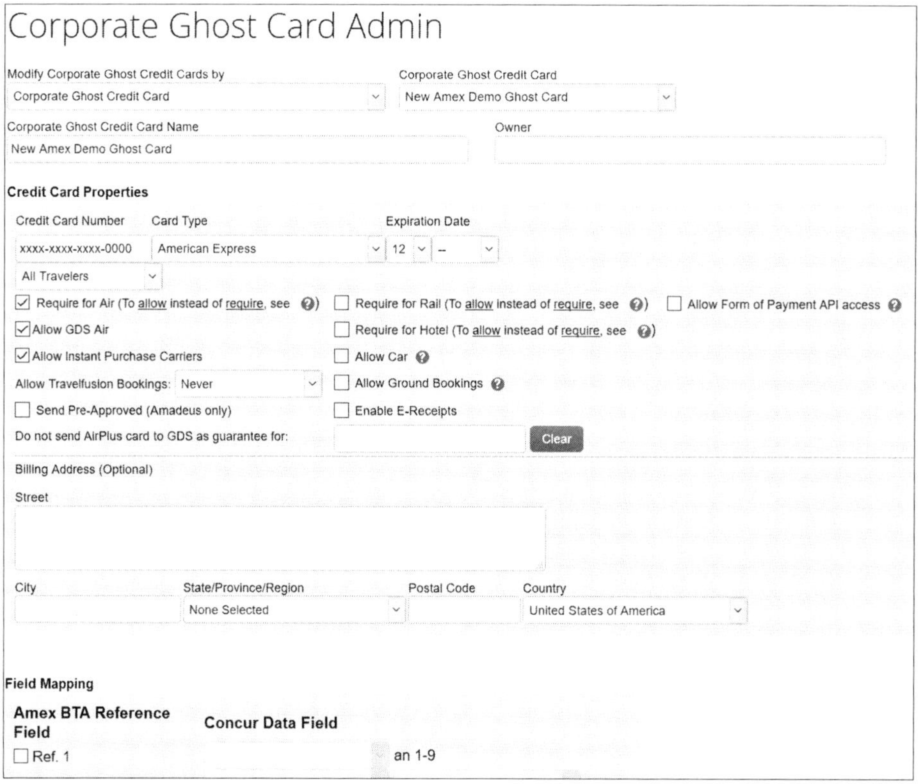

Figure 3.43 Ghost/BTA Cards Can Be Set as Payment Method

3.4.10 Credit Card BIN Restrictions

To ensure that employees can add only their corporate credit cards to their Concur Profile as a payment method and not their personal credit cards, you can set up BIN restriction via TRAVEL ADMIN • CREDIT CARD BIN RESTRICTIONS (see Figure 3.44). To do so, add the first four or five digits of your company's corporate card program (those digits are the same for all cards issued in your company's corporate card program).

Figure 3.44 Credit Cards Can Be Limited to Specific Range of Numbers

3.4.11 Reporting Requirements

Although most Concur clients will deploy Concur Travel alongside Concur Expense and use reporting mainly based on the data gathered during the expense entry and reimbursement process, Concur Travel also provides powerful data for travel management. It can be accessed through Concur Travel-specific reports or through Concur Intelligence, depending on the package bought by the client.

We commonly see clients set up custom fields in Concur Travel to capture data during the booking process rather than waiting until the data is available in Concur Expense. Custom fields can be automatically populated with data from the employee import (e.g., profile fields), including the following:

- PERSONNEL ID
- COST CENTER
- BUSINESS UNIT
- LEGAL ENTITY

Often, companies also require employees to allocate a trip to different cost centers, business units, or legal entities or declare the purpose of a trip. Some possible values for the TRIP PURPOSE dropdown menu include the following:

- INTERNAL MEETING
- EXTERNAL MEETING (CUSTOMER/SUPPLIER)
- COMPANY SPONSORED EVENT/TRADE SHOW
- EXTERNAL CONFERENCE/CONVENTION/TRADE SHOW
- RELOCATION/RECRUITING/SHORT TERM ASSIGNMENT

Finally, whenever one of the rules set up in the system is triggered (e.g., an employee booking a different booking class than expected), the system will store the corresponding reason code, making it also available for reporting (see Table 3.1).

Reason	Booking Type
STAYING WITH FAMILY OR FRIENDS	I—Itinerary
CONFERENCE/CONVENTION/MEETING/TRADE SHOW	I—Itinerary
TRAVELING WITH A CUSTOMER OR SUPPLIER	I—Itinerary
LLA DECLINED-TRAVELING WITH CLIENT/SNR MANAGEMENT	A—Air
LLA DECLINED-DUE TO SCHEDULE	A—Air
LLA DECLINED-PERSONAL PREFERENCE	A—Air
HIGHER CLASS OF SERVICE APPROVED	A—Air
TRAVELING WITH A CUSTOMER OR CLIENT	H—Hotel
NO COMPANY HOTELS NEAR DESTINATION	H—Hotel

Table 3.1 Reason Codes

Reason	Booking Type
COMPANY PREFERRED HOTELS SOLD OUT	H—Hotel
PREFERRED HOTEL BOOKED-WITHIN POLICY	H—Hotel
CONFERENCE/CONVENTION/MEETING/TRADE SHOW	H—Hotel

Table 3.1 Reason Codes (Cont.)

3.4.12 Your T&E Policy

Any business has rules and regulations in place that define what guidelines are in place for booking travel—usually found in a *travel and expense policy* (occasionally also called a *travel and entertainment policy*). Items related to travel booking that are commonly included in such policies will be discussed in the following subsections.

Lowest Logical Fare

In the various subsections of a rule class, click on EDIT next to FLIGHT (see Figure 3.45), to define the rules for lowest logical fare (LLF).

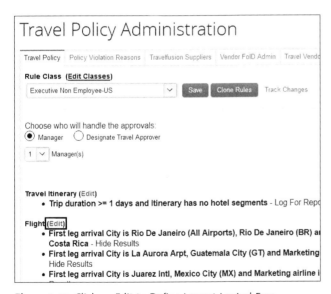

Figure 3.45 Click on Edit to Define Lowest Logical Fare

This defines (per the travel rule class) how the lowest logical airfare is to be calculated. The LLF can then be used to set limits (e.g., employees are not allowed to book flights that are over $100 more expensive than the LLF).

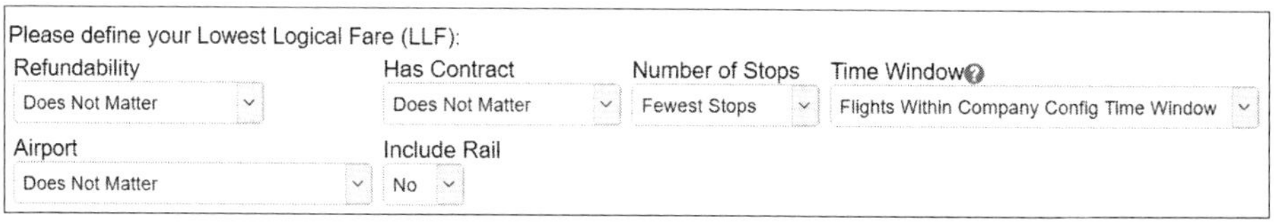

Figure 3.46 Definition of Lowest Logical Fare in Concur

Classes of Flight Allowed/Disallowed

Concur Travel is highly customizable in regards to rules (see Section 3.4.2), which is convenient, considering that T&E policies can come in many variations. One item almost all policies contain, though, is a definition of when an employee can book specific classes on or tickets for a flight.

The most defining factor used to determine which class of travel is allowed is time—for example:

- Coach if less than four hours overall flight duration (excludes layovers)
- Premium economy if more than four hours but less than eight hours
- Business class if more than eight hours overall flight duration (excludes layovers)

Distance is also often used—for example:

- Coach if less three thousand miles
- Business class if more than three thousand miles

Region is used as a factor often as well—for example:

- Always coach if domestic
- Business class allowed if international
- Business class if interregional and more than an eight-hour actual flight time (in this case, an example combining region and time)

How far in advance travel should be booked can also be defined:

▸ Fourteen days for domestic travel or travel within a region

▸ Twenty-one days for international travel outside of region (or international travel altogether in a single-country configuration)

You can also set whether employees are allowed to buy refundable tickets:

▸ Do not allow or allow, based on policy

▸ Can be turned off as a search option in Concur altogether

Many of these examples are already predefined in Concur and simply have to be activated, and others can be configured by the TMC, Concur, or yourself in the RULE BUILDER (see Section 3.4.2).

Type/Class of Hotels Allowed

Rules for hotels are generally set based on price and on company preference (preferred vendors are covered in the next section).

Price limits are simple to set in Concur; the rules are preset in Concur and can simply be activated (and a price set). When using price limits, differences between high-cost cities and non-high-cost cities should always be considered. To do so, one can either make use of the regional rates (see Section 3.4.7) or set up one travel rule that applies to a list of cities (e.g., New York, Chicago, San Francisco, Boston, Paris, London, Zurich, etc.) and another rule that applies to all other places. Having one rule or limit globally is not recommended.

Companies typically guide their employees towards using hotel properties or hotel chains with which they have contracts. The smaller a company is, the more likely it is that they only have contracts with individual hotel properties, whereas bigger companies with higher travel spending have contracts with hotel chains or even super chains (e.g., all Hilton brands, all Starwood brands, or all IHG brands). Either way, the golden rule is to have as few preferred properties per location as possible. Although it's convenient for employees to be able to select from as many hotels as possible, the goal should always be to spread spending as narrowly as possible (as with airlines and rental cars).

Another, less frequently used option is to set limits based on a hotel's star rating. Concur uses Northstar Travel's rating system, which defines the classes as shown in Figure 3.47.

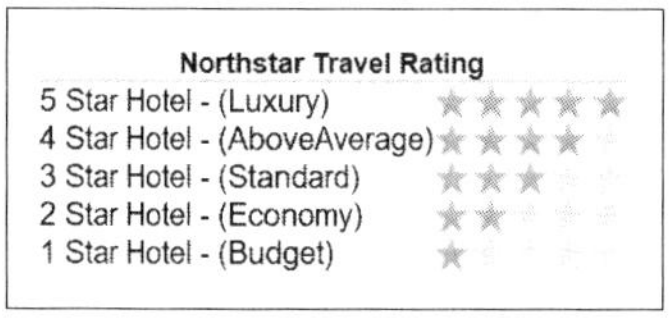

Figure 3.47 Northstar Travel Ratings

3.4.13 Managing Preferred Vendors in Concur

Concur Travel gives clients the ability to configure their preferred vendors such that they clearly stand out to employees during the booking process. It also allows for a company's discount codes with a vendor to be set up so that the employee sees the reduced prices (or additional amenities) negotiated with the vendor.

The preferred vendors in Concur can be configured by airline (see Figure 3.48), hotel (see Figure 3.49), hotel consortium, rental car agency, or railway (see Figure 3.50).

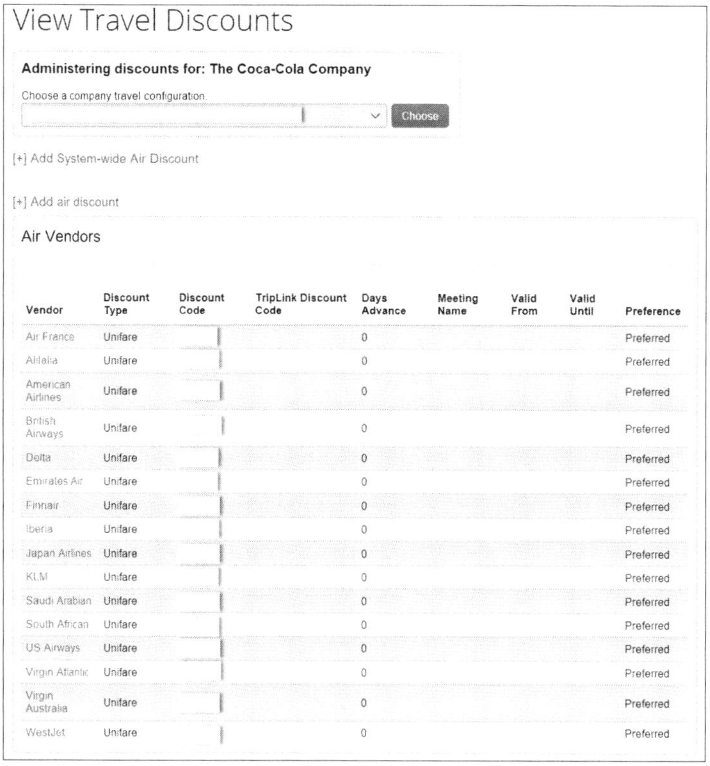
View Travel Discounts

Administering discounts for: The Coca-Cola Company

Choose a company travel configuration

Choose

[+] Add System-wide Air Discount

[+] Add air discount

Air Vendors

Vendor	Discount Type	Discount Code	TripLink Discount Code	Days Advance	Meeting Name	Valid From	Valid Until	Preference
Air France	Unifare			0				Preferred
Alitalia	Unifare			0				Preferred
American Airlines	Unifare			0				Preferred
British Airways	Unifare			0				Preferred
Delta	Unifare			0				Preferred
Emirates Air	Unifare			0				Preferred
Finnair	Unifare			0				Preferred
Iberia	Unifare			0				Preferred
Japan Airlines	Unifare			0				Preferred
KLM	Unifare			0				Preferred
Saudi Arabian	Unifare			0				Preferred
South African	Unifare			0				Preferred
US Airways	Unifare			0				Preferred
Virgin Atlantic	Unifare			0				Preferred
Virgin Australia	Unifare			0				Preferred
WestJet	Unifare			0				Preferred

Figure 3.48 Preferred Airfare Vendors

[+] Add property-specific hotel discount   Import Properties

Hotel Properties

Records 1 - 1000 of 2045 Records   Next >> 1000   All

Vendor	Hotel Reference Name	Discount Code	CD Number	Property ID	Contract Rate	Preference
AC Hotels	AC Hotel Madrid Feria			ARMADFER	95.00	
AC Hotels	AC Hotel Oviedo Forum			AROVDFOR	66.00	
AccorHotels	Novotel Abidjan			RTABJNOV	105,000.00	Most Preferred
AccorHotels	Mercure Brisbane			RTBNEGAT	210.00	Most Preferred
AccorHotels	Mercure Brisbane King George Square			RTBNEMRC	200.00	Most Preferred
AccorHotels	The Sebel Suites Brisbane			RTBNESEB	180.00	Most Preferred
AccorHotels	Adagio Brussels Centre Monnaie			RTBRUABA	102.00	Most Preferred
AccorHotels	Mercure Brasilia Eixo			RTBSBMIL	333.00	Most Preferred
AccorHotels	Mercure Budapest Korona			RTBUDCOR	75.00	Most Preferred
AccorHotels	Novotel Kolkata Hotel and Residences			RTCCUNOV	6,000.00	Most Preferred
AccorHotels	Ibis Gurgaon			RTDELIBI	3,500.00	Most Preferred
AccorHotels	Mercure Fortaleza Meireles			RTFORMEI	269.00	Most Preferred
AccorHotels	Mercure Goiania Hotel			RTGYNMER	213.00	Most Preferred
AccorHotels	Novotel Hildesheim			RTHAJHIL	94.97	Most Preferred
AccorHotels	Caesar Business Manaus Amazonas			RTMAOCBM	238.00	Most Preferred

Figure 3.49 Most Preferred Hotel Vendors

Preferred vendors are usually loaded by the TMC or Concur based on contracts provided by the client, but they can also be manually added (or maintained) by the client itself. Vendors can be defined as MOST PREFERRED, PREFERRED, LESS PREFERRED, or NOT PREFERRED.

The different preference levels can be used in travel rules or simply used to signal to an employee which vendors to choose if multiple options are available.

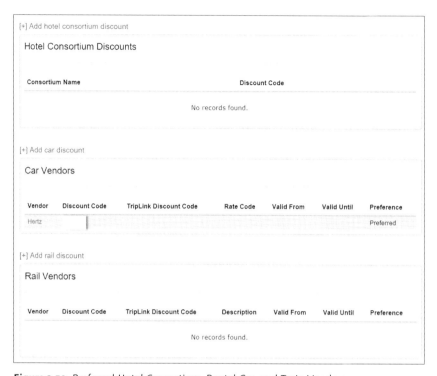

Figure 3.50 Preferred Hotel Consortium, Rental Car, and Train Vendors

3.5 Advanced Configuration Options for Concur Travel

Additional options in the Concur Travel setup can be configured by Concur or your TMC. The following are some of the more useful ones and short descriptions of their impact:

▸ **Airfare**

   ▸ DOMESTIC DEFAULT SEARCH WINDOW
   Defines +/- hours (from what the employee enters) within which flights are presented as results for domestic flights (we recommend a two-hour window).

   ▸ INTERNATIONAL (INTERREGIONAL) DEFAULT SEARCH WINDOW
   Defines +/- hours (from what the employee enters) within which flights are presented as results for international flights (we recommend an eight-hour window).

- HIDE MULTI-SEGMENT
  Concur offers the option to allow employees to book multisegment flights. Some companies prefer employees to do this on the phone with an agent due to the potential of employees spending too much (work) time on this process (we recommend multisegment options to be shown, but employees told during training that they should only use it for domestic routes and to book more complicated international flights through an agent).

- DEFAULT SEARCH TYPE (SCHEDULE OR FARES)
  Indicates whether the flight search results are initially sorted by PRICE or by SCHEDULE (we usually see PRICE as the chosen option).

- VIEW MORE AIRFARES
  Once enabled, this option allows an employee to not only see the fare that Concur originally presents (e.g., basic economy) but also additional available fares (economy, premium economy, business, etc.; we recommend turning this on).

- SHOW REFUNDABLE TICKET CHECKBOX
  Indicates whether Concur shows a checkbox in the search box for flights that allows employees to limit searches to refundable tickets only (we strongly recommend not showing this checkbox).

▶ **Direct connects**

- AIR CANADA
  This direct connect tool occasionally has issues but is generally worth exploring; it provides the full fare catalogue of Air Canada. The fares Air Canada lists in the GDS are not comprehensive.

- SOUTHWEST
  Best option to book Southwest and definitely a must for US clients that often utilize Southwest.

- ALLOW EARLY-BIRD CHECK-IN
  Allows employees to add the early-bird check-in option with Southwest during the actual booking process in Concur.

▶ **Hotel**

- DEFAULT SEARCH RADIUS
  Determines how wide the default search radius should be from the address or airport that an employee entered/selected as a starting point (we recommend five miles).

- ▷ RADIUS FOR PREFERRED HOTELS
  Determines how wide the default search radius for company-preferred hotels should be from the address or airport that an employee entered/selected as starting point (we recommend twenty miles).

- ▷ RADIUS FOR COMPANY LOCATIONS
  Determines how wide the default search radius should be if an employee selects a company location as starting point (we recommend thirty miles).

- ▷ NUMBER OF HOTEL RESULTS TO SHOP
  Determines how many hotels should be listed in the search results with room rates displayed; all other results will only show with a GET RATE button, which the employee must click on for Concur to look up the rate.

- ▷ ALLOW RATES THAT REQUIRE A DEPOSIT
  This is a very important setting—which we recommend you do not activate. Business travel is too dynamic and undergoes too many changes for this option be financially viable.

- ▷ ALLOW RATES THAT ARE NONREFUNDABLE
  This is a very important setting—which we again recommend you do not activate. Business travel is too dynamic and undergoes too many changes for this option be financially viable.

- ▶ **Car rental** (these items are self-explanatory and will be discussed with you by Concur or the TMC during the implementation process):

  - ▷ ALLOWABLE CAR TYPES

  - ▷ DEFAULT CAR TYPE

  - ▷ VENDORS TO DISPLAY

- ▶ **Direct connect options for trains:**

  - ▷ Amtrak Direct connect

  - ▷ Deutsche Bahn

  - ▷ SNCF

  - ▷ UK Rail (Evolvi)

  - ▷ UK Rail (Trainline)

  - ▷ VIA Rail

- **Direct connect options for other travel-related vendors:**
  - Limos.com
  - Groundspan
  - GroundScope
  - Park 'N Fly
  - Gogo Wi-Fi icon activation

3.6   Summary

In this chapter, we looked at the business principles behind Concur Travel, discussed how an employee can book various trip segments, and talked about Concur TripLink/Concur TripIt. We also covered the basic configuration options, from rules classes and travel rules to reporting requirements and preferred vendor. We also took a quick look at some advanced configuration options available to Concur customers.

In the next chapter, we'll talk about Concur Expense with information on its basic and advanced configuration options as well as some country-specific information.

Concur Expense provides an end-to-end solution for claiming expenses, from the point at which the expense was incurred through to reimbursement. In this chapter, we cover the expense process within Concur and basic and advanced configuration options to optimize Concur.

4 Concur Expense

In the previous chapter, you learned how to book travel through Concur. Now, we'll walk through how travel and associated expenses are claimed, processed, and reimbursed to employees via Concur Expense.

We'll start by looking at the business principles that should apply to an expense process. Then, we'll walk through the specifics of the Concur expense process—from the initial expense captures and entry by travelers and employees, through approval and authorization process steps, to the payment options Concur offers for employee reimbursement. To support this process, we'll then cover the basic configuration required in Concur before taking a more in-depth look at the advanced configuration options that Concur offers, including ensuring that your Concur configuration is mapped as closely as possible to your company's expense policy. We'll then look at the Concur Expense Pay Global solution for employee reimbursement. Finally, we'll examine some of the country-specific requirements across various countries' tax authorities and how these requirements are supported and achieved using configuration options in Concur.

4.1 Business Principles

A good expense policy should document the full expense process in place within your company, from initial expense incursion through to employee reimbursement payments. Each step within the process flow should be clearly documented for employees claiming expenses, administrators supporting and processing the expenses, and audit and regulatory services, which need a clear understanding of the safeguards and audit procedures built into your expense process.

An expense policy should have a clear definition of *what* constitutes an expense, in *what* circumstances an expense can be incurred, and by *whom*. As a general rule, expenses should be incurred by direct employees of your company while carrying out their duties to the organization. You should also think about other types of employees or applicants and whether they can claim expenses directly from your organization, such as expenses for interview attendees if your company reimburses the cost of attending an interview. As for what can be considered as an allowable expense under your policy, this should include the details that are specific to your company; you can also take guidance from any regulatory information for your company's industry, as well as from legislative guidance in your respective country.

Once the details of what can be claimed are established, an expense process should then cover the functional process of *how* the expenses are claimed. This process flow should provide process steps for how expenses are captured and submitted by employees, the approval and authorization steps and processes that govern expenses, and payment and/or reimbursement steps.

A key task of your expense policy will be to define the methods of payment that your company will employ and how these might apply to employees claiming expenses. Different methods of payment can be considered, including expense payment via employee reimbursement through options such as your Accounts Payable processes or through payroll, corporate card programs with payments made either by employees or the company, or a combination of some or all of these elements. For each payment method, it's useful to document the payment frequency expected and any relevant deadlines; for example, if your employees are reimbursed via payroll, the processing deadlines for expense submission for each payroll frequency should be duly noted to enable employees to process and submit their expenses on time for payment. Clearly stating deadlines can be effective in helping to manage the payment processes, especially in the case of short turnarounds, such as for weekly or fortnightly reimbursements.

The overall expense process will need to be considered in terms of the compliances that it will need to adhere to and achieve, ranging from legislative and tax requirements to fraud detection and protection to industry standards and regulations. Building more automation into your expense solution to support these compliances will promote compliancy and consistency in expense claims. Building compliances and regulations directly into your expense solution will mean that your company can be safe in the knowledge that the expenses being claimed are within company policy and legislative, industry, and tax standards and regulations. Your employees will benefit from time efficiencies by being able to enter their expenses correctly the first time. Being mobile and active will enable employees to capture their expenses on the go, leading to timesavings for both the employee and your company. Having a modern and efficient expense process will also increase your attractiveness as an employer, by no means an insignificant benefit. Note that employees are used to using their smartphones and apps in their daily life for all kinds of tasks, so they expect the same options for tools that they use for their work tasks.

Finally, in addition to everything else, your expense policy needs to be implemented in a manner that is easy and efficient for your travelers and employees to understand, use, and adhere to. Having an overcomplicated or onerous expense process will produce negative effects, such as causing confusion and errors, producing difficulties in demonstrating policy compliance, and increasing employee dissatisfaction due to a complex, archaic process.

4.2 Using Concur Expense to Settle Expenses

The expense process in Concur follows a standard process flow that we'll discuss in greater detail in this section. The expense process starts with an employee entering business expenses, progresses through different stages of approvals and authorization and through the payment of the reimbursed expenses to the employee, and ends with settling the amounts in the accounting system (see Figure 4.1).

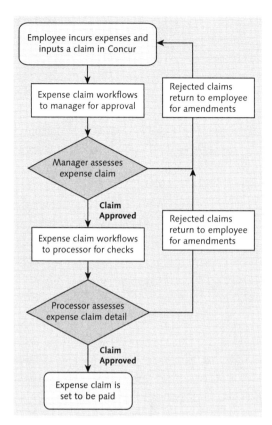

Figure 4.1 Typical Expense Workflow

The process begins with an employee incurring a business expense of some kind. This could be complex, like a business trip with expenses for hotels stays, meals, airfare, and train tickets, or simple, like a single expense item, such mileage incurred traveling to a remote business site. The employee's first step for reimbursement is to create an *expense claim* for all incurred expenses (see Figure 4.2).

From the Concur Expense home page, a user can create a new claim via the CREATE NEW CLAIM button shown in Figure 4.2. The CLAIM HEADER screen will open; this screen can be customized to capture the information relevant to your company, including the addition of further custom fields. Figure 4.3 shows the standard CLAIM HEADER screen, with REPORT NAME, REPORT DATE, and COMMENT fields.

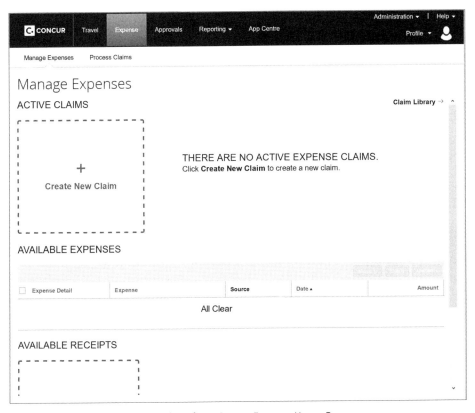

Figure 4.2 Create New Expense Claim from Concur Expense Home Page

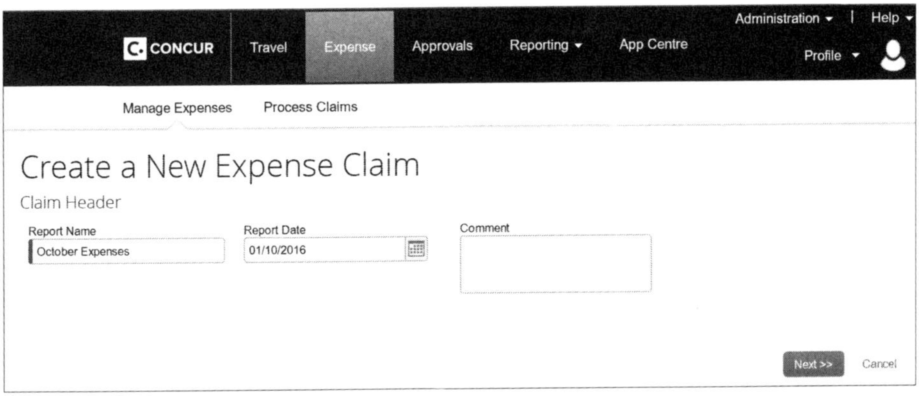

Figure 4.3 New Claim Header Screen

Expenses can then be added to the expense claim via several methods of capture, such as input using the Concur desktop, mobile apps, and integrated services offering options to make the expense capture process as efficient as possible for travelers.

Expenses can be created directly in the claim using the Concur web login, as shown in Figure 4.4. Each expense type has an input form configuration, defining the fields that a user must complete for that expense type. Figure 4.4 shows an expense type for which several fields have been defined as mandatory for input; once completed, the user can save the expense entry using the SAVE button. The user can also access the itemize feature, if configured for an expense type, via the SAVE & ITEMIZE button.

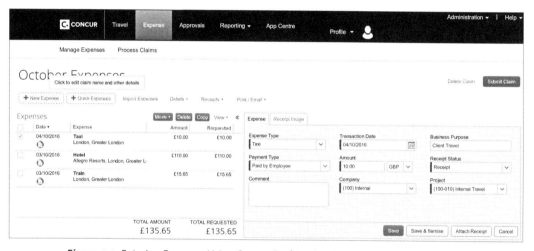

Figure 4.4 Entering Expenses Using Concur Desktop Login

Expenses may require receipts to substantiate the expense incurred. To attach a receipt to an expense item, click on the ATTACH RECEIPT button on the expense entry screen. Receipt images from the receipt store on the expense home page, as seen in Figure 4.5, can then be attached to expense entries.

The Concur receipt store seen in Figure 4.5 on the Concur home page under AVAILABLE RECEIPTS collects receipt images for the user. The images can be uploaded directly, emailed into Concur, or captured using the Concur mobile app. The receipt image then can be attached to an expense entry.

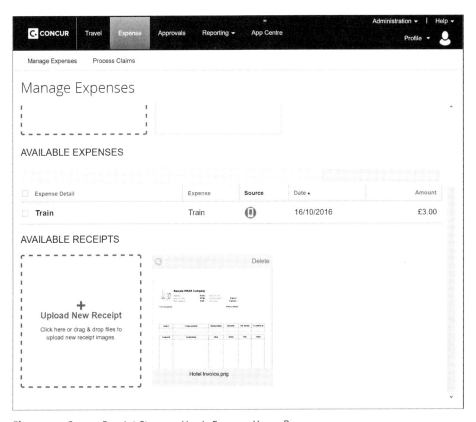

Figure 4.5 Concur Receipt Store on User's Expense Home Page

Users will also see AVAILABLE EXPENSES on the expense home page; these are expenses either fed into Concur from card feeds (see Section 4.3.11 for further information on company card transactions) or created by the user from the Concur app but not yet associated with an expense claim. The user can add these to an expense claim from the expense home page with the MOVE button. These expenses can also be imported into a specific claim from the claim's screen using the IMPORT EXPENSES LINK button, as shown in Figure 4.6.

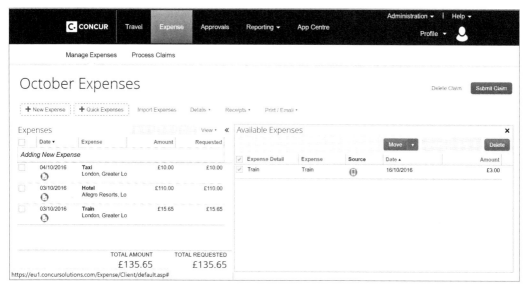

Figure 4.6 Importing Available Expenses into Claim

Once all the required expenses have been added to the claim and details completed, the claim is then submitted by the employee to her *approving manager* using the SUBMIT CLAIM button. Depending on the receipt policy configured, the claim submission process may include a receipt reminder for the user or a missing receipt declaration if a user is missing any expense receipts, depending on the receipt configurations in your expense policy.

Once submitted for approval, the claim status will update on the user's expense home page to a SUBMITTED status (see Figure 4.7), with the name of the approving manager assigned to the claim shown. The claim status updates for each processing step, as shown in Figure 4.7, to keep the user informed of the expense claim's progress through the approval workflow.

The approving manager can be alerted that there is an expense claim awaiting approval if email notifications have been activated; she will also be informed of a claim awaiting approval on her Concur home page, where it will be shown as a task requiring action, as in Figure 4.8.

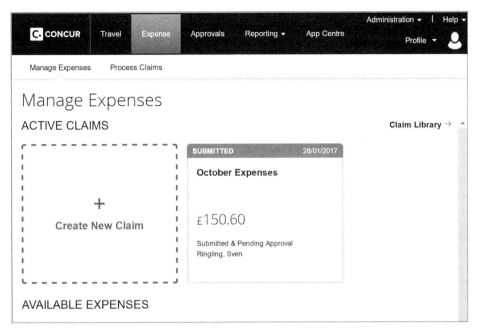

Figure 4.7 Claim Status Updates to Keep User Informed

Figure 4.8 Task Tiles on Concur Home Page for Approval Actions Required

An approving manager can be directly assigned to the employee user record in Concur, or a more detailed organizational structure can be replicated in Concur from your HR system by using the *list management* configurations. The approving manager can check the expense claim entries; any policy violations are clearly highlighted for the manager to review. He must then either approve the claim for payment or reject the expense claim, returning it to the employee for amendment. The approvals view for expense types is a separately configurable form;

additional fields can be configured for approver only view. The approval view, shown in Figure 4.9, may include uneditable fields or require additional inputs.

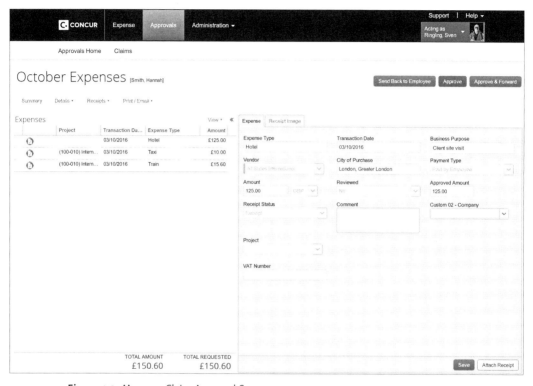

Figure 4.9 Manager Claim Approval Screen

The approving manager has three choices to take action on the claim, activated by clicking on one of three buttons:

▶ SEND BACK TO EMPLOYEE
Reject the claim, returning it to the employee for amendment.

▶ APPROVE
Approve the claim for payment.

▶ APPROVE & FORWARD
Approve the claim and forward it to another approver to provide a secondary approval.

Following managerial approval, the expense claim will then move through the workflow to the *expense processor*; the claim status will also update on the user's claim overview. The role of the expense processor is to check all the details of the expense entries, ensuring that the expenses claimed and approved adhere to the company's expense policy and to the country's legislation. The expense processor also aims to maximize the possible tax reclaims. To support the processor another expense form is configured which shows the processor, the PROCESS CLAIMS areas with fields that show tax details for each expense. In this view, the VAT TAX section shows the processor all the tax-relevant information for the expense type (see Figure 4.10).

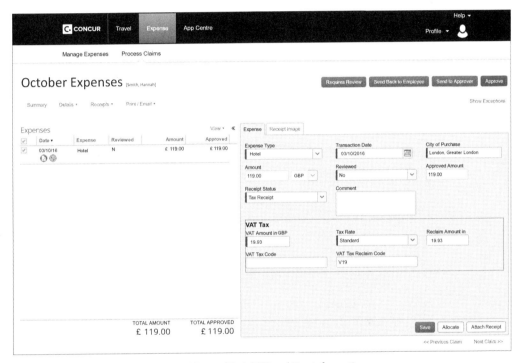

Figure 4.10 Expense Claim Processor View with Additional Tax Information

The VAT TAX section of the expense processing form shows the following tax information:

▶ VAT AMOUNT
The amount of the tax on the expense type depending on the tax configuration for the expense type

▶ TAX RATE
Tax rate applied to the expense type

- TAX RECLAIM AMOUNT
  Amount of tax from the expense available for reclaim processing

- VAT TAX CODE
  Contains the relevant tax code

- VAT TAX RECLAIM CODE
  Reclaim code assigned to the expense type in tax configuration

The tax information is driven by the tax configuration assigned to an expense type and the expense RECEIPT STATUS field. A processor can check the expense entry detail and the matching receipt image captured to ensure that the maximum amount of tax can be reclaimed on expenses from the relevant tax authority. If necessary, a processor can amend expense entries, such as the receipt type assigned to an entry, to drive the correct reclamation calculations.

Once thoroughly checked, a claim can be approved by the processor or assigned different checks, including the following:

- REQUIRES REVIEW marks the claim as requiring review by another processor.

- SEND BACK TO EMPLOYEE rejects a claim, returning it to an employee for amendment.

- SEND TO APPROVER sends a claim to another approver for secondary approval.

- APPROVE approves the claim for payment.

When a claim is returned to an employee for correction, it must pass through the submission and manager approval steps again before reaching the expense processor for approval again.

Once through all approval steps, an expense claim is then available for payment via an interface with your accounting system, payment manager processing, or the Concur Expense Pay Global module. Section 4.5 of this chapter will cover the Concur Expense Pay Global module in detail; for now, we'll discuss the batch processing payment options using the payment manager tools and the Concur SAE.

When several expense claims are ready to be paid, they are entered into a payment batch file that contains all the expense transactions approved for payment. The payment batch file can be closed and transferred into an Excel file, which can then be manually downloaded and moved to the payment solution software for your company.

The SAE is an automated, scheduled extraction of expense claim information that is approved and ready for payment. The extract job will run daily but will only extract expense data approved for payment. When extracted, the expense data is written to a text file to a specified location, which can then be imported into an accounting system to process the employee reimbursement. SAE exports run on an automated schedule; their processing overview can be viewed from COMPANY ADMINISTRATION • TOOLS • IMPORT/EXTRACT MONITOR (see Figure 4.11).

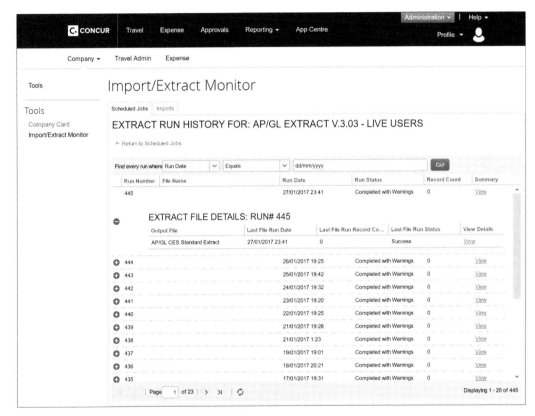

Figure 4.11 Overview of SAE Export Batch Job in Import/Extract Monitor

4.3   Basic Configuration for Concur Expense

In this section, we'll discuss the basic configuration components of your expense policy and processes in Concur. This section will focus on Concur configuration using the standard Concur version. To access the configuration for

Concur, navigate to the EXPENSE menu, under the ADMINISTRATION menu on the Concur home page. The EXPENSE ADMINISTRATION page will then show all the aspects of Concur that you can configure for your company.

4.3.1 Policy Group

Expense policy in Concur comprises several settings that define how expenses apply to a specified group of users. A *policy group* is created to group together users subject to the same expense policy rules and requirements; up to a maximum of five different policy groups can be configured.

Expense types and their associated settings, such as account codes, expense limits, and form configuration, can then be configured for each policy group individually to capture differing expense requirements for different groups of users. A user policy group assignment is defined by direct assignment in a user record via the EXPENSE POLICY GROUP field, as shown in Figure 4.12.

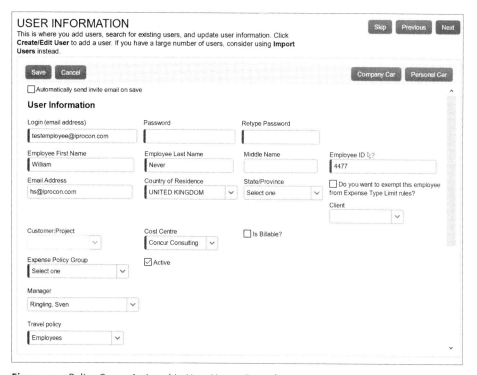

Figure 4.12 Policy Group Assigned in User Master Record

4.3.2   Expense Types

Concur provides several predefined common expense types that can be activated and configured for use in your expense policy, as well as the option to add new custom expense types for your company. Configuring explicit expense types will allow you to track and manage employee expense spending in these areas. You can configure different expense types for different policy groups or different settings for the same expense types across different policy groups, as shown in Figure 4.13; we'll discuss each configuration option ahead.

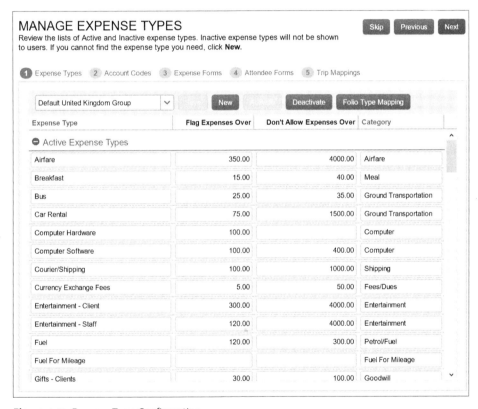

Figure 4.13 Expense Type Configuration

For each expense type, the expense can be assigned the following elements:

- ▶ ACTIVATED or DEACTIVATED status per expense policy
- ▶ Expense type limits, as follows:
  - ▹ FLAG EXPENSE OVER value, to flag a warning on any expenses submitted of this type over the limit defined
  - ▹ DON'T ALLOW EXPENSE OVER limit, to disallow any expense over a set limit
- ▶ FOLIO TYPE MAPPING, to map expense types to spend categories from a hotel folio

4.3.3 Account Codes

Account codes are assigned to each expense type and map between the Concur expense type and the ledger codes in your accounting system. If you've activated an expense code for use in Concur, then it must have an account code assigned; otherwise, users will receive an error when trying to enter expenses of that type.

For each expense type, the relevant account code is simply entered into the corresponding field on the ACCOUNT CODE DEFINITION screen of the EXPENSE configuration menu.

Using Alternate Account Codes

If you use an alternate account code structure, these codes are assigned in the ACCOUNT CODE screen. The option to configure such codes is only available if the alternate account codes are provided in the initial company configuration options.

4.3.4 Forms

The screens for expense entry, claim header entry, and the approvals view are referred to as *forms* in Concur. Each of the form layouts for the expense item entry and attendee information can be customized in Concur to fit your business processes. Fields on these forms can be set as mandatory or optional for completion or hidden from view entirely. The settings you make here will carry over for your employees, approvers, and processors. Standard Concur provides configuration for two types of forms:

1. *Expense forms* for expense information and details

2. *Attendee forms* to capture attendee information when adding or viewing attendees on expense entries

Customizing Expense Forms

Customize the fields that appear on expense forms to streamline the expense input and processing in Concur. For data required by your company's expense policy, make the these fields mandatory for input; hide from view any fields for data that your company does not required to save time and effort for your employees when completing and checking these fields.

Each expense type is assigned to a category, which in turn has a form. To change the behavior of a form field, assign the HIDDEN, OPTIONAL, or REQUIRED status (you must choose one; see Figure 4.14) to the relevant field on the form, then click on the NEXT button to enter the next screen and save the changes made.

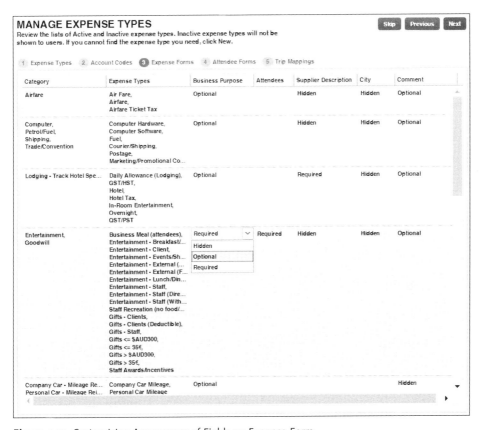

Figure 4.14 Customizing Appearance of Fields on Expense Form

Certain expense types will be configured to include attendees; depending on the attendee type, specific information may need to be captured for that attendee. The same field control that we just discussed can be applied to the attendee form to ensure that the expense captures all the required information about that expense attendee. If your company must meet certain regulatory standards for attendee information, such as in the healthcare/pharmaceutical industry, there may be unique forms (such as Healthcare Professional attendee) available for use.

4.3.5   Trip Mappings

If you're using the Concur Travel module, then as part of the expense type configuration you can map travel segment spending to specific expense types. Configuring the mapping of these segment types to expense types will ensure consistency and continuity in expense type usage across your company.

4.3.6   Taxation

Concur has a flexible tax configuration to help support effective expense tax processing and to maximize the tax reclamation amount for your company. When expense entries are created, different tax reclaim logic is driven by the entry that the user selects in the RECEIPT TYPE field and the reclaim condition configured. Each possible combination of receipt type and tax reclaim rate can be configured in the taxation configuration so that all possible tax scenarios can be automated.

Before we look at the configuration steps, we'll review the terminology involved.

▶ Tax authority refers to a country-specific tax configuration.

▶ Rate is the rate of taxation—for example, standard-rated, zero-rated, partial-rated, etc.

▶ Tax rate is the numerical value of the tax rate: 20%, 5%, etc.

▶ Tax groups are groups of similar expense types that have the same tax rates.

▶ Tax condition is a naming condition referencing how tax is applied to the expense type.

▶ Reclaim rate describes the percentage of tax that is reclaimable for the specific type of expense.

▸ Reclaim condition describes the reclaim scenario.

▸ Reclaim code is a pass-through code for your accounting system for the reclaim information to be reported and processed.

Concur localization will deliver the solution according to the tax rules of your relevant tax authority. However, as you activate any new expense types, you will need to complete the correct tax configuration as part of the expense configuration.

Each expense type is included in a tax group (Figure 4.15), and the different tax reclaim codes are assigned to each receipt type scenario (Figure 4.16).

Figure 4.15 Assigning Expense Types to Tax Group

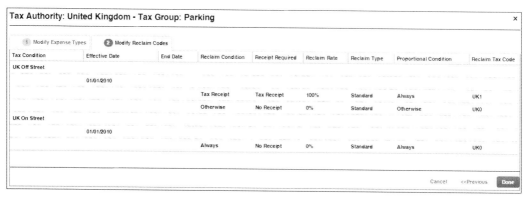

Figure 4.16 Configuring Tax Reclaim Codes per Receipt Type

4.3.7 Approval Workflows

Expense reports should be subject to an appropriate approval routing for the expenses claimed to be authorized for reimbursement to the employee and for any out-of-policy spending to be agreed upon and approved.

As we discussed in Section 4.2, an expense claim will be subject to two types of approvals: managerial authorization and expense processor approval. The approval routing options will define the process flow that the expense claim will follow once submitted by the employee to his manager(s) and then the expense processor. The initial managerial approval will be defined by the approving manager assigned to the user on his user record, and further managers can be included in the approval workflow, as follows:

▶ The *basic approval routing* is Employee → Manager → Processor. Once submitted by the employee, the claim will move through the workflow to the employee's approving manager as defined in the employee record and then to the processor for that same expense policy group as the employee.

▶ The *approval routing with authorization limits* is Employee → Manager → Authorized Limit Approver → Processor. Once submitted by the employee, the claim will move through the workflow to the approving manager defined on the employee record, then to an approving manager with authority for the expense claim limit, then to the processor for that same expense policy group. If you use approval limits in your workflow, the expense processors are not subject to approval limits and can approve any value of expense claim.

- The *second approver* workflow is Employee → Manager → Second Manager → Processor. Once submitted by the employee, the claim will move through the workflow to the approving manager as defined in the user master record, then to the second approver defined for the employee, then to the processor for the same policy group.

- The *manager's manager* workflow is Employee → Manager 1 → Manager 2 → Manager 3 → Manager 4 → Manager 5 → Processor. This workflow allows for up to five levels of managerial approval; it's based on using approval limits defined in the manager user's master record. Each manager will have an approval value limit; when an expense claim has a higher value than that of the approving manager, the claim will flow to the next level of approving manager until it reaches a manager with an approval limit higher than that of the expense claim. The next two boxes provide examples of this process.

Example 1: Expense Claim Value $2,500.00

An employee submits an expense claim with a total value of $2,500.00. This expense claim flows to Manager 1, who has an expense approval limit of $5,00.00; she approves the expense claim but doesn't have an approval limit equal to or higher than the value of the expense claim, so the claim flows to Manager 2. Manager 2 has an approval limit of $2,000.00 and approves the claim, but he doesn't have an approval limit equal to or higher than the value of the expense claim, so the claim flows to Manager 3, who has an approval limit of $5,000.00. Manager 3 approves the expense claim, and because her approval limit is equal to or higher than the value of the expense claim, the managerial approvals for the expense claim are complete, and the claim flows to the processor for final processing.

Example 2: Expense Claim Value $505.00

An employee submits an expense claim with a total value claimed of $505.00. This expense claim flows to Manager 1, who has an expense approvals limit of $500.00 and who approves the expense claim. Manager 1 doesn't have an approval limit equal to or higher than the value of the expense claim, so the claim flows to Manager 2. Manager 2 has an approval limit of $2,000.00 and approves the claim. Because the approval limit of Manager 2 is equal to or higher than the value of the expense claim submitted, the claim does not require approval from Manager 3, and the claim flows to the processor for final processing.

Once the approval flow is specified and any value limits assigned, configuration settings for the workflow preferences can be configured for additional approvers, workflow times, and expense claim recalls.

ADDITIONAL APPROVERS can be allowed for workflows and added by either an employee or a manager. When the initial manager in the workflow completes his approval step, a button will be available to send the claim to another approver—for example, if certain expenses have been allocated to a specific budget or project of which the budget holder is not the employee's approving manager. Enabling this option will allow your approvers to approve an expense claim and then forward the claim onto the budget holder or project manager for his approval as well.

The WORKFLOW TIMEOUT option will automatically reroute any expense claim pending approval for 10 days onto the approving manager of the manager it's pending approval with. Enabling this feature can help ensure that expense claims are processed in a timely manner and that any rerouting is clearly documented in the audit trail of an expense claim.

The RECALL feature will allow employees to recall any expense claims that they submitted. Enabling this option will allow users to correct mistakes or add any missed expenses to the appropriate expense claim before the claim is rejected.

Recalling Approved Expense Claims

An expense claim can only be recalled by an employee if it has not yet been approved by the processor and moved to *pending payment* status. No matter how many levels of approval have occurred or where the claim might be in the process flow for approvals, the claim can still be recalled by the employee if it does not yet have the pending payment status.

4.3.8 Compliance Controls

Compliance controls are criteria that you can use to ensure that the expenses applied in Concur adhere to your expense process, including expense value limits, receipt handling options, company card compliance, and more. Compliance controls fall into three configuration areas: COMPLIANCE RULES, RECEIPT HANDLING options, and EXPENSE LIMITS.

Compliance Rules

The configuration tab for COMPLIANCE RULES will allow you to set specific compliance settings for expenses, general compliance, and company card usage. The first section configures some compliance controls for how claims and expenses can be used by travelers. There are a few keys settings if you use the mileage expense types or corporate cards. Mileage expenses can be enabled to be used on the expense mass input grid to allow users to input multiple lines of mileage expenses in one screen. Another key setting allows users to import personal card transaction information to expenses and thus use their card transactions as supporting information for an expense if allowed by your company's expense policy.

General compliance settings will apply more specific compliance rules to your expense types; some key settings can be applied here:

▶ FLAG EXPENSE PER ATTENDEE WITH AMOUNT EXCEEDING (AND MONETARY VALUE)
A limit amount to be applied to each expense attendee can be configured here to control attendee expenditure.

▶ REQUIRE USERS TO INCLUDE ATTENDEES OTHER THAN THEMSELVES
If an expense type has been configured as requiring attendees, configuring this option will require users to include attendees other than themselves on the expense. Enabling this configuration setting will ensure that attendee expenses do in fact include attendee data.

▶ FLAG EXPENSES WITH TRANSACTION DATES OLDER THAN (AND DAY VALUE)
Configuring a number of days here will help employees claim their expenses in a timely manner.

▶ FLAG EXCHANGE RATE VARIANCE (AND PERCENTAGE VALUE)
The value configured here will allow a tolerance for employees to claim a different value of foreign expenses compared to the internal Concur conversion. Configuring a tolerance will enable employees to claim an expense value specific to their transaction exchange, which may differ from the standard OANDA rates or company-specific imported exchange rates.

▶ REQUIRE USER TO ITEMIZE HOTELS EXPENSES
Enabling this option will mandate users to itemize any hotel expense entered. Enabling itemization of the total expense into its component parts will give greater insight into the expenditure details.

▸ REQUIRE EXPENSE TYPE TO REQUIRE COMMENTS
Specific expense types that should include comments can be selected, requiring employees to provide more information about the specific expense type when making a claim. This is a more flexible configuration option than making the comments field mandatory when multiple expenses share the same expense form.

▸ PERCENTAGE OF CLAIMS TO BE RANDOMLY SELECTED FOR PROCESSOR AUDIT
This setting defines the percentage of expense claims that will be flagged for expense processors for rigorous checking. Expense processors will see a message in the processor screen about the flagged expense claims.

Compliance Warning Messages

For each of the general compliance settings, when a user is set to receive a warning message if his expense entry fails the compliance check, the text of the warning message can also be customized per compliance settings to make the warning more relevant to the company's expense policy.

Company card settings define the compliance settings in relation to company card usage in Concur. Two key settings to track and support the usage of a card can be enabled: you can flag expense types that will show a warning when the company card isn't the payment type used and flag any personal use of a company card. Both settings will show warning exception messages to approvers to alert them to follow up with the employee as necessary. The final configuration option for company cards enables an email warning to alert employees to any transactions that have not been associated with an expense entry by selecting a value for the limit on the number of days for which the transaction can stay unassociated; this can help users process their card transactions in a timely manner.

Receipt Handling Options

The receipt handling compliance configuration allows you to configure your receipt policy within Concur and determine how receipts are applied to expense entries. There are several settings available to refine receipt handling:

▸ Define which types of expense do not require a receipt, such as allowances or per diems.

- Define which types of expense always require a receipt, for all other expense types you've activated that aren't already defined as not requiring a receipt.

- Define any value limits below which a receipt is not required for any expense types.

- Set a control to specify that any expense requires a receipt; if the employee doesn't attached a receipt, then the claim can't be submitted for approval.

- Set the default receipt status for all expense types.

- Select whether your users can submit missing receipt affidavits in place of missing receipts; if selected, define the company-specific texts that will appear to users on the MISSING RECEIPT AFFIDAVIT form. You can use these texts to customize the affidavit text and declaration text for your company-specific policy.

Expense Limits

Here, you can assign an upper limit to the value of an expense that can be claimed and the warning text that a user will see when he submits an expense that exceeds this limit.

4.3.9   Company and Personal Mileage Rates for Cars

Concur has easy configuration options to support mileage reimbursement across different reimbursement types and amounts for company and personal cars. Each personal or company car is configured with the same criteria (see Figure 4.19):

- VEHICLE TYPE

- EFFECTIVE DATE and END DATE, to enable different amounts to be applied each year

- RATE of reimbursement

Depending on your locale, you may see additional fields to manage country-specific requirements. Figure 4.17 shows the PERSONAL CAR RATES configuration for reimbursement under the UK tax authority; therefore, fields are shown for the reimbursement rate change over a certain mileage threshold and a rate payable per passenger. These field settings come from the expense policy country assignment.

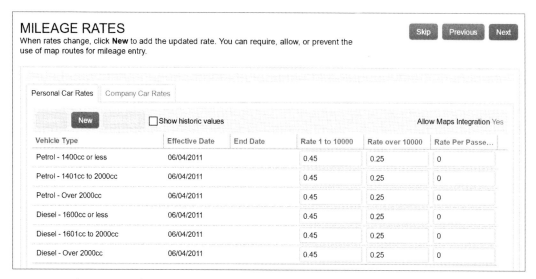

Figure 4.17 Mileage Reimbursement Rates for Personal Cars in United Kingdom

You can also set the option for Google Maps integration when the mileage expense types are being claimed. Google Maps integration enables employees to easily and accurately claim their mileage by entering the *to* and *from* addresses for the claim—Google Maps will calculate the mileage between the address points entered. Using this integration will help standardize the mileage being claimed by your employees when you have multiple employees making the same journey.

The mileage calculator makes claiming mileage easy and efficient and provides the user with a route to his destination. The employee enters the start and destination addresses, and Google Maps will calculate the route between the two waypoints as the total amount of distance traveled. Variables can be included such as the following:

▶ Selecting the DEDUCT COMMUTE checkbox will prompt Concur to ask for the employee's origin address (home address), which will then be used to calculate the distance to the first waypoint. This commute distance is the deducted from the total mileage claim as personal mileage.

▶ The employee can select the MAKE ROUND TRIP checkbox to make the journey a round trip for the mileage to and from the destination.

▸ The route taken can be specified by selecting the NO TOLL ROADS and/or NO HIGHWAYS options to plan a route that avoids tolls and/or highways. In addition, the employee can adjust the suggested route if the route he took or intends to take doesn't match the one suggested.

4.3.10 Employee Reimbursement

The employee reimbursement configuration will specify how your organization reimburses your employees for their expenses, including reimbursement currencies, methods, and frequencies.

For each employee reimbursement country, you can assign a combination reimbursement currency and method. More than one reimbursement currency and method combination can be configured for the same country. This can be useful if you use automated processes such as the Concur Expense Pay Global solution. Reimbursement via Concur Expense Pay Global requires the employee bank information to be entered into the employee profile in Concur. If a situation arises in which an employee doesn't have her bank information in her profile, then Concur Expense Pay Global will have no bank information to process the expense reimbursement. You can create a second configuration for the employee reimbursement via company check as a workaround so that the employee can still be reimbursed via check. The Concur Expense Pay Global solution is covered in more detail in Section 4.5 of this chapter.

Once each employee reimbursement scenario has been configured, you can define the schedule for payment. As each expense claim is approved and the status is set to pending payment, the claim will add the expense data to the open payment batch file. The scheduling defined here will close any open payment batch according the dates set, to process the employee reimbursement via the defined reimbursement methods.

4.3.11 Company Cards

If you have a corporate card solution for your employees to use, you can automate the credit card data feed into Concur to create expense data for your employees. This card feed will import card transactions, which will populate as available expenses in the Concur home page for users to add to their expense claims.

When using card feeds in Concur, you should ensure that there is a dedicated company card administrator to help manage the data. This user will be able to manage the cards, including assigning user cards, managing card transactions, releasing held transactions, and monitoring card imports, among other tasks.

A new card feed is created in the COMPANY CARD configuration step of the EXPENSE menu. Complete the corporate card program information as required, and then specify the batch schedule for that company card (see Figure 4.18).

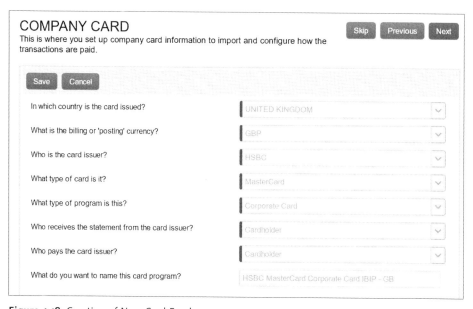

Figure 4.18 Creation of New Card Feed

On the ACCOUNTING tab for the company card configuration, you can assign the accounting codes from your accounting system directly to your card feed.

The company card administrator has access to manage the card program in Concur, including the following tasks:

▶ Creating, deleting, assigning, and unassigning cards to/from your Concur users. Managing card transactions, including releasing any transactions that are held from employees or hiding transactions.

▶ Managing merchant code to expense type mappings.

▸ Configuring settings for how the card transactions will behave.

▸ Monitoring card feed import logs in case of errors.

Hiding Duplicate Card Transactions

Once imported into Concur, card transactions can't be deleted. However, if an expense has already been claimed by an employee without matching the card transaction, the card transaction will appear as a duplicate expense. The MANAGE TRANSACTIONS screen can be used by the card administrator to hide transactions from a user's view so that users won't claim duplicate transactions.

4.3.12 Reporting Configuration

Reporting configuration options allow you to specify fiscal year reporting in Concur, with the year specific to your organization. Standard settings establish the fiscal year as running from January to December; if your organization's fiscal year differs, you can specify the year period here so that Concur's analysis reporting is in line with your fiscal year.

Changes related to reporting won't be available in reporting immediately, but only after the overnight update process has run.

4.4 Advanced Configuration for Concur Expense

The advanced configuration options for Concur give further options to automate and streamline expense processing for your company in Concur; ahead, we'll look at the available options. This section of the chapter will focus on the Concur premium version. Not all configuration settings may be active in your company's Concur instance, so some options may require activation from Concur support.

4.4.1 Policies

The advanced policy configuration will allow you to configure more settings within Concur for your expense policy, allowing you to replicate your company's expense policy a higher level. In the standard configuration, a policy group is created and the expense types, forms, and account codes are applied. In the advanced configuration, you can apply various other settings and features that come with the advanced configuration directly to your expense policy.

Some of the advanced components of an expense policy include the following:

▶ EXPENSE CLAIM FORM
The default form an employee will see when creating an expense report.

▶ WORKFLOW DEFINITION
The workflow process steps that will apply to an expense claim once submitted by an employee.

▶ SCAN CONFIGURATION
If your company tracks paper receipts using barcode technology, then this functionality can be enabled.

▶ IMAGING CONFIGURATION
If your company tracks receipt images received by fax or receipt image upload, this functionality can be enabled.

▶ EXPENSE DETAIL VIEW
Define the columns here that an employee will see in the EXPENSES section of an expense claim.

▶ ALLOCATION SETTINGS
Set the options for the form that an employee will see when allocating an expense, the print format to be used when viewing a summary of all allocations, and the allocation separator symbol.

▶ ROOM RATE AND TAX OPTIONS
Define how the room rate and tax values are shown: combined or separated.

▶ FRINGE BENEFIT TAX
The status of the fringe benefit tax will show.

▶ EMAIL APPROVALS
Set whether email approvals are enabled for a policy or note.

▶ FLIGHT FEES MAPPING
Here, you can enable settings to recognize fees related to airline expenses, such as baggage or preferential boarding fees, separately from the actual costs of tickets. You can set the currency for such fees, set any value limits to apply to the expense type, and specify the expense type to capture this spending.

▶ ALLOCATIONS FROM REQUESTS

If you use Concur Request, this setting determines whether and how allocations can be copied from Concur Request to Concur Expense.

▶ EXPENSE TYPES

Set the expense types applicable to this expense policy.

Fringe Benefit Tax Enablement Settings

The fringe benefit tax will only show as enabled after a configuration for fringe benefit tax has been created and saved.

To create a new expense policy, select the POLICIES configuration step under the EXPENSE administration menu. A new policy is created by selecting an existing policy and amending details to reflect the new policy.

The wizard will then navigate through the steps to create the policy: editing the general policy settings, assigning the usable expense types, and setting the print format for policy reports.

The first step is to assign the general settings of the policy application and behavior for users. Some settings are mandatory, and others will only apply if you're using modules such as Concur Travel or Concur Request.

After changing the new policy settings as required, as seen in the example policy shown in Figure 4.19, click on the NEXT button to assign the necessary expense types to your new policy. When each expense type is activated for a policy, you can define the way that the expense behaves, appears, and any mappings it may need.

As part of the policy configuration, the individual behaviors for expense types can be specified. Different expense properties can be defined for different expense policies so that users who can claim expenses differently from one another can use the same expense types, but with differing configurations, as shown in Figure 4.20.

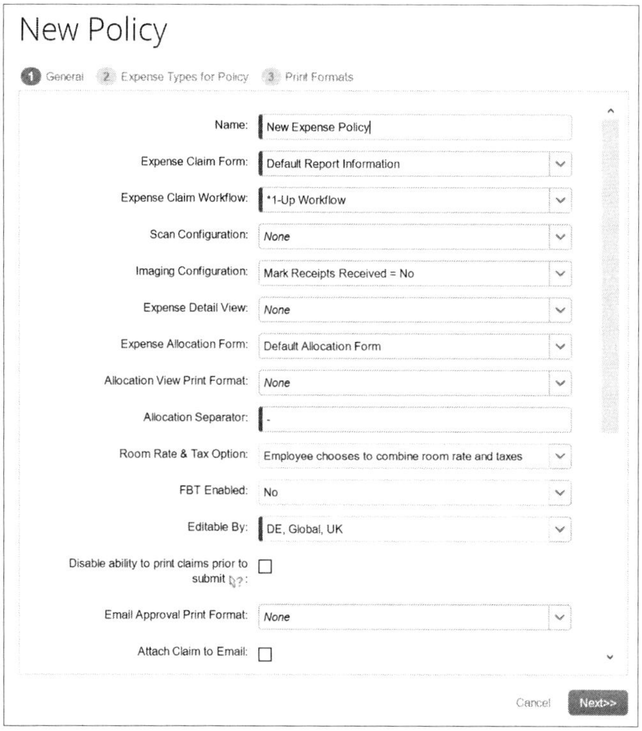

Figure 4.19 Creating New Expense Policy

Figure 4.20 Expense Properties Specific to Expense Policy

The final step in configuring a new expense policy is to define report print formats for the expense policy. Each print format can be activated for an expense policy and its appearance adjusted.

Once configured, an expense policy can be assigned to one expense group or to many expense groups. An expense group can also have multiple policies assigned. If multiple policies apply to an expense group, then the administrator must set one policy as the default, but a user can choose any other assigned expense policy to apply to a claim in the claim header.

4.4.2 Expense Types

Advanced expense type configuration in Concur allows you to activate, deactivate, and modify the behavior of expense types that your company will use. Concur provides several predefined, standard expense types; any others specific to your company can be defined during your implementation. However, as the Concur solution matures in your organization, new expense types may be required, existing types retired, or changes to expense type properties required. Advanced configuration options will allow you to configure expense types in greater detail than in the standard configuration steps.

Expense types can be activated for use, assigned warnings and upper value limits, and have accounting codes assigned, as per standard configuration options. Advanced configuration of expense types allows you to apply more settings, including the use of itemization, changing parent expense types, restricting mobile device usage, and adding formulas for amount calculations. The configuration options for expense types are grouped into five categories:

1. GENERAL SETTINGS define how users can use expense types. This includes assignment of the expense type to a parent expense, spend category for reporting, and whether the expense type should be available for use in the mobile app. The itemization options can also be enabled under the general settings.

   In standard configuration, some expense types are preset to be itemized; with advanced configuration, you can set your own itemizations. Setting an expense type to use itemization will require the expense type costs to be broken down into component parts, such as for a hotel expense in which the overall expense value may have individual amounts for the room cost, room tax, room service, and additional costs like Wi-Fi or phone calls. Requiring itemization of the total expense amounts will provide greater detail and clarity into explicit expense spend categories.

2. On the POLICIES tab, assign expense types configured for use in the applicable expense policies.

3. FORMULAS can be applied to expense types to enforce amount restrictions against expense types, applied per policy.

4. The ATTENDEES tab allows configuration of how attendee counts and costs can be used for a specific expense type. The expense type can be set to show the cost distribution per attendee, for no shows to be included on the expense, and to indicate whether the expense user should be included on the expense by default.

Including No-Show Attendees

Including Concur on meeting invitations will allow expenses with attendees to be created easily and quickly, but invited attendees could miss the meeting. Enabling no show attendees to be included will allow employees to easily manage any no shows on the expense entry created from the meeting invitation.

5. On the ACCOUNTING tab, accounting codes are assigned to individual expense types.

Expense limits can be configured for each expense type, including setting warning and block amount limits via the EXPENSE LIMITS tab in the EXPENSE configuration step.

If itemization has been activated for any expense types, an itemization wizard can be created. This wizard will set the primary expense type itemized and the expense types that can be used for the itemization splits. For example, to use itemization for tip amounts added to taxi fares, the parent expense type for the wizard would be TAXI, and the secondary expense types will be TAXI and TIPS/GRATUITIES so that the full fare amount can be broken down into the separate taxi and tip amounts.

4.4.3   Group Configurations

Advanced configuration contains two types of group configurations: *employee groups* and *expense groups*. These groups will define how expense policies and other details are applied for each type of employee in your organization.

Employee Groups

The employee group configuration is used to define a set of users to which the same expense policy, limits, and allowances apply. Across your business, you will have different levels and types of employees with different types and limits applied to the expenses that they can claim, varying classes of services that can be claimed, different budget levels, and so on; defining employee groups will allow different expense policies to be applied to each group.

Concur uses hierarchical groups to categorize employees into these different groupings. This structural provides inheritance of attributes so that a general policy can be assigned to a group, such as for a company-wide set of protocols, and further criteria and restrictions can be assigned to a subsection of employees. This inheritance of attributes also assists the Concur administrator in reducing the configuration overhead when enabling common shared configurations that can be defined once and then applied to many employee groups. For example, the simple company structure shown in Figure 4.21 includes operations in Europe, Asia, and South America, and the countries within each area are individual country business units; each country is created as a group within Concur.

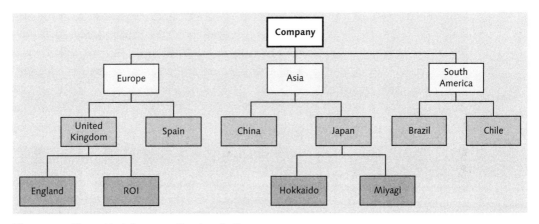

Figure 4.21 Hierarchical Company Structure in Concur

The global group will be assigned to the highest level of the structure—that is, the company level—and this global group can access data that affects any company level below; for example, a user with global-level permissions can view, and possibly change, any group-related configurations below the company level for Europe or Asia, down to the individual countries.

Inheritance allows configurations to flow down the structure from the point that the configuration is assigned to; for example, an expense policy assigned to the UK level of the company structure can have attributes set as inheritable for England, and Republic of Ireland business units below it will share the same policy requirements.

Various factors can influence the design of groups within your organization, including geography (each country can define a different group) and companies (different companies that form a larger global group can define a group structure). A group definition should be based on two key factors: employees who share the same expense policy and are managed by the same authority.

Expense Groups

Once different employee groups are defined, these groups enable you to apply different expense policies, payment types, and attendee type policies to each grouping. An *expense policy* is assigned to each active expense group, can be selected as the default policy for that group. You can decide whether the expense policy's settings are inheritable by groups below the assigned group in the organization structure in Concur. The relevant *payment types* in use for the group also can be selected. The last expense group setting indicates which *attendee types* are active for each expense group. Applying this definition to expense groups will ensure that different types of attendee expenses are only claimed by the appropriately authorized user groups.

4.4.4 Audit Rules and Exceptions

Audit rules in Concur are used to monitor and manage expenses, providing usage restrictions, monitoring information, and data validation, among other things. Rules can be created to enforce certain behaviors when using Concur Expense, such as applying expense limits with hard stop exceptions so that a user can't submit expenses beyond the set limit, or to provide information for management, such as monitoring use of preferred vendors. Rules require certain criteria to trigger, and an exception must be assigned. Audit rules should be used to map the details of your expense policy in Concur.

An *exception* is a message triggered by each audit rule; they're configured in the EXCEPTIONS configuration step of the EXPENSE menu and then assigned to an audit rule when it's created. An exception has a priority level value from 1 to 99. Any exception with a priority level of 99 is considered a *hard-stop rule*. These exceptions cannot pass an audit; the user must correct his input data to align with the rule criteria. Any exception priority level less than 99 is treated as an informative warning to users. Exceptions from 1 to 98 do not have any technical differences but can be used to rate exception priorities, or a number range can be used to group exception types. The actual upper value of a hard-stop exception can be changed under the WORKFLOW configuration menu option to a value other than 99 if necessary, but if these values are changed, ensure that the standard audit rules are checked for any impact.

Audit rules come in three types:

1. *Custom rules* are those specific to a company's Concur configuration or that meet a specific business need. For example, a custom rule might be set for a vendor specific to your company or to support specific aspects of your company's expense policy, such as expense limits. These rules are based on expense data that users enter and are triggered by specific events, such as expense entry save or expense claim submission.

2. *Random rules* allow for a random selection of expense claims for auditing. A random rule is either based on a specific percentage of reports to be audited or on every *n*th report where *n* can be whatever number your company sets.

3. *Validation rules* compare data entered in expense reports against a table of validated entries; if the compared values do not match, an exception is generated. A validation action of the rule is defined to generate an exception, update a specified field, or both when triggered.

The configuration steps for a custom or validation rule are similar; for both, the rule is defined, then the rule criteria are built, and then the exception is assigned. A validation rule will also require definition of what the validation action should be.

Random rules differ in that you only need to activate or deactivate the standard rules for audit options, depending on which report selection your company wants to use.

To create a new audit rule, first create the exception that should be generated by the rule in the exception configuration. Each exception will consist of a short code, priority level from 1 to 99, the group responsible for editing the rule, the Concur product the rule applies to, and text explaining the exception.

Create a new audit rule by clicking on the NEW button from the REQUIRE AUDIT RULE type tab. The first screen defines the new audit rule as seen in Figure 4.22, with the following information:

- ▸ Rule name
- ▸ Event that triggers the rule
- ▸ Editable by group
- ▸ Expense group the rule applies to
- ▸ Whether the rule is active or not

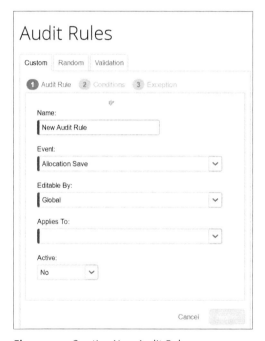

Figure 4.22 Creating New Audit Rules

Various triggering events can be assigned to a rule, including expense entry save, expense entry submission, expense allocation save, or post report submission, to manage and monitor several metrics and behaviors.

Figure 4.23 shows an audit rule with several conditions checked, including the expense amount, the receipt status assigned to the expense, and the country of expense for the rule; the rule will check for any expense type that has a value of more than £250 for the United Kingdom, and an exception will be produced when the rule is triggered.

Figure 4.23 Audit Rule

4.4.5 Expense Forms and Fields

There is a wealth of configuration options in the premium version of Concur for how forms and fields can be displayed to users in your company, including additional forms and fields available to provide further specification for various expense type inputs. Each form is assigned to an expense policy, and so different information can be captured for each expense type by different expense policies.

There are more forms available to provide further customization for different types of expense, and all fields can be individually defined for each form. As with standard Concur, different fields can be set to different access levels; for example, a field could be hidden from an expense user, made mandatory for expense processor input, and then set as read-only for the approving manager.

Other field data types are available, including fields using connected lists. A *connected list* is a multiple-level list of values in which one value influences another. For example, if expenses are billable to customers, then a list of the individual customer projects is required to correctly allocate the project costs. The user will assign a customer to an expense, which will then provide the project list defined for that customer.

Conditional and validation fields can also be used on forms. Conditional fields can be used to ensure that additional information is captured from user decisions. Once the user completes the conditional field, additional fields will appear to capture further information. Validations are assigned to fields to ensure that the data capture in the field is correct and consistent, such as for capturing legal information that needs to be in the correct format or important information like bank data, for which account numbers must fit a prescribed length or format.

4.4.6 Feature Hierarchies

A *feature hierarchy* is a hierarchical structure of data defined for use within a specific Concur module. Features can be used through this structure to determine certain settings for users and processes within Concur. Although connect lists and account code structures are also hierarchies, they are not configured within the feature hierarchies configuration.

There are five areas of feature hierarchies—employee, expense, reporting, request, and invoice, each with different hierarchies available for different uses:

▶ The EMPLOYEE area can be used to administer employee-specific data, such as form selections. The employee hierarchy is also used for hierarchical group selections, such as for delegate criteria.

▶ The EXPENSE area has several hierarchies in use:

 ▹ CLAIMS, used to determine expense group(s) for a user and the relevant expense policies and configurations.

 ▹ AUTHORIZED APPROVER, used to determine an approver when authorized approvers are in use.

▸ COST OBJECT APPROVER, used to determine a cost object approver when they are in use.

▸ TAX, used to determine the tax authority and configured for a user to use, dependent on the user's country and position in the structure.

▸ TRAVEL ALLOWANCE, used to determine the travel allowance configuration for a user.

▸ The REPORTING area determines the reporting data that a user is authorized to view and use.

▸ The REQUEST area has authorized and cost object approver hierarchies, used in the same manner as those in the expense area.

▸ The INVOICE area uses a variety of hierarchies for various aspects of invoice processing, such as invoice routing, authorized payment approvers and cost object approvers separate from those hierarchies in the expense or request area.

4.4.7 Localization

The localization configuration is used to change or update the language localizations that users see within Concur. Settings to change or update localizations will only be available to you in the languages that Concur has been implemented for.

Localizations can be applied to nearly any data type and texts that a user sees in Concur, such as for expense types, audit rules, exceptions, receipts, or payment types, or for administration settings, including locations, time zones, and site settings. Help and tool tips can also be added for different languages to help users.

Localization changes can either be applied individually to correct a one-off entry or made via mass import and export options. To edit an individual localization, simply select the target language of the localization. Each configuration component is then listed in its category, such as expense type or attendee type. Select the component that needs changes, and the translation for the entry can be entered and saved.

If multiple translations are required, then the localizations for a configuration component can be downloaded, amended, and imported back into Concur en masse using a text file.

After choosing the target language for the localization, a file of each configuration component can be downloaded from Concur; the text file will resemble the file shown in Figure 4.24. The file will provide the details all text for the required configuration component, including details of the character length of the data type, the data type, key, and localized text. Any changes, such as to localizations, should be made to the left of the equals sign (=) only.

```
File  Edit  Format  View  Help

Ausgangssprache : English(en)
Zielsprache : German(de)

Translate : en : de

Overwrite : N
Hide Language Mismatch Detail : N

TableJoin : CT_EXPENSE_TYPE_LANG:CT_EXPENSE_TYPE,EXP_KEY

64.CT_EXPENSE_TYPE_LANG.NAME.EXP_KEY.'01000'=Non Reimbursable/Personal Expense
64.CT_EXPENSE_TYPE_LANG.NAME.EXP_KEY.'01001'=Incidentals Allowance
64.CT_EXPENSE_TYPE_LANG.NAME.EXP_KEY.'01002'=Fahrzeuginstandhaltung/Reparaturen
64.CT_EXPENSE_TYPE_LANG.NAME.EXP_KEY.'01003'=Erfrischungen
64.CT_EXPENSE_TYPE_LANG.NAME.EXP_KEY.'01004'=Interne Bewirtung - Mitarbeiter
64.CT_EXPENSE_TYPE_LANG.NAME.EXP_KEY.'01005'=Kurier/Versand/Fracht
64.CT_EXPENSE_TYPE_LANG.NAME.EXP_KEY.'01006'=Drucken/Fotokopien/Büromaterial
64.CT_EXPENSE_TYPE_LANG.NAME.EXP_KEY.'01007'=Büromaterial/Software
64.CT_EXPENSE_TYPE_LANG.NAME.EXP_KEY.'01008'=Reisepass/Visagebühren
64.CT_EXPENSE_TYPE_LANG.NAME.EXP_KEY.'01009'=Trinkgelder/Gratifikation
64.CT_EXPENSE_TYPE_LANG.NAME.EXP_KEY.'01010'=Auswanderungskosten
64.CT_EXPENSE_TYPE_LANG.NAME.EXP_KEY.'01011'=Arzt/Heilgebühren
64.CT_EXPENSE_TYPE_LANG.NAME.EXP_KEY.'01012'=Schulung/Weiterbildung
64.CT_EXPENSE_TYPE_LANG.NAME.EXP_KEY.'01013'=Betriebsmittel - Auslandseinsatz
64.CT_EXPENSE_TYPE_LANG.NAME.EXP_KEY.'01014'=Tageszeitung/Magazine/Bücher
64.CT_EXPENSE_TYPE_LANG.NAME.EXP_KEY.'01015'=09. Versetzung/Auslandseinsatz
64.CT_EXPENSE_TYPE_LANG.NAME.EXP_KEY.'01016'=Versetzungen - Unterkunft
64.CT_EXPENSE_TYPE_LANG.NAME.EXP_KEY.'01017'=Versetzungskosten
64.CT_EXPENSE_TYPE_LANG.NAME.EXP_KEY.'01018'=Versetzungen - Umzugskosten
64.CT_EXPENSE_TYPE_LANG.NAME.EXP_KEY.'01019'=Versetzungen - Reisekosten
64.CT_EXPENSE_TYPE_LANG.NAME.EXP_KEY.'01020'=05. Büro Aufwendungen
64.CT_EXPENSE_TYPE_LANG.NAME.EXP_KEY.'01021'=07. Gebühren
64.CT_EXPENSE_TYPE_LANG.NAME.EXP_KEY.'01022'=zNot Used-Fax
64.CT_EXPENSE_TYPE_LANG.NAME.EXP_KEY.'01023'=Friends & Family Allowance
64.CT_EXPENSE_TYPE_LANG.NAME.EXP_KEY.'01024'=Währungs-Wechselgebühren
64.CT_EXPENSE_TYPE_LANG.NAME.EXP_KEY.'01025'=Bahn - OLD
64.CT_EXPENSE_TYPE_LANG.NAME.EXP_KEY.'01026'=Gebühren der Fluggesellschaft
64.CT_EXPENSE_TYPE_LANG.NAME.EXP_KEY.'01027'=Arbeitsessen (mit Teilnehmern)
64.CT_EXPENSE_TYPE_LANG.NAME.EXP_KEY.'01028'=Eigene Mahlzeiten
64.CT_EXPENSE_TYPE_LANG.NAME.EXP_KEY.'01029'=Interne Bewirtung - Mitarbeiter (Mit Kunden)
64.CT_EXPENSE_TYPE_LANG.NAME.EXP_KEY.'01030'=Externe Bewirtung (Inland)
64.CT_EXPENSE_TYPE_LANG.NAME.EXP_KEY.'01031'=Externe Bewirtung (Ausland)
64.CT_EXPENSE_TYPE_LANG.NAME.EXP_KEY.'01032'=Geschenke > 35€
64.CT_EXPENSE_TYPE_LANG.NAME.EXP_KEY.'01033'=Geschenke <= 35€
```

Figure 4.24 Mass Maintenance of Expense Types for German Localization

Once all desired changes have been made, the file can be imported into Concur using the IMPORT tab in the LOCALIZATIONS configuration tab. Any localization changes made will take immediate effect.

4.4.8   Currency Administration

Concur offers a standard exchange rate framework based on OANDA rates, but you can also import your specific exchanges rates using the currency administration configuration; the reimbursement currencies available in your Concur instances also can be activated or deactivated here. Activating and deactivating currencies is as straightforward as flagging or unflagging a specific currency in this configuration step.

Using company-specific exchange rates requires a feed of the company specific exchange rates to populate Concur; these rates will then be used for the expense entries to convert expense item amounts to the employee reimbursement currency, audit rules, and company card transactions. The rates file will need to contain a currency pair for all possible combinations of expense claim and reimbursement currency.

The Exchange Rate Source field on the Currency Administration configuration tab has three options:

1. Search Local then External Source
   Concur will check for a company-specific exchange rate, then use the OANDA source if a currency pair cannot be found.

2. Use Local Exchange Rates Only
   Concur will only use the currency exchange rate from the company-specific currency conversions.

3. Use External Exchange Rates Only
   Concur will only use the OANDA exchange rates populated in the system.

There is also an option in the Currency Administration tab to allow users to adjust the currency conversion if it doesn't match the value of the expense within a certain percentage. If your expense policy allows users to claim the value of a converted expense from credit card information instead of the suggested rates in the system, you should assign a tolerance percentage here.

4.4.9   Mapping Concept Fields

The mapping concept fields configuration option will allow you to map fields from Concur to general business reporting concepts, such as department, cost center, or business unit, producing more standardized reporting results.

There are several concept fields available, with mapping for each different form type across the employee, expense report header, entry, and allocation forms. Different forms will have different fields available and may require different mappings to the same concept. For each concept field, choose the field on each form that represents the concept.

Mapping Concept Fields: Archiving Update Process

Any new or changed mappings in the concept fields will require a nightly archive process to be run before updating the field mappings present in reporting.

4.4.10 Receipt Handling

Concur offers several aspects of receipt handling to fit any configuration requirements that your company expense policy may have. We have touched upon methods to capture receipts when using the Concur receipt store, mobile apps, and e-receipt options; now we'll look at some of the other methods of receipt capture and processing and some of the other features available for receipt handling in the advanced configuration options.

RECEIPT LIMITS apply limits and conditions for claiming expenses to support the correct receipt submission for each expense type. A limit scenario for a receipt can be based upon submission of the original paper receipt, a receipt image, or both for each expense type in use. Receipt limits are assigned to an expense policy, allowing flexibility in receipt requirement configurations per policy.

PAYMENT HOLD CONFIGURATIONS can put payment of an expense claim on hold if certain receipt limit threshold criteria are exceeded. Once an expense claim is processed through to the payment stage, the claim is evaluated by Concur to check if receipts are required and whether those receipts have been received to see if the claim payment status should be put on hold. Claims can be put on hold for two reasons:

1. REPORT LIMITS WITHOUT RECEIPTS
   A number of reports that can proceed to payment without the required receipts.

2. REPORT GRACE PERIOD
   A number of days of grace period in which a user can add missing receipts; the report will continue through the workflow to payment if approved within the

defined grace period. If the user doesn't add the missing receipts within the grace period, any other claims within the user's queue will also be held for payment.

Both payment hold types can be used within the same payment hold configuration. If both are used, Concur will evaluate either condition for an expense claim, not both. A payment hold is removed from an expense claim by an expense processor.

The RECEIPT IMAGING configuration can govern the way that your Concur users can use the receipt store. Users can upload and email receipt images to the receipt store to be attached to their expense entries or expense claim headers. The configuration can be used to restrict user upload of images to the receipt store, allow receipt images to be attached to a claim header, and for Concur to mark a claim as successfully having received receipts in the expense processor view if they have indeed been received. A RECEIPT IMAGING configuration is then assigned to each expense policy, allowing for different imaging configurations to be applied to different expense policies.

A list of *approved senders* can be used added to Concur for third parties to email receipts into the receipt store for a user. The central email address for the receipts to be sent from needs to be added to the approved senders lists, along with a description and contact info of the approved senders; then the sender can forward a receipt to *receipts@Concur.com* with the email address of the expense user in the email subject line, and the receipt will appear in that user's receipt store. This can be particularly useful if you use Concur Travel, because your TMC can email travel and ticket receipts into users' receipt stores.

Part of receipt handling is the SCAN configuration. SCAN configurations allow expense reports to be submitted without receipt images; these reports will then move to an expense processor, the receipts will then attach the scanned images to the expense entries. This may be necessary if not all employees in your company can capture receipt images themselves. A scan configuration will be created for each required scenario and then assigned to an expense policy.

If you use Concur in Mexico, Concur has functionality to support the use of CFDi XML files for expense claims.

4.4.11 Workflow

The advanced configuration options for workflows include standard settings for the type of workflow that an expense claim is subject to. Different workflow types can be assigned to either an expense claim or to a cash advance request.

In addition to the workflow types mentioned in the standard configuration discussions, the advanced workflow configuration will allow you to create a custom workflow to fit your company's expense policy workflow requirements. To create a new workflow process flow for your company, Concur has two workflow types that can be copied and then adjusted:

1. The CES standard report workflow follows the *employee to approving manager to expense processor* workflow.

2. Exception-based workflows are the same as the standard report workflow, but have an additional rule: If the expense claim has a report exception level of less than 50, the managerial approval step is skipped and the claim goes directly to the expense processor as approved.

There are different settings and processes depending on whether your company chooses to use *authorized approvers* or *cost object approvers*. An *authorized approver* is defined to authorize a specific kind of report, such as for specified approval limits or certain types of exceptions. A *cost object approver* is assigned to a specific accounting object. When using an approval hierarchy for either approval type, the hierarchy is configured in the FEATURE HIERARCHIES step. Approval limits can either be assigned directly to the user in the user profile or defined as part of an assignment in the feature hierarchy.

Using a cost object approval workflow will allow a specific budget's owner to approve all expenses attributed to that budget; if the expense claim contains more than one cost object, each budget approver can approve the costs for her budget in parallel, preventing the need to go through each process flow step one after the other. The approval selection can then be configured to be based on either sequential position of a manager in the organization or value limits assigned to each approver. If at any point in the workflow process an approver rejected the expense claim, then any of the workflow processes currently in process will terminate, and the expense claim will be returned to the employee to start the workflow process from the point of initiation.

An authorized approver workflow follows the default approval checks and then performs an additional check to ensure that the approver identified is authorized for approvals.

4.5 Concur Expense Pay Global

Most companies that use Concur (or any other T&E platform) reimburse their employees through Accounts Payable, Payroll, or third-party financial systems. Most also have a separate process to pay credit card accounts. There's usually a lot of manpower, time, and money that goes into this process—and it often still results in occasional errors, delayed payments to employees, or even employees not getting paid at all.

This is where Concur steps in with Concur Expense Pay Global, an automated employee and credit card reimbursement solution. Concur Expense Pay Global automatically pays employees and corporate credit cards based on the expense reports previously entered by employees. In the following sections, we'll look at the processes, configuration, and maintenance of Concur Expense Pay Global.

4.5.1 Processes

Every expense report that an employee submits can contain three possible types of charges:

1. Cash (or personal credit card) transactions that must be reimbursed to the employee.
2. Corporate credit card transactions, either to be reimbursed to the employee to balance the card account (INDIVIDUALLY BILLED/INDIVIDUALLY PAID) or to be paid directly to the card issuing bank (INDIVIDUALLY BILLED/COMPANY PAID or COMPANY BILLED/COMPANY PAID—or any form of purchasing card and meeting card should they be processed through Concur Expense instead of Concur Invoice).
3. Expenses prepaid by the company (e.g., when a BTA/ghost card, (discussed in Chapter 3, Section 3.4.9) is used in Concur Travel to pay for bookings), which are only required to be entered in Concur Expense to go through the appropriate approval flow.

Concur Expense Pay Global looks at expense reports that have been approved and processed, and ignores the third type of charges, which doesn't require any action. Then, it separates the first two types of charges and puts them into two different batches: one batch to contain the overall cash amount to be reimbursed to employees, and the other containing the amounts due to the credit card issuing bank.

At a specific time during the day (usually early afternoon), Concur sums up the open amounts in both batches and sends a transfer request to the company's funding account. Once the correct amounts are available to Concur, it electronically pays employees with deposits to their own bank accounts and the card issuing bank into its bank account. Within a couple of days, both parties will have received settlement (see Figure 4.25).

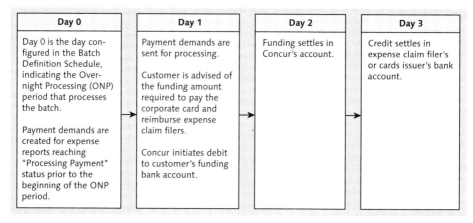

Figure 4.25 Settlement Process Timeline

When organizations use this end-to-end system to monitor their entire expense reimbursement process, their administrative and management costs associated with payments are reduced. No integration with other payment systems is required, which means electronic payments clear fast (in two or three bank-processing days for most countries).

4.5.2   Configuration

To begin, ensure that all employees either have a bank account (and are willing to enter the bank account information in an online platform such as Concur) or a prepaid card with a correlating bank account for funding transfers. In addition, requiring employees to use electronic payment must be in accordance with the HR department. Once these administrative hurdles are passed and Concur Expense Pay Global is purchased, the configuration itself is comparatively simple.

Concur Expense Pay Global can set up batches differently per expense group. This is very important if you have groups of employees that can't be paid electronically but require payment through Payroll, have multiple legal entities or business units with different bank accounts to be used to fund the reimbursement of expenses, or if your company operates in multiple countries, in which case you want to ensure that Concur Expense Pay Global doesn't try to pay a Canadian employee from a US bank account or a German employee from a British bank account.

Employee groups must be set up to split the company/employees into different subsets. The correct group will then have to be assigned to each employee either manually in Concur (in the USER ADMINISTRATION area) or via employee import from the HR system.

Each employee group is linked to an expense group (usually with the same name)—and each expense group is then assigned to one (or more) of the payment batches in Concur Expense Pay Global. The next two subsections will explain how the funding accounts are set up and the payment batches configured.

Funding Accounts

In the PAYMENT MANAGER in Concur, click on FUNDING ACCOUNTS and add as many accounts as you need—usually one per legal entity, business unit, or country in which you're using Concur Expense Pay Global (see Figure 4.26).

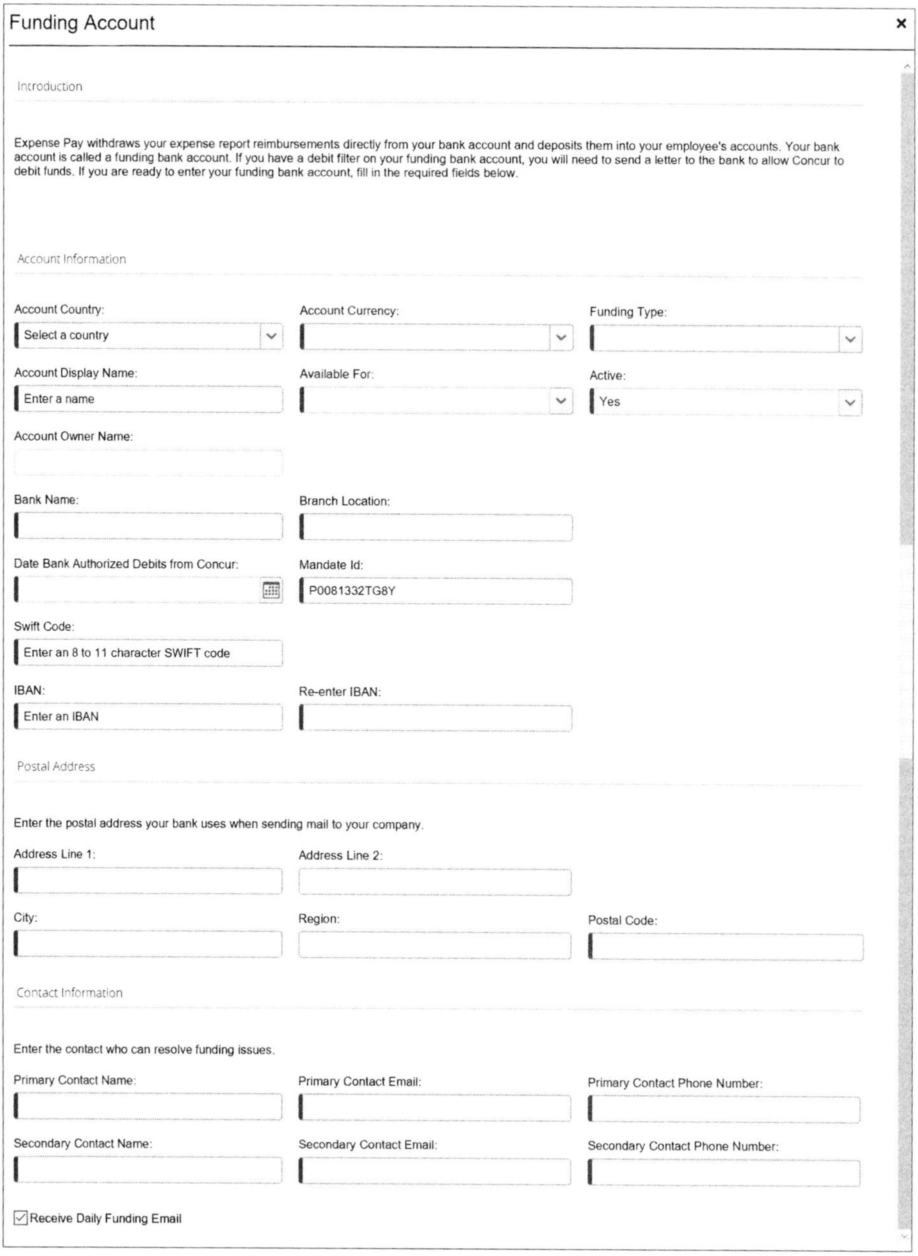

Funding Account   ✕

Introduction

Expense Pay withdraws your expense report reimbursements directly from your bank account and deposits them into your employee's accounts. Your bank account is called a funding bank account. If you have a debit filter on your funding bank account, you will need to send a letter to the bank to allow Concur to debit funds. If you are ready to enter your funding bank account, fill in the required fields below.

Account Information

Account Country:	Account Currency:	Funding Type:
Select a country		
Account Display Name:	Available For:	Active:
Enter a name		Yes
Account Owner Name:		
Bank Name:	Branch Location:	
Date Bank Authorized Debits from Concur:	Mandate Id:	
	P0081332TG8Y	

Swift Code:

Enter an 8 to 11 character SWIFT code

IBAN:	Re-enter IBAN:
Enter an IBAN	

Postal Address

Enter the postal address your bank uses when sending mail to your company.

Address Line 1:	Address Line 2:	
City:	Region:	Postal Code:

Contact Information

Enter the contact who can resolve funding issues.

Primary Contact Name:	Primary Contact Email:	Primary Contact Phone Number:
Secondary Contact Name:	Secondary Contact Email:	Secondary Contact Phone Number:

☑ Receive Daily Funding Email

Figure 4.26 All Information Needed to Set Up Funding Account in Payment Manager

Once the setup of the funding accounts has been completed, Concur will run a *penny test* (depositing a very small amount in an employee's account to ensure it can connect to the specified bank accounts). We highly recommend that your contact at the bank (the person added to the PRIMARY CONTACT NAME field in the screen shown in Figure 4.26) is notified about this step to ensure the penny test isn't prevented by security measures (see Figure 4.27).

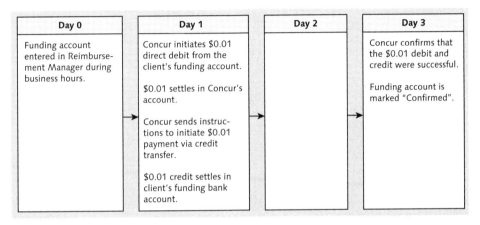

Day 0	Day 1	Day 2	Day 3
Funding account entered in Reimbursement Manager during business hours.	Concur initiates $0.01 direct debit from the client's funding account. $0.01 settles in Concur's account. Concur sends instructions to initiate $0.01 payment via credit transfer. $0.01 credit settles in client's funding bank account.		Concur confirms that the $0.01 debit and credit were successful. Funding account is marked "Confirmed".

Figure 4.27 Process Timeline for Concur Penny Test for a Funding Account

Create Payment Batches

Payment batches are simple to set up. To do so, start by answering the following questions:

▸ To which expense group does the payment batch apply?

▸ What's the payment type to be covered by this batch?

▸ Which funding account is to be used?

▸ How often is this batch to run?

There are different configuration pages for an employee batch (see Figure 4.28) and a card batch (see Figure 4.29).

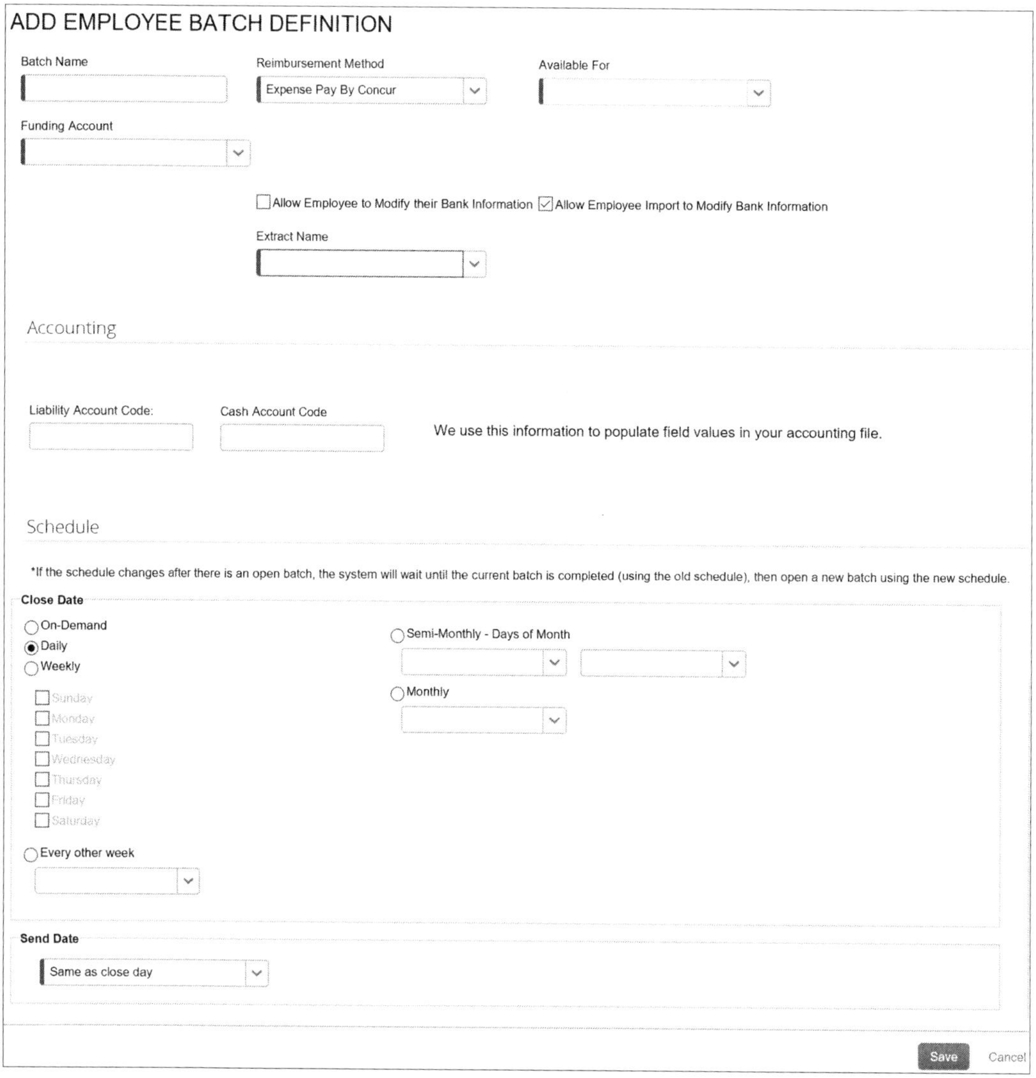

ADD EMPLOYEE BATCH DEFINITION

Batch Name

Reimbursement Method
Expense Pay By Concur

Available For

Funding Account

☐ Allow Employee to Modify their Bank Information   ☑ Allow Employee Import to Modify Bank Information

Extract Name

Accounting

Liability Account Code:

Cash Account Code

We use this information to populate field values in your accounting file.

Schedule

*If the schedule changes after there is an open batch, the system will wait until the current batch is completed (using the old schedule), then open a new batch using the new schedule.

Close Date

○ On-Demand
◉ Daily
○ Weekly

☐ Sunday
☐ Monday
☐ Tuesday
☐ Wednesday
☐ Thursday
☐ Friday
☐ Saturday

○ Every other week

○ Semi-Monthly - Days of Month

○ Monthly

Send Date

Same as close day

Save   Cancel

Figure 4.28 Setup for Employee Batch

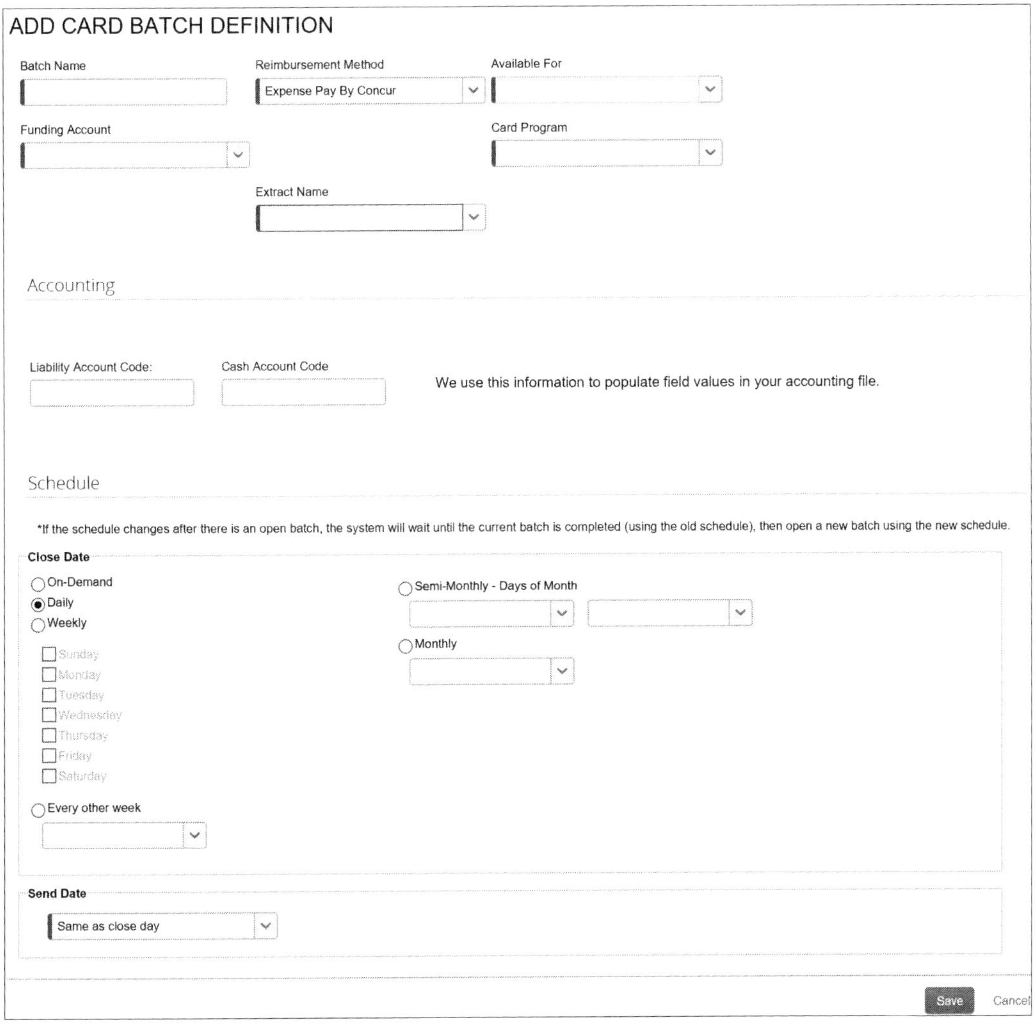

ADD CARD BATCH DEFINITION

Batch Name

Reimbursement Method
Expense Pay By Concur

Available For

Funding Account

Card Program

Extract Name

Accounting

Liability Account Code:

Cash Account Code

We use this information to populate field values in your accounting file.

Schedule

*If the schedule changes after there is an open batch, the system will wait until the current batch is completed (using the old schedule), then open a new batch using the new schedule.

Close Date

- ○ On-Demand
- ● Daily
- ○ Weekly
  - ☐ Sunday
  - ☐ Monday
  - ☐ Tuesday
  - ☐ Wednesday
  - ☐ Thursday
  - ☐ Friday
  - ☐ Saturday
- ○ Every other week

- ○ Semi-Monthly - Days of Month

- ○ Monthly

Send Date

Same as close day

Save   Cancel

Figure 4.29 Setup for Card Batch

The only remaining step is for employees to log into Concur and enter their bank information in the profile settings (see Figure 4.30).

Bank Information

Bank Country	Bank Currency
UNITED STATES ⌄	US. Dollar

Routing Number	Bank Account Number	Re-Type Bank Account Number

Bank Name	Branch Location	Account Type
		Checking ⌄

Status	Active
	Yes ⌄

Save And Agree

By entering your bank account information you are authorizing direct deposit using electronic funds transfer into this account for amounts due to you. If you do not want to authorize direct deposit then you should not enter your bank account information.

John Q. Public
1358 Main St.
Sometown, OH 98765
_____ 20 ___   1001

Pay to the order of _____
_____ Dollars ⌷

VOID

Bank of Sometown

⦙: 234123987 ⦙:   001234567891 ⫿• 1001

Bank Routing Number   Bank Account Number   Check Number (Do not use)

Routing Number is usually located between the ⦙: symbols on your check and is 9 digits.

Account Number is usually located before the ⫿• symbol on your check and is 3-17 digits.

Figure 4.30 Bank Information Page in Concur Profile Settings

Once the required information is added, Concur will perform a penny test to verify the employee's bank account, which usually takes two days (see Figure 4.31).

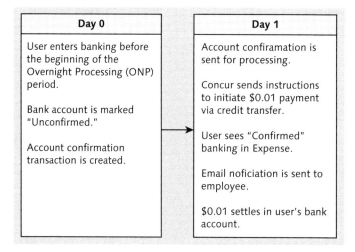

Day 0	Day 1
User enters banking before the beginning of the Overnight Processing (ONP) period.	Account confiramation is sent for processing.
Bank account is marked "Unconfirmed."	Concur sends instructions to initiate $0.01 payment via credit transfer.
Account confirmation transaction is created.	User sees "Confirmed" banking in Expense.
	Email noficiation is sent to employee.
	$0.01 settles in user's bank account.

Figure 4.31 Timeline for Confirmation of Employee's Bank Account

Concur will not allow expense reports to be submitted without bank information available (unless an employee is set up in a non-Concur Expense Pay Global employee group and therefore not required to provide banking information to Concur).

4.5.3 Maintenance of Concur Expense Pay Global

The most common issue faced in Concur Expense Pay Global arises when employees enter their bank account details incorrectly in Concur. In such a case, Concur's penny test can't positively verify the existence of the bank account and will restrict an employee from submitting an expense report (see Figure 4.32).

If an employee complains to your support team or accounting department that he still can't submit expense reports despite having entered his bank information, it's possible to verify where the issue lies quickly. To do so, open PAYMENT MANAGER, then click on MONITOR PAYEES and check the entries on the EMPLOYEE BANKING tab.

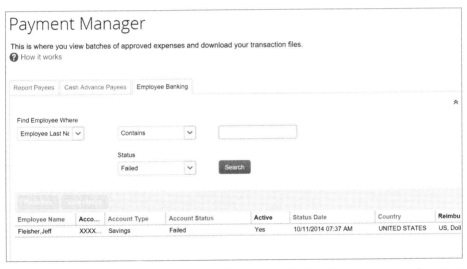

Figure 4.32 Employee Banking Tab Listing All Employees with Failed Bank Account Confirmations

Another question that can come up is about delays in payment. Many employees don't understand that submitting an expense report doesn't result in being paid the next day. In addition to time needed for managers to approve a report and finance departments to take at least have a quick look at a report before processing it, an electronic transfer always takes two to three days from initiation to completion. The status of an expense report can be verified in the Expense Processor module, and the status of an expense payment can be checked in the PAYMENT MANAGER under MONITOR BATCHES (see Figure 4.33 and Figure 4.34).

Figure 4.33 Payment Manager: View Batches

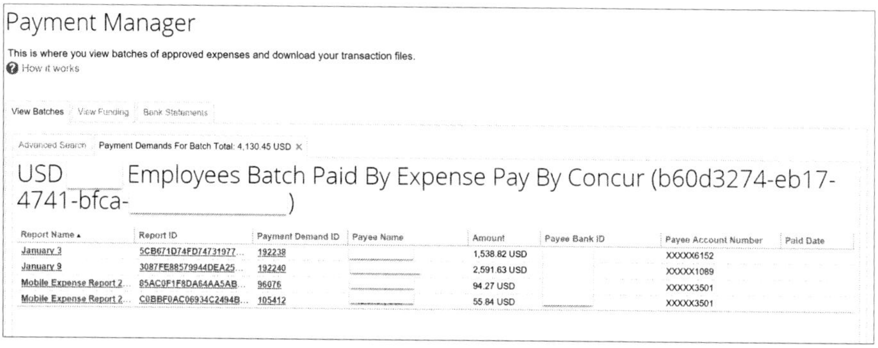

Figure 4.34 Payment Manager: Details of Selected Batch

4.6   Market-Specific Requirements

In this section, we'll look at the key requirements for compliant expenses for the United States, Canada, the United Kingdom, Germany, Australia and New Zealand, as well as some notes on the Asia Pacific region. These configurations will come as part of the standard localization for your Concur implementation; covering each requirement will provide a complete understanding of how Concur supports and enforces these legislative requirements and give you the knowledge to activate these checks within your Concur instance.

4.6.1   United States

The configuration for the United States is relatively simple because no VAT has to be configured. Of the usual information required to be entered by employees, the following elements apply to US employees:

▸ EXPENSE TYPE (for Concur to assign the correct GL account)

▸ TRANSACTION DATE

▸ VENDOR (for the employer to be able to run spend reports per vendor and potentially negotiate discounts)

▸ CITY (discretionary field only required alongside the vendor for vendor discount negotiations)

▸ AMOUNT

Based on IRS rules, employees also must provide a receipt for any expense higher than $75. Most companies decide to apply the $75 limit for credit card charges and $25 for expenses paid in cash. For per diems/travel allowances, GSA rates apply. Any amount over the limit provided by the GSA is technically taxable income and must be reported. To review GSA-provided per diem rates, visit *http://www.gsa.gov/portal/category/104711*.

Concur supports the GSA rates as well and will activate them within the Travel Allowance module that can be purchased during the initial sales process or afterwards from your account manager.

Finally, the usage of personal vehicles for business purposes and reimbursable rates are defined by the government as well. The rates can be found at *http://www.gsa.gov/portal/content/100715*.

4.6.2 Canada

Canada differs from many countries in that it has multiple national and provincial tax rates. This requires a more detailed configuration of the tax module in Concur Expense—which is not made easier by the fact that companies in Canada potentially have multiple options for how to declare/calculate tax through Concur.

In most Canadian provinces, both provincial sales taxes (PSTs) levied by the provinces and the goods and services tax (GST), a value-added tax levied by the federal government, are used. Some provinces do not use a PST, using only the GST. In other provinces, a combined harmonized sales tax (HST, also a value-added tax), a single, blended combination of the PST and GST, is used.

You can find the GST and HST rates at *http://www.cra-arc.gc.ca/tx/bsnss/tpcs/gst-tps/rts-eng.html#rt*. The PST and QST rates of the various provinces can be found at the following sites:

▶ British Columbia: *http://www2.gov.bc.ca/gov/content/taxes/sales-taxes/pst*

▶ Manitoba: *https://www.gov.mb.ca/finance/taxation/taxes/retail.html*

▶ Saskatchewan: *http://www.finance.gov.sk.ca/taxes/pst*

▶ Quebec: *http://www.revenuquebec.ca/en/entreprises/taxes/tpstvhtvq/default.aspx*

If you need the correct taxes and rates to be set up in Concur for Canada, your in-country finance team can provide the required information to Concur. Concur supports tax configuration for multiple provinces within the same country. Instead of one configuration for all of Canada, the provinces in which employees will be incurring expenses need to be set up separately. For provinces that use HST, only one configuration must be set up; for provinces that use a combination of GST and PST/QST, two tax configurations must be added.

There are two more choices for how to set up VAT for Canada:

1. **Extraction factor**

   This Canada calculation method should only be set up if your company decided to use the Canada Revenue Agency's simplified method, commonly called the EXTRACTION FACTOR. The extraction factor entered in a tax configuration in Concur calculates the reclaimable amount based on a percentage of the overall expenses entered in Concur.

Note: This is not an applicable choice for companies that use the Canada Revenue Agency's exact (prescribed) calculation method.

2. **Actual tax amounts per receipt**
Instead of relying on Concur for the calculation of the tax amounts based on the expense amount entered and the rates configured, you can have Concur allow employees to overwrite the calculated tax amount during the expense entry process.

This is usually a functionality only provided for the processor step in Concur, but the fields involved can be set as visible and editable for employees.

You can enter expenses using actual tax amounts per receipt using the following method:

1. An employee enters an expense and clicks on SAVE.
2. The employee opens the expense entry again and compares the tax amount values visible in Concur with the values printed on her receipt.
3. If the values differ, the employee can change the values accordingly and save the amended expense entry.
4. If there is no difference, the employee enters the next expense.
5. Based on the tax amounts saved in the fields at the time an expense entry is saved last, the reclaim amount is calculated.

After expenses have been submitted and approved by a manager, the processor/finance step can change values that an employee might have miscalculated or defined incorrectly (see Figure 4.35).

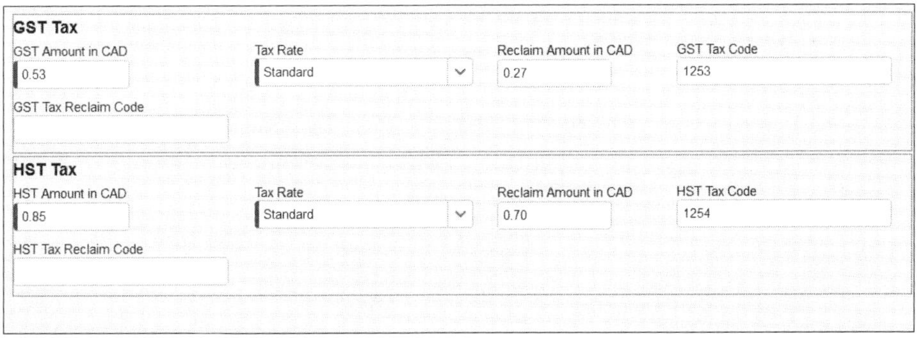

Figure 4.35 Options for Processor to Change Tax-Related Values for Each Expense

> **Personal Car Mileage**
>
> Tax is not the only item that differs by province; car mileage reimbursement does as well. When setting up Canadian employees in Concur, it's important to specify an employee's province of employment; that information will drive the applicable tax rate.
>
> The automobile allowance rates in Canada can be found at *http://www.cra-arc.gc.ca/tx/bsnss/tpcs/pyrll/bnfts/tmbl/llwnc/rts-eng.html*.

4.6.3   United Kingdom

Many of the requirements for the United Kingdom are managed via audit rules, either simple or complex; though they are delivered in your Concur instance, they may not be activated. Activating these rules is straightforward, but you must ensure that you activate the audit rule for the correct UK expense policy and that you test the rule thoroughly to ensure that it meets the requirements of your company's expense policy and legislative rules.

Receipts

In recent years, Her Majesty's Revenue and Customs has confirmed that electronic record versions are indeed acceptable for most records, so long as they contain all the information pertinent to the expense being claimed. This information should include all the information on both the front and back of the document, and it should allow the information to be presented to HMRC in a readable format if it so requested.

Concur meets these criteria, so long as expense images are being taken at a high quality. Providing good guidance and examples for your Concur users in process and FAQ documents will help them understand how best to capture expense images. The processing step in the Concur workflow provides a quality assurance check to determine if an expense image meets the appropriate guidelines; it should alert employees when their expense images do not meet these guidelines.

Fuel and Mileage

Concur has specific configuration features to manage processing of mileage and fuel as part of the UK localization for Concur. Employees will usually claim either mileage or fuel expenses, depending on your expense policy; Concur will allow both types of expense to be recorded but only one to be claimed by the employee, to enable your company to take advantage of VAT reclamation options. Concur will only reimburse an employee for the mileage that he claims.

To ensure that the *fuel for mileage* expense type isn't reimbursed to an employee when they claim it, the expense can be configured as personal using the mileage expense entry form. On the form, configure the PERSONAL EXPENSE field with a default setting value of YES and as read-only in all user views. Then, when an employee inputs this expense type, Concur will automatically set the expense type to not reimburse the employee.

Each mileage rate type, company or personal, is configured in Concur; to claim each mileage type, employees create a record for a car in their profile as either a company or personal car. Each car record type can then only be used with the relevant mileage expense type.

Figure 4.36 Car Configuration Using Variable Rates

For varying mileage rates, Concur uses different CAR TYPES in the CAR CONFIGURATION setup to allow different mileage rates to be applied to employee claims automatically for either mileage type or allow varying rates due to distance and vehicle types. For example, the MILEAGE ALLOWANCE PAYMENT rate for cars and vans reduces to £0.25 per mile claimed over the first 10,000 miles. As shown in Figure 4.36, the UK PERSONAL CAR configuration sets VARIABLE RATES in the CAR TYPE field, which then allows the DISTANCE LIMITS tab to be configured as shown in Figure 4.37. The car configurations must be correctly described as variable to access to the tab to assign the variable details.

Figure 4.37 Distance Variables Assigned to Car Configuration

In the final configuration step to assign reimbursement rates to the car configuration, the distance limits previously configured can be used to configure different reimbursement rates, as shown in Figure 4.38.

Figure 4.38 Two Reimbursement Rates Based on Configured Variables

Each different expense type—fuel for mileage, company car mileage, or personal car mileage—can be assigned to the appropriate tax reclaim group. Then, when an employee claims these expense types, the relevant tax amounts and reclaim codes are applied depending on your company's tax reclaim policy for expenses.

Incidentals

Daily incidental expense types are limited to their upper daily value with an expense limit applied to the expense via an audit rule. A simple limit applied to the expense type itself wouldn't account for the difference in allowance for either domestic or foreign rates. Upon saving an entry, the audit rule will check whether the entry is domestic (i.e., within the United Kingdom) or foreign and will apply the appropriate limit of either £5 or £10, respectively.

P11D Reporting

Concur does not directly provide P11D reporting for your employees, but a standard audit rule also exists in Concur to alert the expense processor that the user has claimed an expense type applicable for P11D processing.

This audit rule will show the expense processor an information exception message noting that the expense type claimed is liable for P11D reporting. The rule merely checks against a set of prepopulated expense types and checks that they have not been claimed as personal expenses. The rule doesn't check the value of any of the specific expense types nor differentiate between the expense types in any way. Therefore, as per the standard configuration, this rule can be considered a usual alert or reminder to the expense processor of this expense type, therefore indicating that the employee has P11D reporting implications.

Yearly Value of Gifts

Concur provides a standard audit rule to manage to VAT requirements on the annual value of gifts, for either internal staff or external clients, and there are some further standard settings that you can use to enhance the way this can be managed.

First, the standard audit rule will check for use of the *gift-client* or *gift-staff* expense type and that the entry is domestic. When these conditions are fulfilled, the traveler, approver, and expense processor all will see a warning level of exception message stating that standard VAT is only reclaimable if the annual value is adhered to. This alerts all levels of user to the annual level VAT reclaim cap. However, this doesn't give the users tools to meet this limitation, if appropriate. There are further settings that can be activated to help users keep track of the year-to-date amounts claimed per attendee.

Within the ATTENDEE CONFIGURATION menu, options are available to enable the management of the annual year-to-date spending for an attendee without having to look after the fact via reporting methods. From the ATTENDEE CONFIGURATION menu, ensure that the expense types used for gifts in your Concur instance are set to be included in the annual total of cost per attendee; then, enable to the DISPLAY ATTENDEE TOTAL FOR THE CALENDAR YEAR option. This will ensure that the attendee's total claimed spending for the calendar year is displayed to the user on the attendee form for the expense type. This totals information is shown for specific attendees across the board—that is, all users who have included this attendee on any expenses, not just the user using the attendee record at the time.

If your company's expense policy has a cap on the total value allowable for any one attendee per year, you can easily add a further additional audit rule that can check on the annual value of expenditure for the attendee. Simply create a copy of the audit rule to check for the VAT conditions as mentioned previously, and add another condition to check on the annual yearly total figures, with a value limit of £50.00.

VAT Invoices for Expenses over £250.00

Maximizing VAT reclamation on expenses over £250.00 is difficult to mandate in Concur, so Concur provides a standard audit rule to highlight requirements for your expense processor.

The rule checks for the value of an expense type, any expense type, over the value of £250.00 submitted with the receipt status of TAX RECEIPT. So long as the country of the expense is the United Kingdom, the processor will see an exception warning on the expense claim, alerting the processor of the requirement to reclaim 100% of the VAT on the expense item.

Vehicle Hire

Car rentals require differing VAT reclaim codes depending on the length of rental and the use of the vehicle. Concur configuration can apply this categorization to the car rental expense type easily with a secondary field to add subdivisions to the expense type. The user selects the expense type of CAR RENTAL, and Concur will then present the user with a new field, NUMBER OF DAYS RENTAL. This is a mandatory field that the user must complete to be able to claim the expense type.

This field presents four options to the user to describe the usage of the expense:

1. HIRE FOR ANY DURATION TO REPLACE A COMPANY CAR

2. HIRE FOR MORE THAN 10 DAYS, BUSINESS USE ONLY

3. HIRE FOR UP TO 10 DAYS, BUSINESS USE ONLY

4. INCLUDES BUSINESS AND PERSONAL USE

This information, in conjunction with the RECEIPT TYPE field, can drive the appropriate VAT reclaim codes for the expense to reclaim 100%, 50%, or 0%.

Taxi Fares

The RECEIPT STATUS field can be used to drive the appropriate tax reclaim status for the expense type of taxis. In the TAXATION customization steps, the receipt types of either TAX RECEIPT or RECEIPT can be mapped to the appropriate tax reclaim codes of UK1 or UK0.

However, you will find that the expense type of TAXI will come assigned as standard to the tax group of NON RECLAIMABLE. Due to the nature of the tax arrangement for VAT reclaim on the cost of taxi fares, this can be considered the easiest option; for most companies, the overhead of vetting the expense details easily outweighs the value of the tax to be reclaimed.

4.6.4 Germany

Germany has a reputation for being very complex in its regulations, and expense reimbursements are not an exception. The rules around travel allowance, the deductions to be applied, and the various tax implications can look daunting, but Concur can be set up to deal with all this quite effectively.

Travel Allowances

The first implementation of a German rule set contains the legal travel allowances for all countries. In the future, if some rates change, you either need to amend the allowances yourself or request an update from Concur support.

If you have configuration rights, you can modify single rates by yourself. You can always download the list to a TXT file and send the amended list to Concur support to upload.

> **Note**
>
> There will be no automation for legal changes of any allowance or deduction rates in the future.

Because Concur is a product born in the United States, allowances were created on top as Concur started to adapt the system to Germany's and other countries' legislative rules. Therefore, most users find the itinerary allowance handling not as user-friendly as the receipts handling.

When creating a new expense claim, the Concur system asks if the trip will include travel allowances rates. If you click on YES, you can maintain itineraries. For multiday itineraries, there is no distinction between domestic trips and trips abroad. You always have to enter one trip in two parts (meaning two forms). First, you enter the date and time of departure and also arrival at the destination, as shown in Figure 4.39, and click on SAVE. Second, you add another stop for the return or for the next destination, and you also state when you left the first location and when you arrived back home or at your next destination.

After you click on NEXT from the EXPENSES & ADJUSTMENTS tab, you can see the calculated allowances and generate expense types for the daily allowances by clicking the UPDATE EXPENSES button.

For one-day trips, choose SINGLE DAY ITINERARIES, as shown in Figure 4.40. This option always shows a whole week in which you can enter your destinations and start and arrival hours. If you select the EXCLUDE checkbox, then no allowance will be generated for that day.

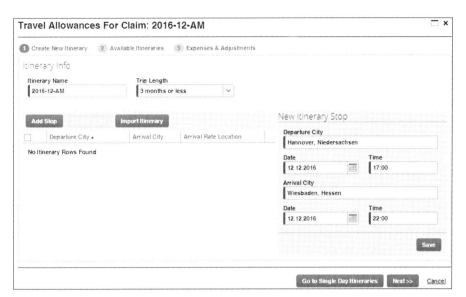

Figure 4.39 First Leg of Multiday Trip

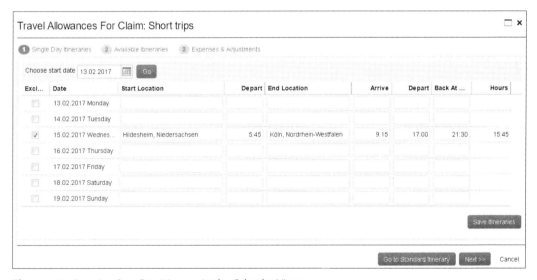

Figure 4.40 Entering One-Day Itinerary in the Calendar View

Overnight Allowance

When an employee has a private stay with friends, an overnight allowance is given. This can be requested on the EXPENSES & ADJUSTMENTS tab.

The lodging rates are delivered in the same area as allowances. The overnight allowance can be handled differently. Depending on the settings, the overnight allowance can be requested by activating the OVERNIGHT checkbox, adding the allowance to the daily allowance for the same expense type. By default, the USE OVERNIGHT option in the travel allowance configuration is deactivated. To get different expense types for overnight and daily allowances, the setting has to be activated, and the accomodation type has to be set to DAILY ALLOWANCE, as in Figure 4.41. Once activated, the dropdown list to select the LODGING TYPE will be available.

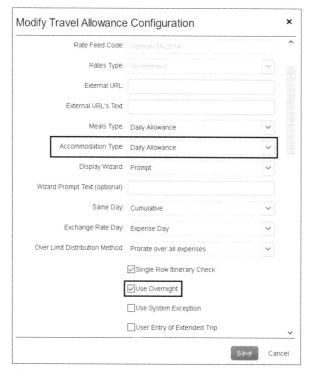

Figure 4.41 Setting for Different Expense Types for Overnight and Daily Allowances

Deductions

On the EXPENSES & ADJUSTMENTS tab, the user also lists meals provided. While setting up the system, you can choose if meals can include benefit-in-kind or if not. If not, you'll see checkboxes like those in Figure 4.42:

▶ BREAKFAST PROVIDED

▶ LUNCH PROVIDED

▶ DINNER PROVIDED

If yes, you either see a dropdown list with the following kind of meals:

▶ BUSINESS ENTERTAINMENT (meal amount will be deducted)

▶ COMPANY EVENT (meal amount will be deducted)

▶ EXTERNAL ACTIVITY (more than eight hours, meal amount will be deducted; less than eight hours, no deduction, for reporting purposes only)

▶ INCENTIVE MEAL (no deduction, reporting purposes only)

▶ WORKING MEAL (meal amount will be deducted)

Or you'll see the deduction list with the following entries:

▶ TAXABLE (meal tax will be deducted)

▶ PROVIDED (meal amount will be deducted)

▶ NOT PROVIDED (no deduction)

Figure 4.42 Overnight as Dropdown and Deductions as Checkboxes

Either way, the user needs to know the legislative rules well to make the correct selection, and taxable meals still need to be handled in a manual, postpayroll process. If you have a different process for handling benefit-in-kind meals, we would recommend using the checkboxes for the deduction of working meals. For any other business meals provided, you can set up your own expense types where the attendees of the meal need to be maintained. This can be reported on as well and handled later in a manual process.

M-Report

German companies must print an "M" in the certificate of wage tax deduction if an employee had meals provided. M-reports also list meals provided if checkboxes are in place. The summarized report contains a list of employees who meet the criteria, as shown in Figure 4.43. The detailed M-report contains all trips and the kinds of meals provided.

Employee ID	Employee Last Name	Employee First Name	Employee Active Flag	M-Flag
224			Y	Yes
1007			Y	Yes
585			Y	Yes
663			Y	Yes
1005			Y	Yes
29			Y	Yes
648			Y	Yes
674			Y	Yes
599			Y	Yes
569			Y	Yes

Figure 4.43 M-Report Summary

The yearly employee report also contains the itinerary duration, allowance paid, total deductions, and overnights. This report can be used to declare the yearly paid allowance in the certificate of wage tax.

Benefit-in-Kind Report

In Germany, if travel allowance is zero because the trip duration was less than eight hours and meals at the external activity were provided, then the employee has to pay tax on benefits in kind. The benefit-in-kind (BIK) report evaluates these and other such cases. If there is no integration to Payroll in SAP ERP HCM, the taxation has to be handled manually afterward.

The BIK report only produces results if benefit-in-kind dropdown lists for meals provided are used. Otherwise, the yearly employee report can be used to calculate tax amounts.

The values for breakfast, lunch, and dinner can be configured in the Travel Allowance section (if a user has configuration rights).

Three-Month Rule

Traveling for a long time to the same location leads to full taxation of travel allowance, because the location is determined to be a regular place of work. The calculation is quite difficult. A three-month period starts when the traveler is on a three-day trip. If there is no break of at least 28 days, where the employee does not work at that same location, then the allowances are fully taxable after three months. The prerequisite for the calculation is to use the exact same address for same destination. The name of the city is not enough, because a traveler can visit different places in the same city.

If the USE ADDRESS LIST checkbox in Concur is active, then the user needs to enter the full address when creating itineraries, including the street, city, and postal code. Later, the user can choose from the list of his addresses.

> **Note**
>
> If the USE ADDRESS LIST checkbox is active, the SINGLE DAY ITINERARIES page is not yet supported.

4.6.5   Australia and New Zealand

Australia and New Zealand have been important markets for Concur for a while, so the solution has achieved a good level of maturity for this locale. The two big topics to watch out for are GST and fringe benefits tax (FBT).

Goods and Services Tax

Prices for typical travel and entertainment expenses include GST in the total price. In Australia, the rate is 10%, and it's 15% in New Zealand (as of January 1, 2017).

GST is not applied to all expenses; for example, fresh food, most medical expenses, exports including international airfare, and accommodations if hotel rooms or apartments are individually owned are exempt.

Concur's global template is preconfigured with typical tax requirements, including three key tax groups:

1. Standard
2. No GST
3. Domestic/international

The *standard* tax group claims the full GST input tax credit if both of the following circumstances are met:

▸ The expense was purchased in the employee's home country.

▸ The user has a tax invoice, or the amount is less than the tax office's threshold for a tax invoice.

Tax invoice thresholds are $82.50 in Australia and $50 in New Zealand.

The *no GST* tax group is configured for expenses that are free of GST.

Expense types configured in the *domestic/international* tax group cater to expenses purchased domestically, but could be of a domestic or international nature; for example, domestic airfares have GST, but international airfares are GST-free. Employees must identify if the expense was domestic or international. Concur will calculate the GST for domestic airfares, but not international airfares.

Receipt Status

Concur uses three receipt statuses:

1. Tax Receipt
2. Receipt
3. No Receipt

GST may be reclaimed when the transaction has the following properties:

▸ In the employee's home country

▸ The expense type is in either of the following:

  ▸ Standard tax group

  ▸ Domestic/international tax group and is a domestic expense.

GST cannot be claimed when the transaction exceeds the tax invoice threshold if the receipt status is Receipt or No Receipt.

E-receipts do not satisfy the requirements of a tax invoice.

Mixed Supplies

Purchases in supermarkets and petrol stations often include mixed supplies. A *mixed supply purchase* includes a mix of goods with GST (e.g., flavored milk) and some that are free of GST (e.g., fresh milk). Company tax teams often approach mixed supply purchases as follows:

▸ Expense types are mapped to the most likely tax group and accept the discrepancies this approach allows, due to the small amounts involved. This results in over reclaiming or under reclaiming GST.

▸ Users are allowed to amend the GST amount. The user can be allowed to change the GST amount, but some finance system ignore the tax calculations and rely on the gross or net amount in conjunction with the tax reclaim code.

▸ Expenses are itemized:

　▹ Multiple expense types clearly identify if they are for expenses that include/don't include GST, such as fresh food (no GST).

　▹ A GST FREE checkbox can be added to the expense form and a tax rule added to not calculate GST when the box is checked. This option is only available in Concur professional edition.

Uber Expenses

Uber does not (as of February 2017) issue tax invoices and there is no GST to reclaim. Uber expenses are typically coded as taxi expenses, as the credit card merchant category code (MCC) for taxis, limousines, and Uber are usually the same (4121). An audit rule identifying when the merchant name contains Uber and the expense type taxi can alert the user to change RECEIPT STATUS to RECEIPT. Custom audit rules must be enabled in Concur standard edition to enable this audit rule. Note that the audit rule is case-sensitive; you should include *Uber*, *UBER*, and *uber*.

Fringe Benefits Tax

Gifts and entertainment expenses can incur FBT for Australia and New Zealand employees. FBT calculation methods include actual expenditure and 50:50; the latter method assumes that 50% of total meals and entertainment expenses are liable for FBT. FBT is payable by the company. Concur's FBT module doesn't calculate the FBT payable but apportions the transaction based on attendee type.

Meal expenses are treated differently depending on whether the employee is traveling. Travel meals are typically deemed to be sustenance and not subject to FBT. Meal and entertainment expenses when not traveling may be subject to FBT depending on the circumstances.

When the FBT module is set up, users are required to identify attendees by type (business guest, employee, spouse, etc.). Employee attendees must be identified as Travelling or Not Travelling (see Figure 4.44).

Figure 4.44 Employee Attendees: Traveling or Not Traveling

As shown in Figure 4.45, Concur's FBT module apportions the expense based on the following:

▶ Ledger

▶ Expense Type

▶ Attendee Type

▶ Attendee Status (Travelling/Not Travelling)

▶ Location of the expense (Foreign or Domestic)

Each combination can have a separate Account Code, tax Reclaim Code, and reclaim treatment. When Reset Reclaim Code to Zero is selected, the GST will be calculated but not reclaimed. Entertainment of business guests cannot usually be reclaimed.

FBT setup must happen in conjunction with the local tax advisor to ensure the setup is consistent with the company's approach to FBT and GST.

Ledger	Expense Type	Attendee Type	Attendee Status	Foreign or Domestic	Account Code	Reclaim Code	Reset Reclaim Amount to Zero
SAP	Off Site Meals	Business Guest	Not Traveling/Not Applicable	Domestic	601111	P5	✓
SAP	Off Site Meals	Spouse/Partner	Not Traveling/Not Applicable	Foreign	601111	P5	✓
SAP	Off Site Meals	Spouse/Partner	Not Traveling/Not Applicable	Domestic	601111	P1	☐
SAP	Off Site Meals	No Shows	Not Traveling/Not Applicable	Domestic	601111	P5	✓
SAP	Off Site Meals	No Shows	Traveling	Domestic	601111	P5	✓
SAP	Off Site Meals	Employees	Not Traveling/Not Applicable	Foreign	601111	P5	✓
SAP	Off Site Meals	Employees	Traveling	Foreign	601111	P5	✓
SAP	Off Site Meals	Employees	Not Traveling/Not Applicable	Domestic	601111	P1	☐
SAP	Off Site Meals	Employees	Traveling	Domestic	601111	P1	☐
SAP	Off Site Meals	Healthcare Profe...	Not Traveling/Not Applicable	Foreign	601111	P5	✓
SAP	Off Site Meals	Healthcare Profe...	Not Traveling/Not Applicable	Domestic	601111	P5	✓

Figure 4.45 FBT Setup for Entertainment Expenses

FBT Reports

Companies with Concur Intelligence can run the following premium reports:

▸ Australian Fringe Benefit Tax Analytics Dashboard

▸ Australian Fringe Benefit Tax Details

The FBT dashboard provides a comparative analysis of the actual versus 50:50 methodologies to determine the most advantageous methodology. This may need to be interpreted in conjunction with other gifts and entertainment expenditures not processed in Concur.

Users select prompts, and the report estimates FBT and identifies the most advantageous method of calculation and details of the potential FBT events. Prompts include the following:

▸ TRANSACTION DATE range

▸ ATTENDEE STATUS (TRAVELLING/NOT TRAVELLING)

▸ ATTENDEE TYPE

▸ EXPENSE TYPE(S)

▸ GROSS UP FACTOR

▸ TAX RATE

▸ MINOR BENEFIT EXEMPTION AMOUNT

Travel Diary

The Australian Taxation Office (ATO) requires a travel diary when an employee travels away from home for more than five consecutive nights. Concur's TRAVEL DIARY (see Figure 4.46), accessible from the expense claim header, can record details of locations, dates, times, and purpose of travel. The Travel Diary is independent of itinerary data from itineraries in Concur Travel or Concur TripLink. The diary can be included on a printed summary of expenses, can be used in audit rules, and is available in reporting.

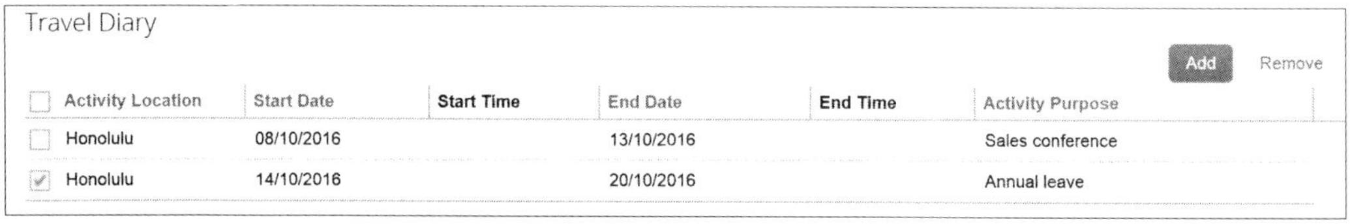

Travel Diary

	Activity Location	Start Date	Start Time	End Date	End Time	Activity Purpose
☐	Honolulu	08/10/2016		13/10/2016		Sales conference
☑	Honolulu	14/10/2016		20/10/2016		Annual leave

Add   Remove

Figure 4.46 Concur Travel Diary

Although designed for Australian regulatory requirements, the diary can be used in any country and provides a good overview of the locations and purpose of expenses.

Personal Car Mileage

The ATO's maximum rate for mileage reimbursement is $0.66 AUD/km. Companies can choose to reimburse at a higher rate, but any amount above $0.66 is taxable. Mileage per vehicle greater than 5,000 km per year may be taxable. Concur does not calculate any taxes that might be applicable on mileage expenses.

Travel Allowance

Most companies reimburse actual expenses and do not pay travel allowances. Travel allowances for part-day travel (i.e., no overnight stay) may be taxable and are often not reimbursed. The ATO specifies maximum reasonable amounts that can be paid without being declared as income and are exempt from substantiation requirements. Rates vary by salary range and location of the expense.

Instant Purchase Airfare

The cheaper classes of domestic and trans-Tasman (Australia to New Zealand and vice versa) airfares are typically instant purchase or require same-day payment and ticketing. Same-day preapproval of such travel is difficult to obtain, and itineraries not approved prior to expiration of the ticketing time limit (TTL) will be cancelled.

The recommended approach is to allow Concur Travel's configuration for travel policy and the use of visual guilt to guide a booker to compliant travel. Concur Travel or Concur Request can provide alerts to a nominated approver to show what has been booked. The booking is assumed to be approved unless the approver directs it to be canceled. In this model, the traveler is expected to have had an informal discussion with the approver, so the notification shouldn't be a surprise.

Credit Card Liability and Payment

Almost all Visa and MasterCard programs in Australia and New Zealand are company liability and company bill, company pay (CBCP). Banks typically direct-debit the entire balance regardless of whether the employee has submitted his expenses.

Employee Name Change

Employee names recorded in the company's HR system often don't match names on passports. This may be due to marriage, divorce, or the use of anglicized names in the workplace. For companies using Concur Travel, this situation usually requires the employee to be able to amend his name in his Concur profile and configure the name fields so they don't update with each new employee import. This means that name changes made in a company's HR system will not flow to Concur; the profile must be updated manually by the employee, a delegate, or an administrator.

Concur App Center Partner: ingogo taxi Bookings

The ingogo taxi booking app is a Concur App Center partner and can provide e-receipts directly to employee Concur accounts.

E-Receipts

Selected TMC partners can provide e-receipts of itinerary sectors and TMC booking fees directly to an employee's Concur Expense account.

Locale

The EN_AU (Australia), EN_NZ (New Zealand), EN_SG (Singapore), or EN_HK (Hong Kong) locale settings provide UK-based language, date, and number settings.

Flex Faring

Domestic flights in Australia, New Zealand, India, and flights between Australia and New Zealand use *flex faring* (also known as one-way combinable fares). Flex faring allows travelers to mix booking class and airlines on the same itinerary. Travelers will often book the cheapest, most restrictive flight on the outbound leg and book a more flexible return flight.

Flex faring can be configured to prevent more expensive booking classes to save money.

Non-GDS Hotel Partners

Regional hotels can be accessed via non-GDS hotel partners in Australia, including the following:

▶ Lido

▶ AOT

▶ Hotel Network

▶ Booking.com

4.6.6 Asia Pacific

Some countries, including India and China, have varying VAT/GST rates that can't readily be automated in Concur. This may require users to manually select VAT/GST rates from a dropdown menu to reflect rates shown on their receipts.

> **Note**
>
> Press reports indicate that India may implement a national GST, which may allow automation based on expense type in the future.

The JAPAN PUBLIC TRANSPORTATION expense type allows users to import trip information from their travel cards by using any card reader available in the market. Users can also manually search for stations and add details accordingly.

Some companies in Asia request complicated approval workflows that may require custom workflow creation from Concur. Complex workflows add considerable testing effort.

Hard-copy receipts are required in most countries in Asia, except Australia, New Zealand, and Singapore.

4.7 Summary

Concur Expense is an efficient, accurate, and easy-to-use expense solution. In this chapter, we discussed an effective expense process, including related business benefits, and looked at the configuration required for Concur and some advanced configuration options. We also walked through some country-specific requirements, and how they can be implemented in Concur.

In the next chapter, we'll talk about Concur Request, which is primarily used for getting and giving approvals for business trips and other travel.

Concur Request is designed to help businesses control expenses by requiring employees to obtain approval before incurring expenses.

5   Concur Request

Concur Request integrates directly into your travel booking and expense processes. Concur provides a complete T&E solution, which allows information to flow directly from Concur Travel to Concur Request—and from there into the expense report.

Concur Request is available as a standalone product, integrated with Concur Travel or with Concur Expense, or integrated with Concur Travel and Concur Expense. Your travel agency or travel management company (TMC) can also be integrated into the travel planning and approval process and will automatically receive alerts once travel is approved. Concur Request will also allow you to do the following:

▶ **Streamline trip preparation for employees**
Concur Request integrates with Concur Travel and Expense and connects with TMCs, meaning that travelers potentially only need to enter trip details once to cover both the request and the actual booking.

▶ **Control expenses before they occur**
Concur Request allows your managers to compare estimated costs of business travel and other expenses with their budget to make smarter decisions, ensure internal policies are adhered to, and eliminate unnecessary spending.

▶ **Integrated cash advances**
By integrating cash advance requests into the Concur Request process, companies can track planned versus actual advances. An additional option can carry over unspent funds from one trip to another.

▶ **Track planned and actual spending**
Concur Request itinerary data can be matched with actual credit card charges and hotel receipts. This allows to companies to track the difference between what employees are planning/budgeting and what they're actually spending.

In this chapter, we'll first take a quick look at the business principles involved with Concur Request, then walk through the process of getting and giving approvals, discuss the configuration and deployment of Concur Request, and conclude with a short section on how Concur Request integrates with Concur Travel and Concur Expense.

5.1 Business Principles

In medium to large companies, standard operating procedures (SOPs) for business travel often define the processes an employee must follow after being asked to travel to other cities or other countries on company business and prior to booking trip segments. Those procedures will include justification for (and eventually approval of) the business trip, how to prepare for the trip, and how to report business expenses that occurred during the trip.

If approval prior to the business trip is required, companies often will ask for a travel request form to be completed/submitted/approved as a precondition to issuing a cash advance/allowance—but in most companies (and in the age of individual corporate credit cards), this pretrip request is mandatory not so much for issuing cash but for budgeting reasons (and to follow the chart of approval).

5.2 Getting and Giving Approvals with Concur Request

To begin the approval process, you first create a request (usually for a trip), which includes the departure and arrival dates, the reason for the trip, and the details of the different segments, such as air, car rental, and hotel, and the details of expected spending (meals, other expenses). The process follows these steps:

1. On the Concur start page, go to REQUESTS • NEW REQUEST.

2. On the REQUEST HEADER tab, enter the necessary information, such as REQUEST NAME, COA REQUEST POLICY, START DATE, END DATE, and PURPOSE (see Figure 5.1). The actual fields requiring information to be entered or selected by an employee are based on a client's needs—like they are on the Concur Expense side, for which expense report headers or expense entry forms ask for information relevant to a specific client.

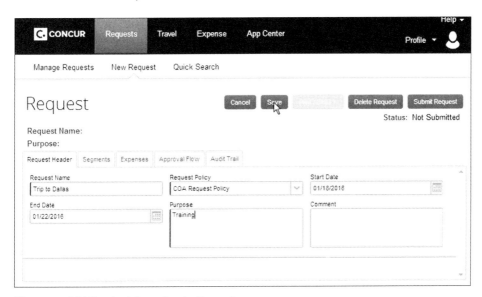

Figure 5.1 Add Header Information to Request

3. On the SEGMENTS tab, fill in the information for each part of your trip (referred to as a *segment* in Concur). The most common segments are as follows:

 ▷ FLIGHT (see Figure 5.2, also applies to TRAIN)
  Here, fill in the flight or train details planned. The information required for each part of the segment is FROM/TO (airport/train station), DATE, and DEPARTURE TIME. VENDOR NAME and COMMENTS can be entered as well.

 ▷ CAR RENTAL (see Figure 5.3)
  Here, fill in the details of the rental car reservation planned. The information required for each part of the segment is CITY, DATE, time, and DETAIL (booking class/drop-off location), under the PICK-UP/DROP-OFF sections.

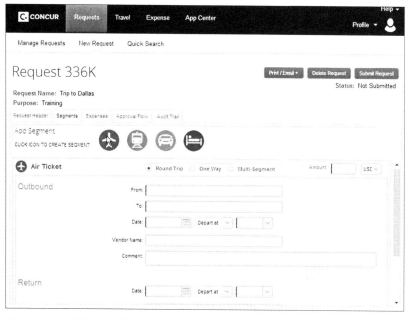

Figure 5.2 Add Flight Information, If Applicable

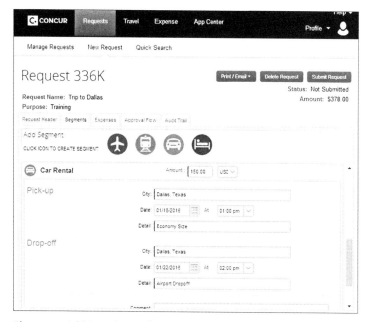

Figure 5.3 Add Rental Car Information, If Applicable

▸ HOTEL RESERVATION (see Figure 5.4)
Here, fill in the details of the hotel stay that your trip demands. The information required for each part of the segment is CITY, DATE, and CHECK-IN/CHECK-OUT time. DETAIL and COMMENTS can be entered as well.

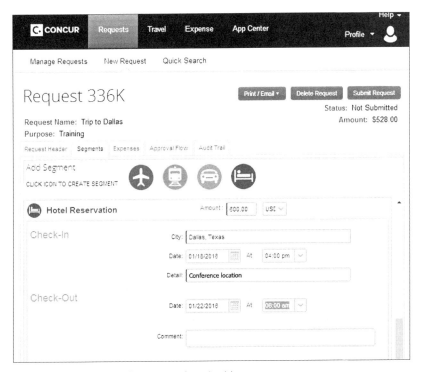

Figure 5.4 Add Hotel Information, If Applicable

4. On the EXPENSES tab, fill in the details of the additional expenses that you foresee needing during the trip. Based on a company's chosen setup, a limited number of expense types are available to choose from and for which to add potential expenses to.

The entry forms are highly customizable, as in Concur Expense, but usually require the following information (see Figure 5.5): EXPENSE TYPE (to be selected from list), CITY (where the expense will occur), transaction DATE, and transaction AMOUNT/CURRENCY. DETAIL/DESCRIPTION and COMMENTS can be entered as well.

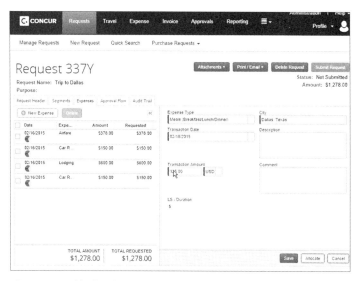

Figure 5.5 Add All Other Anticipated Expenses

Once a user submits a request, it's routed to that user's request approver. When the approver logs into Concur, he performs the following steps:

1. Goes to APPROVALS and clicks on the REQUESTS tab

2. From the list of open requests, selects the request needing approval (see Figure 5.6)

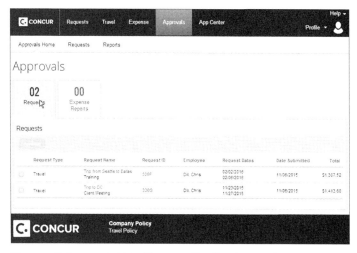

Figure 5.6 Approver's List of Requests Pending Approval

Once an approver has opened a request, she opens each tab to analyze and verify the content provided by the employee, as follows:

1. She ensures that the REQUEST HEADER tab contains all sufficient information related to the overall trip, as per the company's requirements.

2. She ensures that the EXPENSE SUMMARY tab shows all expenses that could potentially occur during the business trip, both related to travel items (AIRFARE/TRAIN, CAR RENTAL, and LODGING/HOTEL) and additional expenses, such as MEALS, PARKING, TAXI, TOLLS, and so on (see Figure 5.7).

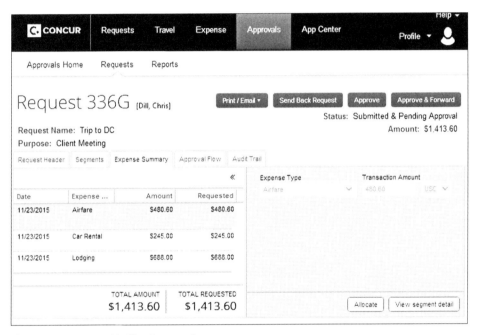

Figure 5.7 Approver Verifies Expense Summary

3. She ensures that the trip details shown on the SEGMENTS tab correlate with the instructions given to the employee regarding the travel schedule to adhere to (and, potentially, the vendors to be chosen; see Figure 5.8).

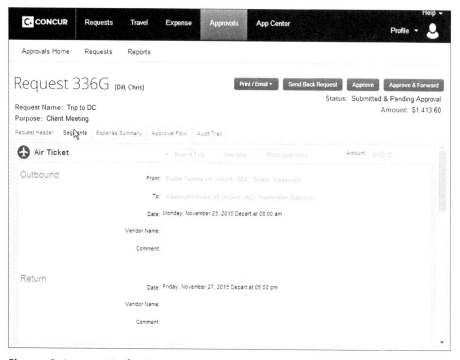

Figure 5.8 Approver Verifies Trip Segments

After reviewing the request, the approver can take one of the following actions:

▶ APPROVE

▶ APPROVE & FORWARD the request to another approver (if this feature was chosen as part of the workflow setup)

▶ SEND BACK REQUEST to the user (with a comment highlighting what changes must be made for approval)

If the request is approved, the employee books the trip segments, goes on the trip, and, upon return, creates an expense report to associate with the approved request, which provides proof that the expenses were preapproved.

5.3 Concur Request Configuration

The overall structure of Concur Request is very similar to that of Concur Expense. Having already explored a Concur Expense implementation in Chapter 4, you know and understand most of the configuration items to be set up for Concur Request. The following parts of Concur Request are similar to or the same as in Concur Expense; they won't be shown in detail so as to avoid duplicating information from Chapter 4:

- ALLOCATION SETTINGS
- ATTENDEES
- AUDIT RULES
- AUDIT RULES—VALIDATION RULES
- EXCEPTIONS
- EXPECTED EXPENSES (in Concur Expense, these are the EXPENSE TYPES)
- FEATURE HIERARCHIES (shared)
- Forms and fields
- Group configurations for employees (shared)
- List management (shared)
- LOCALIZATIONS (shared)
- Locations (shared)
- Policies and groups
- Processor (configuration)
- Site settings
- Validations (shared)
- WORKFLOW—AUTHORIZED APPROVALS
- WORKFLOW—COST OBJECT APPROVALS

Other configuration items are specific to Concur Request; we'll look at these other items in the following subsections.

5.3.1 Agency Proposals

The main difference between a generic Concur Request setup and one configured to utilize the agency proposals feature is that when the user submits a request using said feature, the request goes first to the travel agency. The travel agency provides up to three trip proposals, and the user chooses one before submitting the request for approval.

This feature is explained in more detail ahead (see Section 5.5), but it's the same as option that requires employees to book a trip prior to an automatic request approval with the exceptions that it doesn't require an employee to go through the booking process and also doesn't put the request approver under the pressure of having to approve within 24 hours.

Setting up this option requires two steps:

1. Concur enables agency proposal in the backend for American Express, CWT, or all others.

2. The client's Concur administrator activates the ENABLE AIRFARE MULTI-LEG FORM IN REQUEST setting (see Figure 5.9) via ADMINISTRATION • REQUEST • SITE SETTINGS.

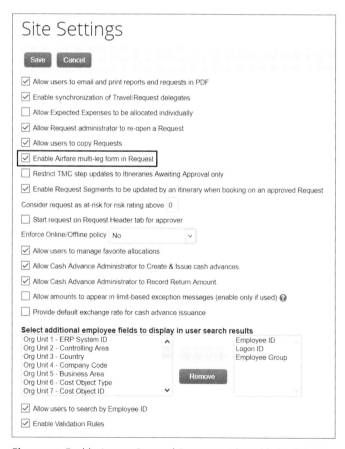

Figure 5.9 Enable Agency Proposal Function with Highlighted Setting

5.3.2   Booking Switch

Turning this functionality on means that whenever an employee uses the Travel Wizard from the Concur home page to search for flights or other trip items, Concur verifies if those trip segments require approval or not.

If they don't require approval, the employee can go ahead and book the trip (unaware of any mechanisms having taken place at all).

If they do require approval, the following process begins:

1. Concur will automatically create a Concur Request item based on the itinerary information the employee entered in the trip search.
2. The employee reviews and potentially edits the Concur Request item.
3. The employee submits the request to the request approver.
4. Once approved, the request is sent to the agency, and the agency completes the booking.

This functionality can only be activated if Concur Request is connected/integrated with Concur Travel.

To enable the booking switch functionality, the travel management company (TMC) or Concur itself must activate it in the TRAVEL SYSTEM ADMIN settings. In the WIZARD OPTIONS part of the TRAVEL CONFIGURATION page, the TMC or Concur admin must check the ENABLE REQUEST BOOKING SWITCH box.

Once enabled, the module will appear in the REQUEST ADMIN • BOOKING SWITCH options (see Figure 5.10).

Figure 5.10 Booking Switch Options in Request Admin Settings

The configuration of the booking switch functionality is based on *criteria*, pre-defined sets of rules based on which the Booking Switch will route an employee to either self-book a trip or submit a request in Concur that will (if approved) result in an agency booking.

To set up a criterion, the admin clicks on NEW in the BOOKING SWITCH page (see Figure 5.10), which will lead to the page shown in Figure 5.11.

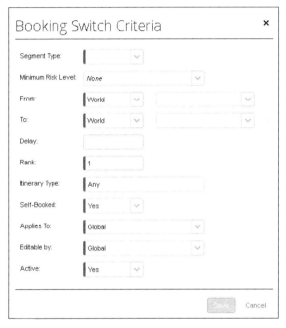

Figure 5.11 Criteria Parameters

The following list provides a short explanation of each selection on the page:

▶ SEGMENT TYPE
   To which trip segment type the criteria applies: air, rail, car rental, or hotel

▶ MINIMUM RISK LEVEL
   Only appears if Concur Messaging is configured for this client as well

▶ FROM and TO
   Whether the criteria apply to the FROM and TO entries of the employee's search; can be set to WORLD, COUNTRY GROUP, or COUNTRY

▶ DELAY
Time frame can be defined to steer toward self-booking or agency booking depending on how close (or far off) the trip start time is from the time the employee is searching for trip segment options

▶ RANK
If multiple criteria apply to an employee's search, this number defines in which order they are applied, with smallest rank applied first

▶ ITINERARY TYPE
If SEGMENT TYPE is AIR or RAIL, this dropdown allows selection of ANY, ONE-WAY, ROUND TRIP, or MULTIPLE SEGMENTS

▶ SELF-BOOKED
Either YES (self-booked) or NO (agency-booked)

▶ APPLIES TO
The group of people the criteria apply to (the same option that can be set for AUDIT RULES)

▶ EDITABLE BY
The group of administrators allowed to change the criteria (the same option that can be set for AUDIT RULES)

▶ ACTIVE
Either YES or NO

5.3.3 Budget Insight

Budget Insight is an additional Concur service that can be configured with Concur Request. Budget Insight gives approvers the option to see budget information alongside every request. If multiple budget approvers are affected by a request, they also can all see the request at the same time for approval.

Budget Insight also gives budget approvers access to view their budget information whenever they want—not only when there's a request to be approved.

Because this is a purchasable module, a contract must be signed with Concur first before it's activated in the backend by Concur. Concur will also assign a Budget Insight specialist to help a client during the setup process.

5.3.4   Country Groups

Country groups can be set up in Concur Request to be used for audit and workflow rules and for email reminders.

Some country groups are already predefined by Concur out of the box, but administrators can change them at will—or delete existing groups and create new ones.

Access to this feature must be granted by Concur, after which it will be listed in ADMINISTRATION • REQUEST (see Figure 5.12).

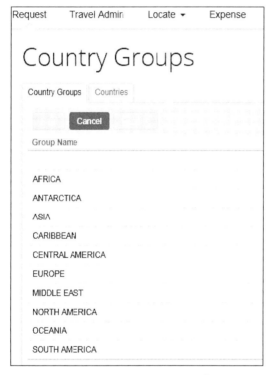

Figure 5.12 Country Groups in Request Admin

5.3.5   Event Requests

In a company in which assistants work for multiple employees, most likely there are time when several of those employees attend the same event. Those assistants normally would have to create a separate Concur Request for each of the employees they work for, but event requests allows assistants to create one request template that lists all employees; Concur then automatically duplicates the same request for each of the employees listed.

This feature requires the REQUEST EVENT MANAGER and REQUEST PROXY LOGON user permissions to be assigned to assistants.

5.3.6 Risk Management

Concur Messaging, which handles risk management, is another Concur service that must be purchased separately within Concur Request. It allows clients to manage all aspects of duty of care for their employees, be they reminders about visas, warnings regarding travel documentation and vaccinations, or risk updates concerning political or weather-related issues.

Risk management information is provided to both the employee herself and the approver. It's based on the location to which the employee is planning to travel. Companies can set up different workflows based on risk level and audit rules within those workflows.

Because this is a purchasable module, a contract has to be signed with Concur before it's activated in the backend by Concur. Concur will also assign a risk management specialist to help a client during the setup process.

5.3.7 Segment Types

Segment types are travel-related types of expenses that an employee can use in a Concur Request, such as air/rail tickets, car rentals, hotel reservations, and so on. Some segments—air subscription, insurance, rail subscription, and travel visa—can be used with the agency proposals feature described earlier (see Section 5.3.1).

For every segment, an administrator can set an icon and a default display order. The employee will see the icon while creating a Concur Request, and the various segments are shown in the order defined.

Segment types (see Figure 5.13) can be found via ADMINISTRATION • REQUEST.

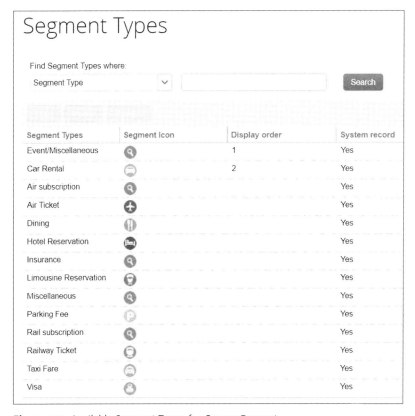

Figure 5.13 Available Segment Types for Concur Request

5.4 Deploying Concur Request

Usually, Concur Request is not set up during the original implementation of Concur Travel or Concur Travel and Concur Expense but instead added after the initial go-live. Although it would be better (from a change management perspective) to deploy Concur Travel, Concur Expense, and Concur Request at the same time, we commonly see Concur Request requested by parts of a company (or some executives) that require better budgeting and cost control, after Concur Travel or Concur Expense have been deployed.

A Concur Request implementation project takes an average of nine weeks to complete—which can be extended due to changes in scope, additional requirements, or resource constraints. These are, as with all other Concur products, remote implementations based on a series of prescheduled conference calls with the project team, ad hoc calls with Concur resources, and interactions by email.

For a Concur Request project, we recommend clients to work with the project team that originally deployed Concur Expense, because that team will be familiar with the current configuration, the T&E policies in play within the organization, and applicable business processes. This will result in a much simpler project, especially because many configuration items (and project tasks) are like those in the original Concur Expense implementation.

Table 5.1 presents a typical Concur Request project implementation schedule.

	Week 1	Weeks 2-3	Weeks 4-8	Week 9
Pre-project work	**Getting started**	**Analysis and design**	**Configuration, review, and validation**	**Deployment**
1. Send client Concur Request questionnaire.	1. Project kick-off call. 2. Define project deliverables, schedule, and client resources.	1. Refreshed test entity with a copy of product data. 2. Design call to review the Concur Request questionnaire document and additional Concur Request requirements. 3. Clients make decisions related to configuration of Concur Request.	1. Concur will configure the system, facilitate meetings to support the customer's testing iterations, and configure changes identified during the testing process. 2. Customer will test the configuration and note any changes or issues via the issue log.	1. The customer will provide training and change management for employees. 2. Concur will move the configuration into production. 3. After go-live, Concur will close the project and transition the customer to Concur Client Support.

Table 5.1 Detailed Nine-Week Overview of Concur Request Implementation

5.5   Integration with Concur Travel and Concur Expense

If Concur Request is to be integrated with Concur Travel, assuming Concur Travel is already configured and in production, a company can select one of two options for the process. First, the company can require employees to ask for approval prior to booking a trip. This option makes the employee go through the process outlined before (see Section 5.2) and—once the request is approved—allows the employee to open the request and click on the BOOK WITH CONCUR TRAVEL button to start the actual trip booking process.

The longer a request approver takes to approve the original request, the more the prices will have changed since the employee looked them up prior to adding segments to the request.

Second, the company can require employees to book a trip prior to an automatic request approval. This option should only be chosen if a company is certain that request approvers will always approve requests within 24 hours if the request contains one or more flights. That's because when an employee enters the segments into Concur Request, Concur will automatically search for actual flights, trains, rental cars, and hotels and have the employee go through the reservation process—just as if he was actually booking a trip. Once all parts of the trip are reserved, the actual cost at that time is added to the Concur Request form and eventually submitted to the request approver.

Although hotels and car rentals generally do not require cancellations until the day before check-in/pick-up and the request approver therefore would have plenty of time to make up his mind, flight and train tickets can only be reserved for a maximum of 24 hours, thus producing the time window within which the request approver must approve a request utilizing this feature.

On the Concur Expense side, once a request has been approved, the trip booked, and the employee returned, the employee can create a new expense report as usual.

On the report header form, the employee can add a Concur Request form by clicking on the ADD button under the REQUESTS section (see Figure 5.14).

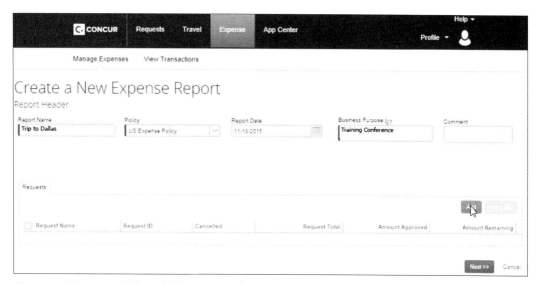

Figure 5.14 Expense Header with Option to Add Approved Request

The employee can select an existing and approved request (see Figure 5.15).

Figure 5.15 Select Any Approved Request Not Yet Assigned to Expense Report

Once that's done, the request is added to the report—after which the employee clicks on NEXT to start the report and add expenses (see Figure 5.16).

Figure 5.16 Create New Expense Report

Concur will automatically add the request form to the expense report and pre-populate the expense list in the report with available data from the request (and travel-related data if the trip was booked in Concur Travel).

5.6   Summary

Concur Request is a great solution to control a company's spending before it actually happens (and, therefore, before it's too late to control). It prevents unnecessary spending and allow for comparing budgeted against actual spending. We looked at the Concur Request process and the related configuration options, in addition to some available modules.

In the next chapter, we'll talk about Concur's reporting capabilities.

Concur's reporting capabilities provide detailed insight into your T&E spending, allowing for both cost savings and increased efficiency for your organization.

6   Concur Reporting

Concur's reporting solution offers comprehensive insight into all your T&E data. Concur's reporting uses IBM's Cognos reporting solution, a web-based tool that allows you to create queries, reports, and dashboards that can be run and viewed on desktops and mobile devices. It also allows you to extract and share reports in multiple ways.

The Cognos tool can report using simple queries; more complex, structured management-style ones; and interactive dashboards. Reports and queries can be exported into multiple formats, such as HTML, Excel, PDF, or CSV, and shared using distribution options such as report bursting. Data is updated from Concur into Cognos by nightly batch jobs; thus, the data available in Concur reports will always be correct as of the previous day. This process also includes permission assignments and changes.

Concur's reporting uses a hierarchical structure to restrict users to reporting on data that is relevant to them and their teams. The one exception to the application of the hierarchical structure authorizations arises when a user has been directly assigned to a user's profile as a *BI Manager*. Regardless of the hierarchical structure, BI managers will be able to report on the Concur data of any of their assigned users.

During your Concur implementation, one standard reporting currency will be selected for all countries using Concur. This currency may be different than the currency that your country uses in Concur. All standard reports will show values in this reporting currency; to report in your country's relevant currency, different currencies can be added to the report by your report administrator.

In this chapter, we take a look at the reporting features available in standard Concur Analysis and Concur Intelligence, including a look at the standard reports available in Concur, creating your own queries and reports using Query Studio and Report Studio, and dashboards.

6.1   T&E Analysis vs. Concur Intelligence Tools

The reporting options for your T&E data in Concur come in two versions: the standard Concur Analysis offering and the premium version known as Concur Intelligence. There are several differences between the two reporting versions, including the following:

▶ Number of standard reports available across the Concur Travel and Concur Expense modules

▶ Number of user licences

▶ Studio tools provided to build custom reports

▶ Report scheduling and automated distribution options (known as *report bursting*)

▶ Availability of integrated T&E reporting

▶ Presence of reporting dashboards

Concur comes with access to the standard Concur Analysis reporting; Concur Intelligence reporting can be purchased as an add-on feature. In the following sections, we'll first discuss features common to both reporting options before diving into some tools exclusive to Concur Intelligence.

6.1.1   Concur Analysis and Concur Intelligence: Shared Tools

Concur Intelligence and Concur Analysis share several standard features and tools, as we'll explore in the following subsections. In some cases, Concur Intelligence includes additional functionality.

Default Reports

The number of standard prebuilt reports varies between Concur Analysis and Concur Intelligence, with the latter containing all the reports available in Concur Analysis and more. As of December 2016, this includes 138 standard Concur

Analysis reports and 187 Concur Intelligence reports. These standard prebuilt reports are based on Concur's key T&E reporting metrics and data. In order to manage the large number of standard reports available, Concur has comprehensive catalogues that provide a definition, for each report, its data, and its intended audience. This information can be found under the HELP menu on the CONCUR CONNECT homepage, as shown in Figure 6.1.

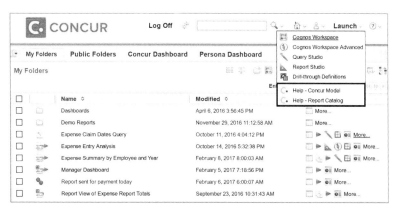

Figure 6.1 Concur Report Catalog

Report Design Tools

There are two report design tools available in Concur: Query Studio and Report Studio. Query Studio is available in both Concur Analysis and Concur Intelligence; Report Studio is available in Concur Intelligence. Both are flexible tools that you can use to design new queries and reports, in addition to the standard prebuilt reports available in Concur. In addition, extra user licences for Query Studio come with Concur Intelligence; Concur Intelligence provides twenty licences standard, versus five licences in standard Concur Analysis.

Because each reporting option provides access to different studio tools, the ability to modify the standard Concur reports will depend on whether the report was made with Query Studio or Report Studio. The appropriate studio tool access is required to modify a standard report; for example, if you have the standard Concur Analysis reporting feature, you do not have access to the Report Studio tool and therefore can't modify any standard reports built in Report Studio. If you have Concur Intelligence but only a user licence for the Query Studio, then you can access all the reports that Concur has to offer, but you can only amend those standard reports that have been built in Query Studio.

We'll cover the using the Query Studio and Report Studio tools in greater detail in Section 6.3 and Section 6.4.

User Roles and Licences

The Concur Analysis and Concur Intelligence offerings each allow for a different type and number of user licences. The different types of licences are as follows:

▶ The *consumer* licence allows a user to run any of the prebuilt and customer reports available.

▶ The *business author* licence allows a user to run all the reports available and gives access to the Query Studio to build simple reports.

▶ The *professional author* licence allows a user to run all reports available and gives access to both Query Studio and Report Studio to build a range of reports.

▶ The *manager* licence allows a user access to run the reports available for only their direct and indirect employees.

Table 6.1 provides a summary of the number of users allowed under each license type for both standard Concur Analysis and Concur Intelligence.

User License Type	Concur Analysis	Concur Intelligence
Consumer	10	40
Business author	5	20
Professional author	N/A	10
Manager	Unlimited	Unlimited

Table 6.1 Cognos Reporting Licenses: Numbers and Types

6.1.2 Concur Intelligence-Only Tools

The following reporting features are only available in Concur Intelligence:

▶ **Scheduling and bursting of reports**
Scheduling within Concur reporting allows for the scheduled, automated running and distribution of reports. Bursting is a feature whereby the report scheduled is tailored to the recipient, showing only data relevant to him.

▶ **Reporting dashboards**
Dashboards are an easy data visualization tool with which key metrics and key

performance indicators (KPIs) can be monitored and managed on a single screen specifically configured for a target audience, which can contain up to six reports. Concur offers prebuilt dashboards designed for the most commonly used reports, as well as tools to build your own.

▸ **Alert and exception notifications**
Exception-based highlighting is a tool within Concur's reporting to alert budget managers when important figures in their budgets change in a significant manner. Triggered alerts will alert budget managers to suspicious card transactions for their budget or to budget changes that may require review and correction action to be taken. Concur's reporting uses budget values set in the budget manager's user profile to determine exceptions and alerts.

▸ **Integrated T&E data**
If you use both Concur Travel and Concur Expense, integration of data from both modules in reporting is only available in the Concur Intelligence offering.

6.2   Using Existing Reports

Concur offers several standard reports, providing insight into all aspects of your T&E spending, including integrated reports if you use Concur Travel and Concur Expense.

The standard reports can be found in the Concur Analysis/Concur Intelligence STANDARD REPORT folders and are organized into a folder structure for reporting areas across T&E data, including additional reporting areas for how Concur is being used in your company.

Before we look at how to run the standard reports available, we'll look through the preferences that you can set in Cognos to enhance your reporting.

6.2.1   Set Reporting Preferences

Your reporting preferences can be found in the MY AREA options, as indicated by the person icon, available from the CONCUR CONNECT page. There are three areas of preferences that you can set (see Figure 6.2), each of which will be discussed in the following sections. Any changes that you make to your preferences take effect immediately.

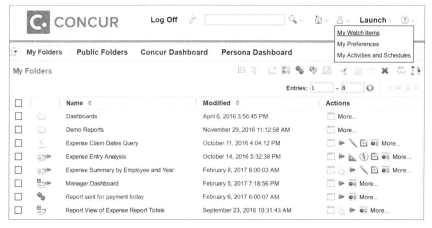

Figure 6.2 User Preferences Menu on Connect Homepage

General Preferences

The GENERAL PREFERENCES tab sets preferences for how reports and queries will be displayed and run. Some of these settings are also available when you select to run a report using the RUN WITH OPTIONS function (for more details, see Section 6.2.2). Table 6.2 lists some of the general preferences options.

Preference Setting	Application
NUMBER OF ENTRIES IN LIST VIEW	The value entered will define the number of entries shown in a list.
REPORT FORMAT	Defines the default format in which a report will be exported from Cognos: ▸ HTML ▸ PDF ▸ EXCEL ▸ CSV
PRODUCT LANGUAGE and CONTENT LANGUAGE	The language used to display Cognos reports and content data can be personalized here to match your local language. However, reports can be created in specific languages other than the default set and will override any preferences set in your profile.

Table 6.2 Preference Settings Available in Cognos

Preference Setting	Application
PORTAL DEFAULT VIEW	The reports and folders in the portal can either be displayed in a simple list view or in a detail view; the latter shows a short description of each folder or report as available for the individual item.
TIME ZONE	Cognos has a default time zone of UTC. The preference set here can change the time zone that your Cognos installation uses. You should change this setting to your local time zone if you want to schedule report jobs to run and be distributed in your local time zone.
ENABLE BI-DIRECTIONAL LANGUAGE SUPPORT	This setting will allow you to view numbers in Arabic, Hebrew, Urdu, and Farsi in the correct left-to-right format while still viewing text in the right-to-left format correct for these languages.

Table 6.2 Preference Settings Available in Cognos (Cont.)

Personal Preferences

The PERSONAL PREFERENCES tab contains logon details for the Cognos connection workspace. Your usual logon details will be listed as your PRIMARY LOGON; if you have additional logon information for any other workspaces, it can be listed under SECONDARY LOGON.

The ALERTS EMAIL field can be used to define an email address that Cognos alerts are sent to for notifications of specific events.

Other preferences include settings to apply CREDENTIALS, GROUPS AND ROLES, and CAPABILITIES. Many of these settings may be read-only for your Cognos connection. These settings perform the following functions:

▶ CREDENTIALS can provide authorizations to other users, groups, or roles to run report entries.

▶ GROUPS AND ROLES will show the groups in Cognos and the Cognos roles that are assigned to your primary and secondary logons as applicable.

▶ CAPABILITIES will show functions and features available based on your primary and secondary logons. This is a useful view to check if you're authorized for specific activities in Cognos reporting.

Portal Tab Preferences

The last tab is for PORTAL TAB PREFERENCES, in which settings can be made for the portal tabs shown on the Cognos connection homepage. Here, you can modify the sequence of the tabs that are shown and add new/hide existing tabs as needed.

6.2.2   Running a Standard Report

The REPORTING tile can be found on the MY CONCUR homepage, and the types of reports shown will depend on the product (either Concur Analysis or Concur Intelligence) that your company uses or the reporting access assigned within Cognos.

Use the REPORTING tile to open the screen shown in Figure 6.3, launching Concur's reporting features.

Figure 6.3 Concur Reporting Homepage

The CONCUR CONNECTION homepage includes the following four main areas:

1. **Folders and dashboard tabs**
   These tabs allow access to folders containing reports and to dashboards.

2. **Report folders**
   All the standard reports and metrics are arranged into a folder structure. For Concur Intelligence, there are four main folders (see Table 6.3); the folders are the same for Concur Analysis reporting, except that the DASHBOARD METRICS folder is not available.

Folder Name	Use
CONCUR DATA WAREHOUSE	Contains the Concur data warehouse model. It will appear empty, but must not be deleted.
▶ INTELLIGENCE—STANDARD REPORTS ▶ ANALYSIS—STANDARD REPORTS	This folder will contain all the standard reports available in either Concur Analysis or Concur Intelligence reporting.
<YOUR COMPANY NAME>	The report folder will be named after your company and customer number. This report folder can be used to share reports between users in your company.
DASHBOARD METRICS	Any metrics that can be added to reporting dashboards will be contained here.

Table 6.3 Reporting Folders in Cognos

3. **Reporting tools**

   Standard tools to create new report folders, schedule report jobs, set folder properties etc.

4. **Homepage navigation**

   Tools to navigate to Cognos help, personal settings and preferences with reporting.

Personal Folders

If you create a report or report view in any tool, and save the new report to your PER-SONAL FOLDER, found under MY FOLDERS, then the report can't be seen or shared with any other reporting administrator. To access the report, another user will need to be set as your delegate.

To share reports across the organization, a reporting administrator should set up a shared folder structure under your company's folder in the public folders.

To run a standard report, navigate via the relevant folder structure to the report and click on it. This will open a report prompt page on which you can enter your report selection criteria. Different prompt fields will appear depending on the data set for your chosen report. Figure 6.4 shows a report that uses both a date-type prompt (SENT FOR PAYMENT DATE:) and a value-type prompt (EMPLOYEE:).

Enter your report criteria, and click FINISH to run the report.

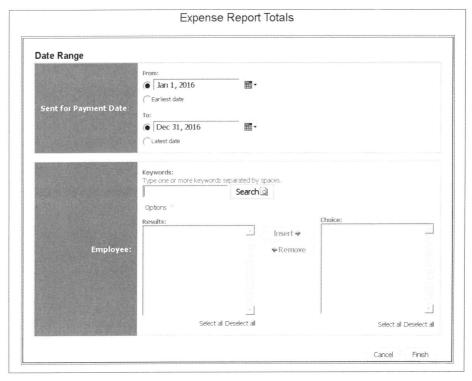

Figure 6.4 Report Prompt Screen Using Different Types of Data Selection Prompts

You can also set a report to run with layout or output options different than your usual default stored values when you run the report by using the RUN WITH OPTIONS selection button under the ACTIONS column on the right-hand side of the screen. Advanced options (see Figure 6.5) also allow you to choose additional formats to run the report in, choose other languages for the report, and schedule the report to run at a specific time and date. To schedule a report to run as a recurring job, use the scheduling feature described in Section 6.4.2.

Using additional options to run your report will also allow the report to be distributed to recipients when the report has been run in the background. When the TIME AND MODE of the report is set as RUN IN THE BACKGROUND, Cognos will show the DELIVERY options. Here, choose SEND BY EMAIL for the report to be sent out to users. The email distribution list, email title, and a message can be included in the email.

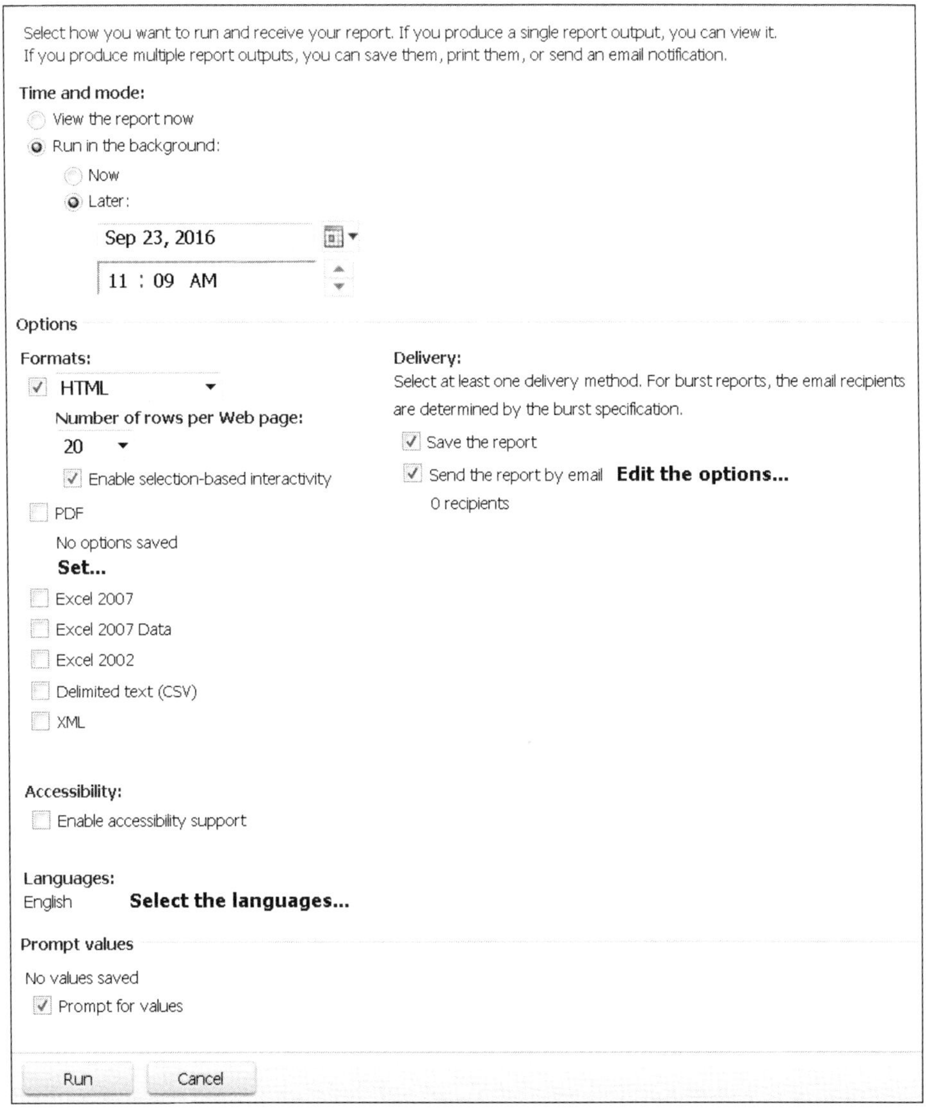

Select how you want to run and receive your report. If you produce a single report output, you can view it.
If you produce multiple report outputs, you can save them, print them, or send an email notification.

Time and mode:

○ View the report now

◉ Run in the background:

    ○ Now

    ◉ Later:

          Sep 23, 2016   ▦ ▾

          11 : 09 AM   ▲▼

Options

Formats:

☑ HTML   ▾

    Number of rows per Web page:

    20 ▾

    ☑ Enable selection-based interactivity

☐ PDF

    No options saved

    Set...

☐ Excel 2007

☐ Excel 2007 Data

☐ Excel 2002

☐ Delimited text (CSV)

☐ XML

Accessibility:

☐ Enable accessibility support

Languages:

English   **Select the languages...**

Prompt values

No values saved

☑ Prompt for values

Delivery:

Select at least one delivery method. For burst reports, the email recipients
are determined by the burst specification.

☑ Save the report

☑ Send the report by email **Edit the options...**

    0 recipients

[Run]   [Cancel]

Figure 6.5 Advanced Options Available when Running Reports

Once a report has been run, a report view can be created to save the report selection parameters and thus make the report output repeatable. The report view can be saved into shared folders to be shared across your organization. To do so, under the KEEP THIS VERSION dropdown (see Figure 6.6), select the SAVE AS

REPORT VIEW... option. Cognos will ask for a save location to be specified; the default save location will be your MY FOLDER area. Once saved, the report view can be accessed quickly from a folder by any user permissioned for the folder. Selecting the report will run it with the saved selections criteria.

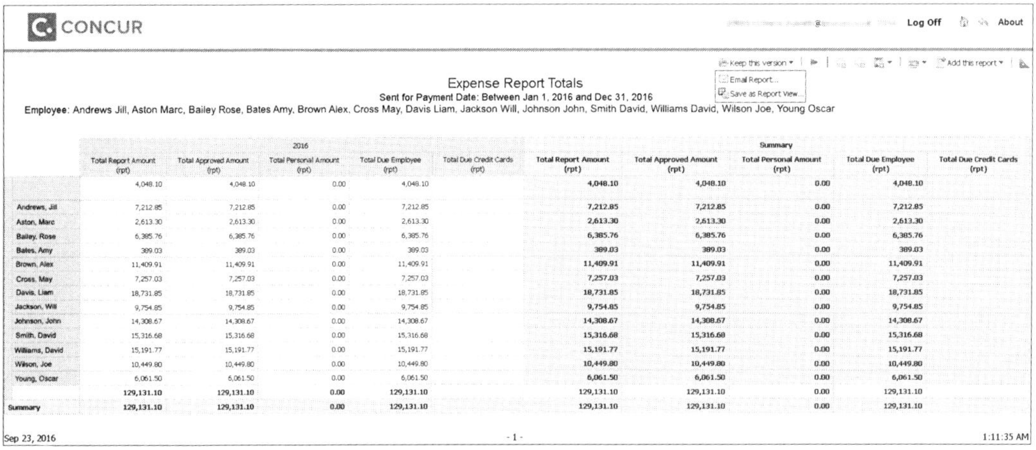

Expense Report Totals

Sent for Payment Date: Between Jan 1, 2016 and Dec 31, 2016

Employee: Andrews Jill, Aston Marc, Bailey Rose, Bates Amy, Brown Alex, Cross May, Davis Liam, Jackson Will, Johnson John, Smith David, Williams David, Wilson Joe, Young Oscar

	2016					Summary				
	Total Report Amount (rpt)	Total Approved Amount (rpt)	Total Personal Amount (rpt)	Total Due Employee (rpt)	Total Due Credit Cards (rpt)	Total Report Amount (rpt)	Total Approved Amount (rpt)	Total Personal Amount (rpt)	Total Due Employee (rpt)	Total Due Credit Cards (rpt)
	4,048.10	4,048.10	0.00	4,048.10		4,048.10	4,048.10	0.00	4,048.10	
Andrews, Jill	7,212.85	7,212.85	0.00	7,212.85		7,212.85	7,212.85	0.00	7,212.85	
Aston, Marc	2,613.30	2,613.30	0.00	2,613.30		2,613.30	2,613.30	0.00	2,613.30	
Bailey, Rose	6,385.76	6,385.76	0.00	6,385.76		6,385.76	6,385.76	0.00	6,385.76	
Bates, Amy	389.03	389.03	0.00	389.03		389.03	389.03	0.00	389.03	
Brown, Alex	11,409.91	11,409.91	0.00	11,409.91		11,409.91	11,409.91	0.00	11,409.91	
Cross, May	7,257.03	7,257.03	0.00	7,257.03		7,257.03	7,257.03	0.00	7,257.03	
Davis, Liam	18,731.85	18,731.85	0.00	18,731.85		18,731.85	18,731.85	0.00	18,731.85	
Jackson, Will	9,754.85	9,754.85	0.00	9,754.85		9,754.85	9,754.85	0.00	9,754.85	
Johnson, John	14,308.67	14,308.67	0.00	14,308.67		14,308.67	14,308.67	0.00	14,308.67	
Smith, David	15,316.68	15,316.68	0.00	15,316.68		15,316.68	15,316.68	0.00	15,316.68	
Williams, David	15,191.77	15,191.77	0.00	15,191.77		15,191.77	15,191.77	0.00	15,191.77	
Wilson, Joe	10,449.80	10,449.80	0.00	10,449.80		10,449.80	10,449.80	0.00	10,449.80	
Young, Oscar	6,061.50	6,061.50	0.00	6,061.50		6,061.50	6,061.50	0.00	6,061.50	
	129,131.10	129,131.10	0.00	129,131.10		129,131.10	129,131.10	0.00	129,131.10	
Summary	129,131.10	129,131.10	0.00	129,131.10		129,131.10	129,131.10	0.00	129,131.10	

Sep 23, 2016 - 1 - 1:11:35 AM

Figure 6.6 The Report View Option Makes a Report Repeatable

6.3 Building and Editing Reports in Query Studio

Query Studio is a lightweight tool that allows you to create simple queries and reports. To launch Query Studio, select the LAUNCH menu, then select QUERY STUDIO.

Cognos will ask you to confirm the data warehouse package to use for Query Studio. For this example, select CONCUR DATA WAREHOUSE.

The QUERY DESIGNER screen contains three main areas (see Figure 6.7):

1. **Data and related functions panel**
   This area to allows you to insert data, edit data, change a report layout, run the report, and manage a file.
2. **Toolbar**
   This area contains the most commonly used report functions in the standard toolbar and font settings in the font toolbar to be used in your report.
3. **Report design panel**
   In this design area, you'll build your report.

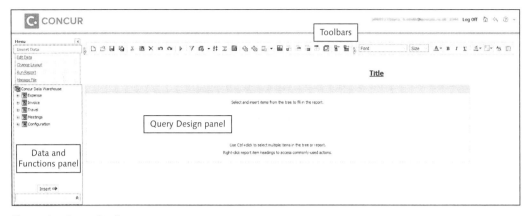

Figure 6.7 Query Studio

Query Studio allows you to create two different types of reports:

▸ A *list* report will show data in simple lists and is best suited to simple value lists of data. List reports show simple queries, such as the total spend for an expense type for the whole company.

▸ A *crosstab* report is a list report with columns and rows of data; a measure at the intersections of each column and row to provides a summary of the data. Crosstab reports can provide more detailed information, such as the total spend of an expense type per country or business unit to provide a more detailed breakdown.

In the following subsections, we'll cover how to create a new report in Query Studio before moving on to manipulating data within reports.

6.3.1   Creating a New Report

Query Studio allows you to create simple, list-style reports, manipulate data, and add charts for visual representation. The first step to create a new report is to select the NEW REPORT button on the toolbar button to open a blank report screen.

From the data menu on the left-hand side of the screen, each piece of data information that can be used in reporting is organized into a comprehensive folder structure within the areas of EXPENSE, INVOICE, TRAVEL, MEETINGS, and CONFIGURATION. To add a new piece of data into your report, simply select the field from the data menu and either double-click on the data item or use the INSERT button found at the bottom of the menu to add the data item to the report. Data items are added from left to right, but you can use drag and drop to drop the data items into specific places. Continue to add data fields to your report until you have all the desired data.

Delete any data field added to the report by selecting the column and clicking on the DELETE button on the toolbar.

Titles can be added to reports by double clicking on the title to select the TITLE option in the report design panel; Cognos will open the EDIT TITLE AREA, providing access to fields for the report title and subtitle and options to show any filters, sorting, or data suppression when applied to the report (see Figure 6.8).

Figure 6.8 Editing Report Title and Subtitle

To save the report created, click the SAVE button on the toolbar; Cognos will then ask for a report NAME, short DESCRIPTION for the report, SCREEN TIP, and a save LOCATION, as shown in Figure 6.9. The save location for a new report will default to your MY FOLDER location. To save the report to another shared location within your company, choose another location. Reports can only be saved to locations a user has permission to access.

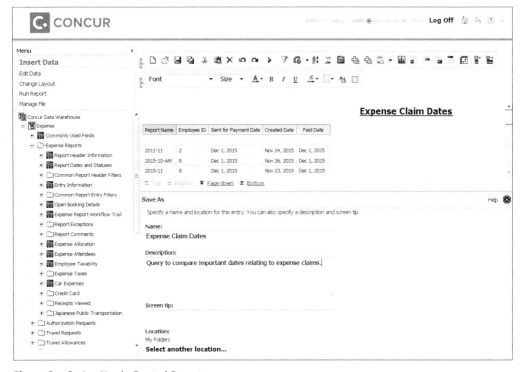

Figure 6.9 Saving Newly Created Report

6.3.2 Manipulating Data within Reports

Several data manipulation techniques are available to make alterations to your report, including renaming data columns, filtering, summaries, and calculations, all of which can be accessed via the toolbar at the top of the report designer page. You can perform the following actions:

▸ Column header names can be renamed to something more specific and informative for your organization by double-clicking on the required column header to open the renaming options.

► Filters can be added to reports to both ensure that only relevant data is being reported and provide performance improvements. When adding a filter value based on a column selection, you can include or exclude data from the report in several ways depending on the data being filtered. Filters can also be combined for more complexity. One common filter to include in reports removes test users from any user administration reports.

► Calculations can be added to your queries to provide sums, averages, and counts for the data of a single column or to multiply values in two columns and provide the resulting value in a third column. Multiplication calculations in reports can be useful for budget-related predictions, such as seeing how a cost increase for a specific expense could affect a budget.

► Reports automatically summarize data to remove the repetition of measure values within the report and to improve the performance, look, and feel of the report. For example, when reporting on the total value of an expense, the summarization of the data will report the total expense type and value rather than reporting each individual line item instance and individual value of that expense type. The option to automatically summarize data and values can be deactivated for a report through the advanced runtime options for the report.

► Suppressing cell options can be used to hide empty cells values from your finished report. The suppression options can be applied to cells, rows, or cells and rows of data within the report from the appropriate button on the toolbar.

Adding Charts

Several chart types can be added to a report for a visual representation of the data and to show patterns and trends in the data.

6.4   Building and Editing Reports in Report Studio

In the previous section, we covered how Query Studio can create simple data queries; now, we'll look at Report Studio and how it can be used to create more complex, management-style reports.

A report created with Report Studio will consist of multiple pages used to define the layout and presentation of the report. The report layout pages will design how the report will look, including how the data is presented with report style and chart options; how the data is formatted, such as font, color, and text options;

and how the data will flow from one page to the next if the report crosses multiple pages. A prompt page for the report can be also be built for report selections. One or multiple queries can be used in the report to provide added levels of detail and complexity or to use key functionalities such as report bursting. Reports created with Report Studio can contain multiple objects, such as charts and lists, and multiple nonreport objects, such as logos and images, to create a more stylized report.

The Report Studio homepage (see Figure 6.10) includes five main areas, as follows:

1. The DATA and RELATED FUNCTION panel allows you to insert data, edit data, change a report layout, run the report, and manage the file.

2. The PROPERTIES panel allows you to configure various properties for data, queries, or report page selections.

3. The most used report functions are in the standard toolbar, and font settings are in the font toolbar.

4. The REPORT DESIGNER panel is where you'll build your report, including sidebar navigation through the different pages and queries that make up your report.

5. EXPLORER BARS can help you navigate the multiple layers that make up the report, including multiple queries or pages in the report; the condition explorer works with different variables that define conditions in your report.

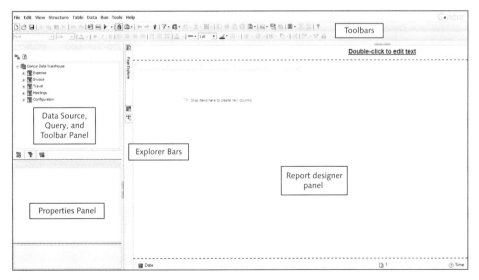

Figure 6.10 Report Studio Homepage

Comparing the Report Studio homepage with the Query Studio homepage shown in Figure 6.7 you'll see many more toolbar options in Report Studio, as well as additional options for manipulation of data parameters.

In the following subsections, we'll provide a quick primer on the types of reports and their structure, discuss creating a report, and then walk through the process of bursting reports.

6.4.1   Report Types and Structures

The report designer offers several report types that can be created to represent the data in the most appropriate manner. Report types available include the basic list to show columns of data, the crosstab to show rows and columns of data with a measure at the intersection of each, and chart reports to show the data graphically. Different report styles will suit different reports best, depending on whether the data being reported on is relational or dimensional. Once the report type has been selected, Cognos will open the Report Studio homepage.

Report Studio can be used to create either relational or dimensional reports, whichever suits the report specification better. The relational reporting style should be used for relational data and is best represented by lists and list reports. Dimensional reporting styles are appropriate for dimensional data, which are best represented by crosstab, map, and chart reports. When authoring a new report, take a moment to consider how you view your data. If you consider your data in list, tables, and columns, then your chosen reporting style is *relational*. If you consider your data using different dimensions and measures and with various cells intersecting, then your reporting style is *dimensional*.

Reports created in Report Studio will consist of at least two components: the report layout and the report query, crossing multiple report pages.

A report *layout* is the set of pages that define how the report appears to the user, including how the data is presented, such as a chart or a crosstab layout; any report formatting and specification for how data should flow from one page to the next if necessary is part of the layout.

The *queries* included in a report will define the data that appears in that report, and multiple queries can be used in a single report. As an example of using multiple queries in a report, you can configure a report that is burst to recipients, in Section 6.4.3, in which one query is used to report data and the second query is used to collate who should receive the report. For a more detailed guide of how to configure a report to be burst to different users, see Section 6.4.3.

A report will consist of one or more report *pages*, which are used to design each step of the report, from the report *prompt* pages used to enter the report selections to the layout of the report itself in the report pages. The page explorer on the EXPLORER BARS bar can be used to navigate between the multiple pages that make up your report.

6.4.2 Creating a New Report

Access Report Studio in the same manner as Query Studio, using the same menu. When asked to confirm the data warehouse package to use, select CONCUR DATA WAREHOUSE.

Report Studio will then offer choices for the type of report to create (see Figure 6.11). Chose the appropriate report type depending the data to be reported on, click the OK button, and the Report Studio homepage will open.

Figure 6.11 Different Report Styles Available in Report Studio

Data items can be added to the report easily by selecting them from the data and related functions panel; either double-click an item, or drag and drop it into the REPORT DESIGNER panel. As with Query Studio, data items are added left to right across the REPORT DESIGNER panel. Many of the features and functions of Report Studio will behave in the same manner as in Query Studio. In the following subsections, we'll cover some of the more advanced and unique features and functions of Report Studio.

Objects in Reports

Several objects can be added to your report to enhance the report features. Charts can be added to reports as individual objects to visually represent specific data and metrics within a wider report. There are several chart types available to represent different the metrics being demonstrated in a report, including straightforward visualizations, such as using line or bar charts to show data trends or pie charts to show percentages or proportions of a whole. You can also use combination charts to highlight the relationships among various sets of data or bubble and quadrant charts to show a comparison of key data metrics with respect to axis and size metrics.

Chart options can be selected from the Chart toolbar button; once you've created a chart in your report, several chart properties are available to be configured. Double-click on any aspect of your chart, and the Properties pane will allow customizations to be made. Figure 6.12 shows an example of some parameter options that can be applied to a data item, including data Type, Label, Expression, and Functions.

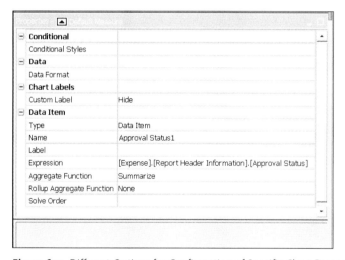

Figure 6.12 Different Options for Configuration of Specific Chart Properties

Scheduling Reports

Reports can be set to be run in the background and distributed to users on a daily, weekly, or monthly schedule. Scheduling reports will ensure that corporate reports are run on a regular basis using constant parameters and will ensure efficiency due to the scheduled job being set up once for multiple outputs. Any report in Cognos can be set to run on a schedule.

From the Cognos connection homepage, select MORE ACTIONS for the specific report, then select the NEW SCHEDULE option to open the NEW SCHEDULE screen (see Figure 6.13).

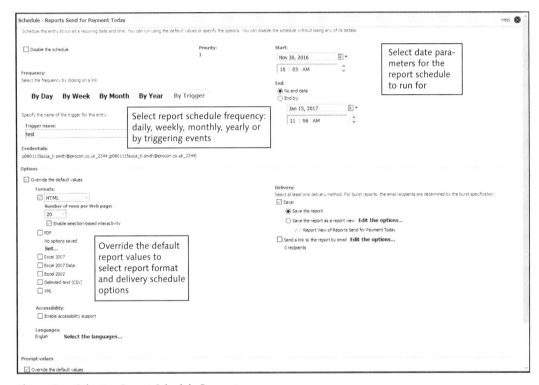

Figure 6.13 Selecting Report Schedule Parameters

In the schedule selection screen, as seen in Figure 6.13, set the following parameters to create the report schedule:

▶ FREQUENCY
   Select the frequency with which the report should be run.

▶ START and END dates
   Enter the date on which the report schedule should first run, and enter an end date if appropriate. The end date can be left set to the default NO END DATE selection for the job to run on an ongoing basis.

▶ OVERRIDE THE DEFAULT VALUES
Select this radio button to override the report's default values for the report output and format to be selected.

▶ DELIVERY
Choose the delivery method required, such as SEND A LINK TO THE REPORT BY EMAIL.

Email Delivery of Schedule Reports

When setting up report schedules, reports can be set to be delivered by email to users once they're run. The default option for the report to be attached to the email sent to users is unchecked. Select this option for the report to be attached to the email, not just contained in the body of the email.

The schedule manager will keep an overview of all schedules that have been set up and their statuses. The manager is useful for seeing an overview of the progress of any scheduled jobs and any outputs.

From the Cognos Connection homepage, launch the schedule manager from the MY PREFERENCES menu by selecting the MY ACTIVITIES AND SCHEDULES menu option. The schedule manager will show all report jobs scheduled and current, past, and upcoming activities. For each job scheduled, the schedule manager will report the status of the job, whether there were any warnings or errors when the job ran, and, if selected, the outputs from each scheduled job run.

6.4.3 Bursting Reports

Bursting of reports allows you to distribute reports to different parts to the business; each part of the business will only see data in the report that is relevant to it. For example, you may have created a standard format for a budget report that your organization requires budget managers to use. By using the bursting feature, the report can be configured and scheduled and delivered to each budget manager, reporting that manager's own budget data only.

Report bursting can be based on the reporting hierarchy or BI managers or by means of a custom field for a more specific audience. The configuration for report bursting and distribution list is built directly into the Cognos report and selected as part of the report properties when the report is run.

Chart- and crosstab-explicit reports cannot be burst, but reports that contain chart or crosstab objects can be. Only the HTML, PDF, and XLS report formats can be burst.

To configure a report to be burst, you will use two queries. The first query will be the *data content* query—that is, identifying the data being reported—and the second query will define the recipients of the report—that is, who it's being reported to.

The criteria by which you wish define your burst recipients must be contained in the content query for your report. For example, to create a report that will be burst to certain BI managers in a reporting group, then the content query must contain the data element reporting group. The recipient query must then contain the users to receive this query. For example, after go-live with Concur, you may want to check the employee uptake of Concur Expense, monitoring the number of expenses claims that employees are raising per reporting month, reported by BI managers for each division within your business. Figure 6.14 and Figure 6.15 illustrate how to create the report bursting configuration and how to schedule the report to send a weekly summary of the claims raised to each BI manager.

To configure a report to be burst, follow these steps:

1. Create and test the content query to ensure that the correct data is being reported.

2. Create a second query, the distribution query. In both queries, a common data element for EMPLOYEE ORG UNIT has been included (see Figure 6.14).

3. In the burst dialog box (see Figure 6.15), under the BURST GROUPS settings (which sets the data to be burst), select the following:

   ▷ QUERY
   Select the content query to be used to define the data to be returned.

   ▷ LABEL
   Enter the selection for the criteria that will be used to burst the report.

   ▷ GROUPS
   Click on the PENCIL icon and create the data element that the burst groups will be grouped by; in this example, the bursting will be grouped by EMPLOYEE ORG UNIT.

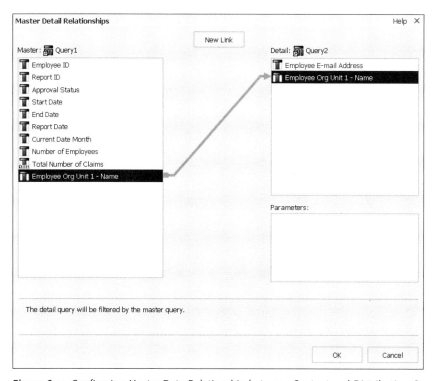

Figure 6.14 Configuring Master Data Relationship between Content and Distribution Queries

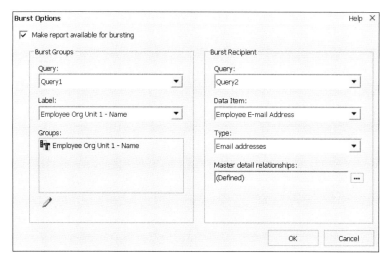

Figure 6.15 Completed Report Bursting Options

4. In the Burst Options dialog box, under the Burst Recipient settings (for the burst recipients' data selections), make the following settings:

▷ Query
Select the query to be used to populate the burst recipients.

▷ Data Item
Enter the item to be used to uniquely identify each recipient, such as an employee email address.

▷ Type
This should always be set as Email Addresses.

▷ Master Detail Relationships
The last setting is to link the content and recipient queries; in this case, the common data item between the two queries is Employee Org Unit.

Your report has now been configured for bursting. This report can now be scheduled to run automatically and distributed to the burst recipients.

From the report folder, select the report and choose Run with Advanced Options to set the report to burst. Under the Time and Mode selection, chose to run the report in the background, either now or at a specified time and date. The option to select the report to burst now can be selected. If a report has been scheduled in a job, then on the Job Scheduling screen ensure that the option to override the default values is checked on the prompt screen selections, enable the Burst The Report checkbox, and chose the checkbox option to Send The Report By Email.

Converting Query Studio Reports

Report Studio can be used to elevate simple Query Studio reports into more complex Report Studio reports, with all the additional features and functions available in Report Studio added to the report.

Any report can be opened in Report Studio, either directly in Report Studio using the Open option in the File menu or from the Cognos connection homepage by using the More option under the Actions column for the individual report. Once the report is opened in Report Studio, the report can be enhanced as required and then saved.

6.5 Dashboards

Dashboards help visualize current performance against various data metrics and KPIs. Concur provides a standard dashboard with six key metrics that can be customized for use in your company. Each metric can be changed to one of 50 other standard metrics that Cognos reporting provides, and any of the metrics available can also be run as standalone reports, found in the INTELLIGENCE • DASHBOARD METRICS folder.

On the Cognos reporting homepage, the reporting dashboards are located on the DASHBOARD NAVIGATION tab.

Concur also provides *actionable analytics*, which are dashboards and alert metrics that can be delivered directly to your BI manager via email for the expense spending that affects their budget. Each BI manager individually can elect to receive reports via the notification settings in her Concur profile, and these reports can map to the budget reporting information that managers can set up in their Concur profiles to give greater insight into the expense spending in their budgets. The BI manager reports are active by default, but each user must opt in to receive notifications and specify the notification frequency.

Each budget manager can specify quarterly budget amounts relevant to his budget in his Concur profile, as shown in Figure 6.16. The actionable analytics reports will then use these figures to track expense spending against the budget and to send alerts when a certain percentage of budget has been reached.

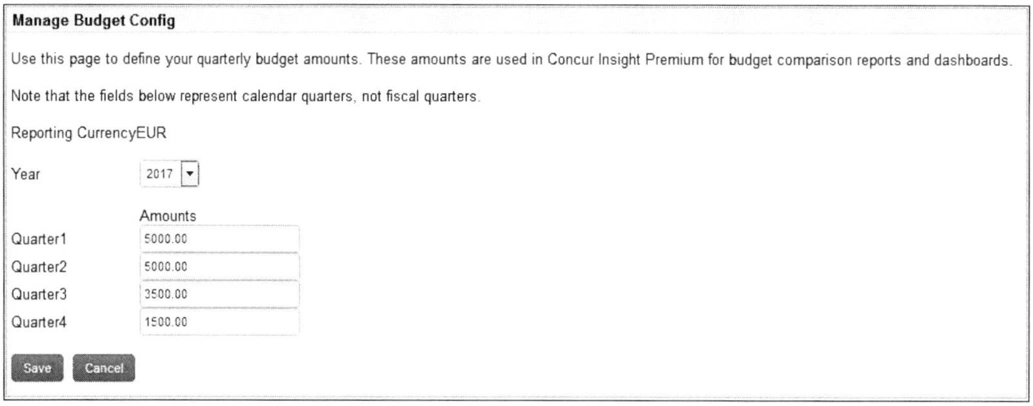

Manage Budget Config

Use this page to define your quarterly budget amounts. These amounts are used in Concur Insight Premium for budget comparison reports and dashboards.

Note that the fields below represent calendar quarters, not fiscal quarters.

Reporting CurrencyEUR

Year   2017 ▾

	Amounts
Quarter1	5000.00
Quarter2	5000.00
Quarter3	3500.00
Quarter4	1500.00

Save   Cancel

Figure 6.16 Setting Budget Thresholds

The actionable analytics alerts are configured to be turned off by default; once enabled, they're enabled for all budget managers across a company. When an administrator activates the alerts, the budget threshold percentage is also specified; individual budget managers can change their threshold percentages as relevant to their individual budgets, as shown in Figure 6.17.

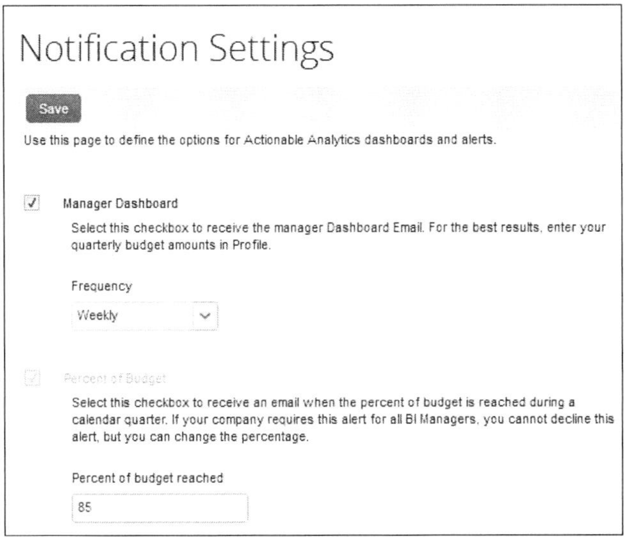

Notification Settings

Save

Use this page to define the options for Actionable Analytics dashboards and alerts.

☑ Manager Dashboard

Select this checkbox to receive the manager Dashboard Email. For the best results, enter your quarterly budget amounts in Profile.

Frequency

Weekly

☑ Percent of Budget

Select this checkbox to receive an email when the percent of budget is reached during a calendar quarter. If your company requires this alert for all BI Managers, you cannot decline this alert, but you can change the percentage.

Percent of budget reached

85

Figure 6.17 Setting Individual Budget Thresholds for Actionable Analytics

The actionable analytics configuration will also allow an upper value for credit card transactions to be defined and an alert sent to budget managers if an employee exceeds this threshold value. As per the budget percentage alert, once an alert for a value threshold on credit card transactions is defined, it will apply for all budget managers, but budget managers can be allowed to configure an individual limit via their profile settings, as shown in Figure 6.17.

6.6 Summary

In this chapter, we discussed the reporting options available in Concur to provide insights into your company's T&E data. We discussed the different reporting options available using either the standard Concur Analysis or Concur Intelligence reporting options and compared the functionalities and options that the two options offer. We also provided an introduction to the Query Studio and Report Studio tools to give you an idea of the powerful queries and reports that can be created. Finally, we discussed the reporting dashboards that Concur provides and how they can be customized for your organization.

In the next chapter, we'll discuss integrating Concur with third-party applications and services.

Concur's many partners provide apps and services that integrate with Concur's solution. Some of these apps are intended for individual business travelers, some for back-office teams, and some create benefits for different stakeholders, like the billing team. These integration capabilities are one of Concur's biggest strengths.

7   Integrating Concur with Third-Party Apps and Services

Integration with third-party apps and services is one of the big value-adding aspects of a modern cloud solution. You can improve the process inside one piece of software only so far; once that reaches perfection, further gains need to be sought outside. *Connectivity* and *network economy* are objectives high on the agenda of digital transformation, and Section 7.1 of this chapter will explain why. We'll then demonstrate how third-party integration can be configured in Concur before discussing e-receipt integration and other integrated apps and services in the following sections.

7.1   The Value of Third-Party Integration

In traditional on-premise systems, the focus of integration has historically been primarily on internal systems. A lot of effort was put into integration with major business partners, such as the use of electronic data interchange (EDI) in the supply chain and automated communication with the authorities, often driven by legislation. However, these interfaces usually require a significant effort to set up and maintain. They are also a constant source of headache for IT departments due to frequent changes in protocols, security, and data formats. The third-party integration scope offered by Concur, in which connections with hundreds of mobile apps, added-value services, e-receipt providers, and travel agencies can be used often within minutes, is practically unfeasible in the on-premise model.

Some of the third-party services offered by Concur can create great value for the right customers (such as the expense billing solution described in Section 7.4.1 for many professional services or engineering companies). Others may just add a bit of extra convenience for the business traveler. The value of the Concur integration model is that these apps can usually be activated and set up quite quickly so that you can realize their potential; in the old days, you might have had to wait for years to get some of the integration projects high enough on the agenda to be implemented. At the current speed of change, particularly in the world of mobile apps, users may already have moved on to better apps and made a new integration worthless on go-live day.

What is it these apps and services help to achieve? Although some benefits are very bespoke, most fall into the following categories:

- Reducing workload for business travelers (e.g., e-receipts)
- Providing better information for business travelers to plan their journey and respond to changes (e.g., Concur TripIt professional for flight delays and cancelations)
- Making business travel more enjoyable (e.g., SeatID for social seat choices)
- Making business travel more effective (e.g., Concur TripIt professional or Lounge Buddy)
- Simplifying booking with vendors or portals not available through the travel management company (TMC) (e.g., Trainline Europe)
- Increasing accuracy of expense data (e.g., mileage tracking apps)
- Reducing manual work in back-office processes (e.g., integration with financial systems or foreign VAT reclamation)
- Reducing compliance risks (e.g., tax audit services like Meridian Global Services or imsHealth for compliance reporting in the life sciences industry)

7.2 General Configuration of Third-Party Apps and Services

Connections to third-party apps are managed in the Concur App Center menu. As shown in Figure 7.1, you'll find an overview of apps for individual users under POPULAR CONNECTIONS and apps and services for the company to be managed by back-office teams under ENTERPRISE APPLICATIONS. In some cases, one vendor will have a connection in both categories; for example, the cab service Uber has an app for individual users to receive e-receipts in their personal Uber app but also allows the corporate travel team to connect to their Uber business account. Concur App Center also includes a search field and allows users to search by category, making it faster to find connections.

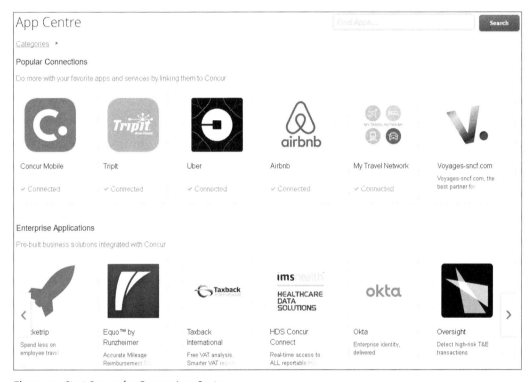

Figure 7.1 Start Screen for Concur App Center

Selecting one of the connections for users provides further information about its features, how to use it, and an option to CONNECT via the button in the upper-right corner (see Figure 7.2).

> **Tip**
>
> Alternately, you can use the CONNECT TO APPS option in the Concur mobile app menu to connect to apps, though not all apps are available there.

Figure 7.2 Details and Connect Button for User App

The description usually explains how to connect the app with a user's Concur account. In many cases, it's as easy as providing the user name for the vendor account (e.g., your Uber user name) and then logging in upon request to authorize the connection once. In other cases, it can be more complicated, particularly for enterprise apps. If it isn't possible to connect directly, the CONNECT button is replaced by a REQUEST INFORMATION button. Enterprise applications often require communication with a vendor.

Although connecting to an individual app is still easy compared to similar connections in traditional systems, it can help to get some advice to develop an app strategy for Concur and to manage the setup. Not all apps work for all countries or policies, and the ever-growing number of apps also can be confusing for users. For example, you often have apps that Concur indicates are available globally, but the respective vendor might not offer any services in your region. You may also not want to encourage users to connect to certain services when your policy prescribes a different preferred vendor in that field. Can you stop users from connecting to apps that you don't want them to use? Let's discuss that topic next.

Connections in Concur App Center are managed through the web services configuration via ADMINISTRATION • COMPANY • WEB SERVICES. Here, you can change the behavior of connections and even create new ones, though this functionality is rarely used. We want to focus here on how to activate or deactivate apps.

Before you can do this, you need to make sure you have WEB SERVICES ADMINISTRATOR rights. To do so, add the corresponding permission to your user account (see Chapter 2) as indicated in Figure 7.3, if it isn't already assigned. Being able to access the WEB SERVICES menu item and being able to open some items doesn't necessarily indicate that you have the correct permissions.

Figure 7.3 Permissions Required to Control Concur App Center

To deactivate user apps, perform the following steps:

1. Go to ADMINISTRATION • COMPANY • WEB SERVICES.

2. Click on MANAGE USER APPLICATIONS.

> **Tip**
>
> This doesn't work with all browser versions. If you see a blank screen, try a different browser. We found issues when using the web services options in Internet Explorer; Firefox has often been the most reliable browser to use.

3. Click on PREVENT USERS FROM CONNECTING (see Figure 7.4) for the apps you want to block. This automatically sets HIDE LISTING DETAILS.

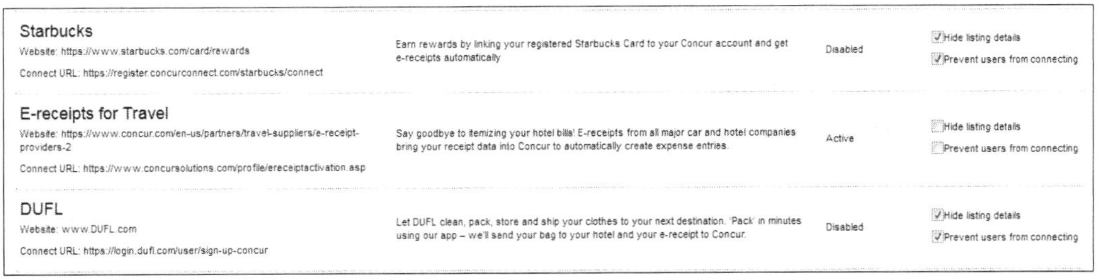

Figure 7.4 Switching On or Off User Apps

4. To one hide the listing, click HIDE LISTING DETAILS. However, this didn't work at the time of writing (February 2017). The connections were still available for users to see, which can create unnecessary confusion.

> **Note**
>
> There is no SAVE button; all changes are saved immediately.

Now, users will no longer see the CONNECT button. Instead, they'll see a note like that shown in Figure 7.5.

This app is unavailable as it is not authorized by your company.

Figure 7.5 Note Indicating User Can't Connect to App

In the CONNECT TO APPS menu of the Concur mobile app, this deactivation has almost the same effect: The CONNECT button is eliminated. However, there is no explanatory note like there is in Concur App Center to indicate that the app deliberately is not authorized.

If a user is connected to the app already when the integration is switched off, the integration stops working once the change has been made. However, although we have tested this with several apps, we recommend checking in every case if you need to be sure. Unfortunately, even apps with switched-off integration are still listed as CONNECTED for the user. This can be confusing and requires good communication to clear up.

Enterprise apps are also configured in the WEB SERVICES menu, using the ENABLE PARTNER APPLICATIONS link. Pick the application from the list as shown in Figure 7.6, then click on the ENABLE or DISABLE button.

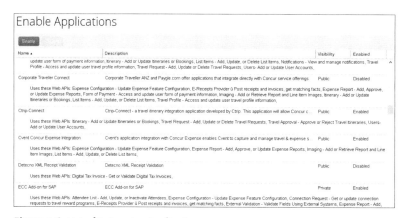

Figure 7.6 List of Enterprise Applications

7.3 E-Receipt Integration

E-receipts are a special category of third-party integrations comprising several vendors, but all follow the same principal: The employee books a service or pays a ticket or incurs any other expense through the vendor's app or website, then an expense item including a receipt image is automatically created in his or her Concur account without any further action.

Apart from third-party integrations managed through Concur App Center, there are two other cases in which e-receipts can be created:

1. E-receipts generated by bookings in Concur Travel
2. Credit card receipts provided by the credit card data import

For all three sources of e-receipts, you need to check whether the data complies with statutory requirements and your internal audit rules. Some vendors' e-receipts lack details such as destination and travel dates for flights. Others lack information required for VAT reclamation (such as VAT ID or VAT amount), which is OK if there's no VAT applicable in the country of purchase, but in other cases it increases the cost of the items purchased significantly.

In this section, we'll focus on integrations managed in Concur App Center. The setup for e-receipt integrations is usually very quick and can be performed by each user as discussed in the previous section, so long as the app is enabled in the web services configuration. E-receipts produce a more efficient process and reduce the number of errors if used properly. Therefore, we recommend that you actively encourage users to set up e-receipt integrations for vendors allowed in your policy and give them a little guidance for each vendor. Some users find most connections intuitive and don't need further guidance, but others can find it difficult and therefore don't use the option or make mistakes initially, which often leads to personal expenses accidentally being transferred to Concur. There are quite a few differences in how transactions related to Concur are managed, as follows:

- Some apps require two separate accounts if you want to use them for business and personal bookings so that all bookings on the business account only are automatically transferred to Concur.

- Other apps require users to select a checkbox to have a transaction sent to Concur.

- ▶ Many apps allow users to pay a tip through the app. Some show the tip separately in the e-receipts, and others don't.

- ▶ Some apps allow for a comment to be captured in the app, which is then also shown on the e-receipt. Figure 7.7 shows an example: The Lyft taxi app allows users to capture a reference and description, which is then displayed on the e-receipt.

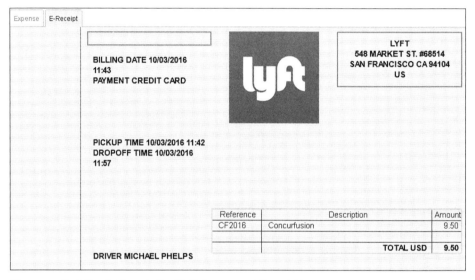

Figure 7.7 Taxi Receipt from Lyft with Reference and Description

The easiest way to connect to apps for e-receipts is often through the mobile app once the vendor app is installed. For example, the following steps connect a user's Concur account to the Gett taxi app:

1. Click CONNECT TO APPS in the Concur mobile app.

2. Select GETT from the list shown in Figure 7.8.

3. Click CONNECT.

4. Accept the terms and conditions.

5. Provide the phone number registered with Gett.

6. Enter the security code sent to that phone number by text message.

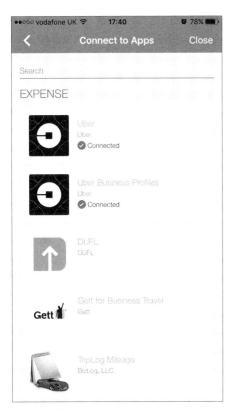

Figure 7.8 Selecting App Connections in Concur Mobile

7.4 Further Selected Solutions

In this chapter so far, we've covered the value and configuration of third-party integrations with Concur in general terms; in this section, we'll discuss a few selected solutions we've found to be particularly valuable, which will provide good examples to further illustrate the idea of third-party integration. For each of the solutions, except the first, we'll provide information for performing the integration and running the solution's main function.

7.4.1 Concur ExpenseIt

Concur ExpenseIt is not technically a third-party app, because Concur acquired it; customers can subscribe to it through their normal Concur subscription contract.

However, we still want to cover it here because it's one of the most important apps for Concur Expense users.

Concur ExpenseIt photographs, scans, and recognizes receipts, autopopulates the most important fields, and creates an expense item in Concur. The autopopulation feature is the most important advantage over using the Concur mobile app only.

Concur ExpenseIt speeds up the T&E process for users, but it doesn't recognize everything—particularly for non-US formats and languages other than English. Its language and localization capabilities have improved in 2016, but there is still more to be expected. As such, we recommend letting users know that this tool is an accelerator, but not perfect, and therefore users should perform a quick check of all data fields before submitting an expense.

> **Note**
>
> Note that the tool is good with dates and even handwritten amounts, which can lead to complacency in not checking these fields. However, on rare occasions amounts have also been recognized incorrectly; for example, a pound sign (£) may be turned into the number 5 added to the amount. This shouldn't stop users from using it, but they need to be aware of it.

Once Concur ExpenseIt is part of your subscription, users can download the app and follow the instructions in the app or in Concur App Center. It's important that the email address used to email receipts is a verified address in the user's Concur user profile.

There are a few settings users can make in Concur ExpenseIt:

- ▶ AUTOMATICALLY EXPORT ANALYZED RECEIPTS TO CONCUR
  If switched off, the user can review and amend the autopopulated fields in Concur ExpenseIt before triggering export to Concur.

- ▶ SAVE RECEIPTS TO PHOTOS
  Switching this on is an easy way for users to keep their own digital record of all receipts by moving them periodically from their smartphone to other storage.

- ▶ CLEAR CACHE
  We recommend using this option every few months to free up storage space on the smartphone.

Once set up, Concur ExpenseIt is easy to use. The process runs as follows:

1. Take a picture of your receipt.

2. Confirm you want to use this picture to submit it for analysis.

3. The receipt will come back from analysis usually within less than three minutes.

4. If automatic export has been switched on, it is then immediately sent to Concur, creates an expense item there, and can be assigned to expense reports and amended.

5. Otherwise, the user can access the receipt data, amend it, and then click on Export to send it to Concur (see Figure 7.9).

Figure 7.9 Reviewing Receipt Data in Concur ExpenseIt

Note a few interesting points about Concur ExpenseIt:

▸ Apart from scanning paper receipts, you can also send e-receipts via email to *receipts@expenseit.com*. This accesses the autopopulate feature and creates expense items as it would with scanned paper receipts, making it more user-friendly than forwarding e-receipts to *receipts@concur.com*.

► Not all of what the app does is tech wizardry; the software sends some receipts for review by human operators to improve the recognition rate.

► Unlike the normal Concur mobile app, Concur ExpenseIt commands an additional subscription fee.

► Concur ExpenseIt can also automatically itemize hotel expenses.

7.4.2 Pivot Prime from Pivot Payables

Pivot Payables provides an easy-to-use expense statement and rebilling solution in the Pivot Prime application. Expense images and data are extracted from Concur Expense and collated into a PDF report or secure encrypted PDF link that can be sent to or shared with your customers. The report generation is automated to include all expenses relevant to a specific customer or project. The application also can be used internally across divisions and projects to recharge costs. Once an expense has been paid in Concur, it's available to be rebilled using Pivot Prime as soon as processing frequencies allow, enabling your company to recoup outstanding monies faster and more efficiently.

Certain expenses may be incurred by your employees that are rebillable to your customers. If you have several employees working on the same project or customer, it can be onerous to identify and amass all the relevant expense data and evidence into a single report. Pivot Prime uses customer and project code information already assigned to the expense entries in Concur. With this automated process, no expenses can be missed from a rebilling report.

A Pivot Prime report has an overall view for all the expenses attributed to the customer or project, including any foreign currency amounts and their conversions, and then full details of each expense entry, including the associated expense image for the customer information. Reports of expense images only also can be generated from Pivot Prime, in addition to creating billing reports.

Integration Setup

The integration setup for Pivot Prime is quick and can be completed in as little as 30 minutes. You need to provide your contact at Pivot Payables with access data for your instance, then the contact sets up the integration for you.

Once an expense has been paid in Concur, it can be rebilled to a customer. A nightly batch job extracts all expense data with a paid status in Concur into the Pivot Prime application. The extraction batch job runs on the PST time zone, so it will have a different report deadline if you're in a different time zone.

Running a Billing Statement

Billing statements can be quickly and easily generated with Pivot Prime in just a few clicks. Expense data can be queried based on three date specifications:

1. Expense report paid dates
2. Expense dates
3. Expense report paid dates with cutoff date

Once the required dates are entered, the expense data is queried, and Pivot Prime will provide a summary of the number of billing reports that are available, including the customer name, the project activity that the expense has been assigned to, and the total number of expense items in the report (see Figure 7.10).

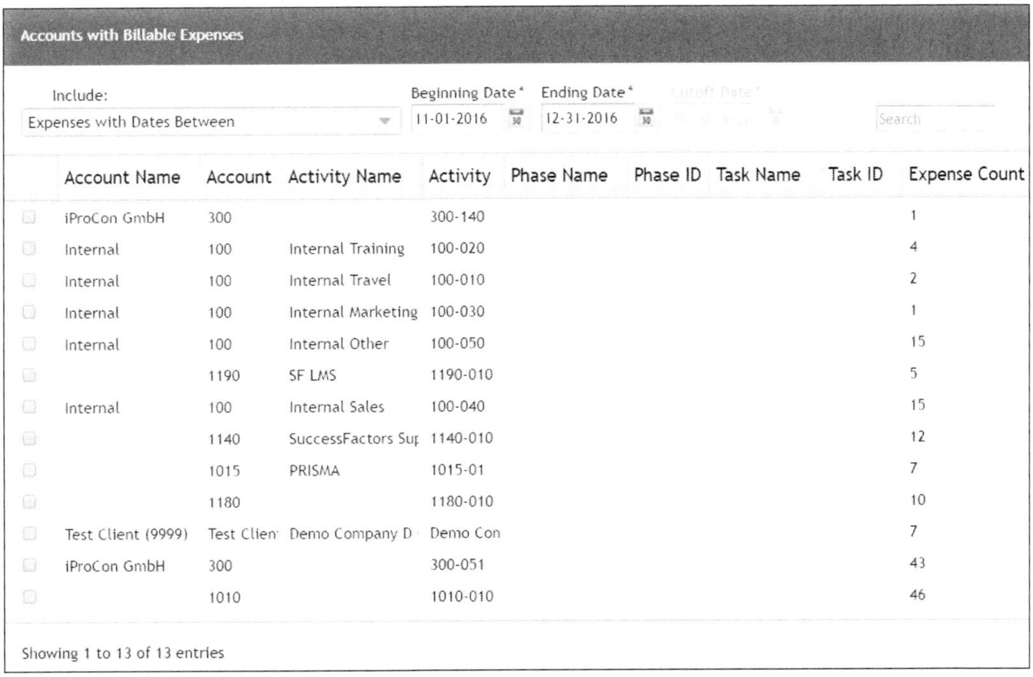

Accounts with Billable Expenses

Include:
Expenses with Dates Between ▾   Beginning Date* 11-01-2016   Ending Date* 12-31-2016   Cutoff Date*   Search

	Account Name	Account	Activity Name	Activity	Phase Name	Phase ID	Task Name	Task ID	Expense Count
☐	iProCon GmbH	300		300-140					1
☐	Internal	100	Internal Training	100-020					4
☐	Internal	100	Internal Travel	100-010					2
☐	Internal	100	Internal Marketing	100-030					1
☐	Internal	100	Internal Other	100-050					15
☐		1190	SF LMS	1190-010					5
☐	Internal	100	Internal Sales	100-040					15
☐		1140	SuccessFactors Sup	1140-010					12
☐		1015	PRISMA	1015-01					7
☐		1180		1180-010					10
☐	Test Client (9999)	Test Clien	Demo Company D	Demo Con					7
☐	iProCon GmbH	300		300-051					43
☐		1010		1010-010					46

Showing 1 to 13 of 13 entries

Figure 7.10 List of Projects for Expense Billing

A report can then be generated for all the required customer account and project specifications.

The Pivot Prime report contains a total overview for all the expenses in the report to be reimbursed, and the individual details of each expense submitted include the associated expense image. This gives the customer a full view of all the expense information and details for the expenses to be agreed upon and approved for reimbursement. The generated reports can be downloaded as PDF documents to be sent to a customer or shared via a secure link to the report.

Pivot Prime can manage different currencies if foreign expenses are due for rebilling. Pivot Prime will use the original amount of the expense, the amount converted to the employees' reimbursement currency, and a billed amount, which can be set to your local currency (see Figure 7.11). The amount conversions are based on the Concur standard currency conversion using the OANDA rates.

Computers R Us Ltd

Statement of Reimbursable Expenses

Expense Reports Paid Between: **08/01/2016** through **09/30/2016**	Total Amount Billed:	£ 1,107.78
Charged to Activity: **100-123**	Billed to Account:	Computers R Us
Activity Identifier: **Customer 123**		

Employee Name	#	Date	Type	Original Amount	Converted Amount	Billed Amount
Will Jackson						
	1	06/15/2016	Taxi	9.60 GBP	£ 9.60	£ 9.60
	2	06/15/2016	Car Rental	148.01 EUR	£ 117.60	£ 117.60
	3	07/07/2016	Airfare	104.95 GBP	£ 104.95	£ 104.95
	4	07/11/2016	Individual Meals	16.75 GBP	£ 16.75	£ 16.75
	5	07/12/2016	Fuel	34.09 EUR	£ 29.08	£ 29.08
	6	07/12/2016	Hotel	61.00 EUR	£ 52.03	£ 52.03
	7	07/12/2016	Car Rental	118.89 EUR	£ 101.41	£ 101.41
	8	07/27/2016	Airfare	172.96 GBP	£ 172.96	£ 172.96

Figure 7.11 Pivot Prime Report Showing Foreign Expenses and Converted Reimbursed Amounts

7.4.3 VAT IT Foreign VAT Reclamation

Many organizations, most notably small and medium enterprises (SMEs), don't reclaim foreign VAT at all because the cost for doing so would be higher than the return for their volume.

VAT IT is one of several Concur partner solutions for foreign tax reclaims. They use the data and receipt images in Concur to maximize the tax reclaims for your company. VAT IT gets a user record assigned to it that allows it to directly connect with your Concur instance and read all your expense, and associated tax, data, as well as access your images. The data is then analyzed and submitted to the appropriate tax authorities. VAT IT is a cloud-based reporting application that can be accessed anywhere on the go to see how much value-added tax is being reclaimed for your company via a dynamic dashboard and click-through navigation for all claims and invoices.

VAT IT is a Concur-certified partner, which ensures that your travel and expense data is secure and stable when being extracted and handled.

Integration Setup

The VAT IT solution uses the *Expense Configuration*, *Expense Report*, and *Update Expense Reports Imaging APIs* to extract expense tax and image data from your Concur instance.

A user record for VAT IT is created in Concur with the web services administration permissions, and the partner application is also enabled under the Web Services Administration configuration menu.

The user record is created with specific naming conventions, parameters, and permissions for the web service administration. User records for partner applications use the *WSAdmin-AppProviderName@YourCompanyDomain.com* naming convention, which enables the administration user to be clearly separated from your usual company users in reports, user management, and so on. The user may require expense or travel permissions, depending on the partner applications being enabled and the assignment of the web services administration authorization.

The partner application is enabled in the Web Services administration menu. Select the Enable Partner Applications submenu and then VAT IT from the list shown in Figure 7.12 and clicking on the ENABLE button (for more detail *see* Section 7.2). Concur will present a disclaimer; if you agree, the partner application can access your company's Concur data.

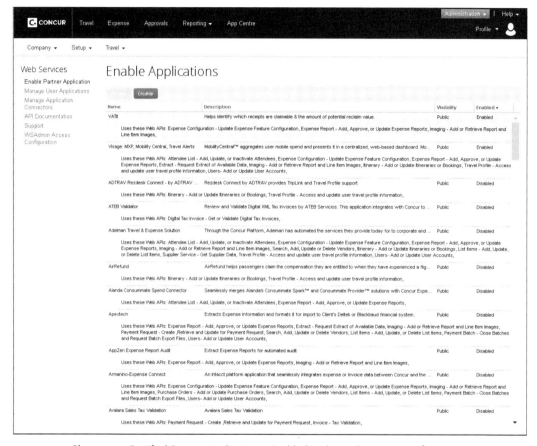

Figure 7.12 Certified Partner Applications, Enabled in the Web Service Configuration Menu

Monitoring Reclaim Amounts and Claims

VAT IT submits all tax claims and data automatically, requiring no user input, and offers a fully automated invoice process with an informative dashboard to alert users to progress and to claims completed.

Data is extracted from Concur and other integration points that you may use, such as for credit cards or ERP systems, and collated into VAT IT's reclaim software, which uses algorithms to identify amounts for possible reclamation and optical character recognition (OCR) technology to assess digital invoices and expense images. This data is then collated into one record claim to be submitted to each appropriate tax authority for its reclamation process.

The VAT IT dashboard provides a comprehensive overview of the status of all VAT-able amounts. Each dashboard tile has click-through navigation to take you to the detail of the claims, showing your totals of claimed and refunded amounts, claims submissions, and refunds by country, as well as the status of all claims. The key figures for all the important values such as total refunded, total claimed, any amounts awaiting refund, or any rejection are all clearly shown for easy management reporting.

Another function of the reclaim service is invoice restyle or reissue. This is a process whereby an invoice is reissued by the vendor if the original doesn't contain required information, such as if the VAT isn't correctly split out from the total amount or if the invoice is marked "Copy," which would not be deemed acceptable by many international tax authorities. One of the key metrics shown on the dashboard, as shown in Figure 7.13, reports the value of invoices being subjected to the restyle/reissue service to enable you to make improvements to your expenses process if necessary.

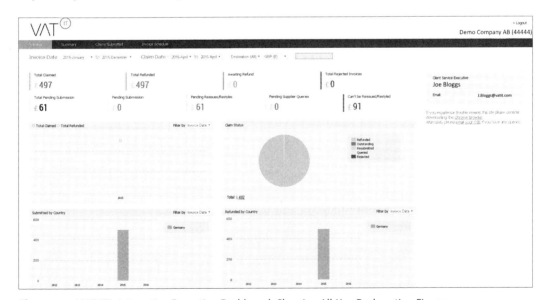

Figure 7.13 VAT IT's Interactive Reporting Dashboard, Showing All Key Reclamation Figures

7.4.4   Visage Mobile International Travel Roaming Alerts (ITRA)

Visage Mobile travel alerts read travel data from Concur Travel to enable your company to effectively manage mobile phone charges for your employees' international travel. Travel alerts are generated in advance of employee travel for the mobile phone administrators in your company to ensure that the employee traveling has the appropriate phone coverage in the country of travel; when that employee returns from travel, the service is disabled again so that roaming mobile costs can be controlled. Having full visibility of your employees' international travel will enable your business to make cost savings and negotiate better corporate supplier arrangements.

Integration Setup

Visage is a certified partner application, and the integration is set up with an authorized user and the partner application enablement under the WEB SERVICES configuration menu.

The user record is created with specific naming conventions, parameters, and permissions for web service administration, with the naming convention *WSAdmin-AppProviderName@YourCompanyDomain.com*.

The application itself is enabled in the WEB SERVICES administration menu by selecting the application in the ENABLE PARTNER APPLICATIONS configuration step, then clicking on the ENABLE button (see Section 7.2 for details).

Monitoring Travel Alerts

The travel alert integrations use the Concur APIs for attendee lists, expense configuration, expense reports, itinerary, and travel profile accesses to extract the full profile of all your employees and their travel details. Alerts like the one shown in Figure 7.14 are then sent to specified users on a periodic basis to alert them to upcoming travel for the week, month, and next month ahead.

Each traveler's full travel itinerary is sent in an Excel file attached to the alert email. The trip itinerary data for each employee includes data such as the trip name, start and end dates, departure and arrival cities and countries, and mobile information associated with the employee, such as mobile phone number, handset information, and plan information. Recommendations are included as part of the travel data to help administrators make the best roaming coverage decisions based on the available plans and covered by various mobile phone carriers.

International Travel Roaming Alerts

0 travelers were identified since the last report was sent to you on 09/17.

1 is traveling internationally this week.

Please refer to the attached spreadsheet for details on each travel itinerary.

Destination	Since 09/17	This week (09/18 - 09/24)	This month (09/01 - 09/30)	Next month (10/01 - 10/31)
Germany	0	1	1	0
Total*	0	1	1	0

*Total of unique international travelers for the specified time period

Please refer to the international traveler coverage map below for the traveler distribution. (Note: Darker color means more travelers.)

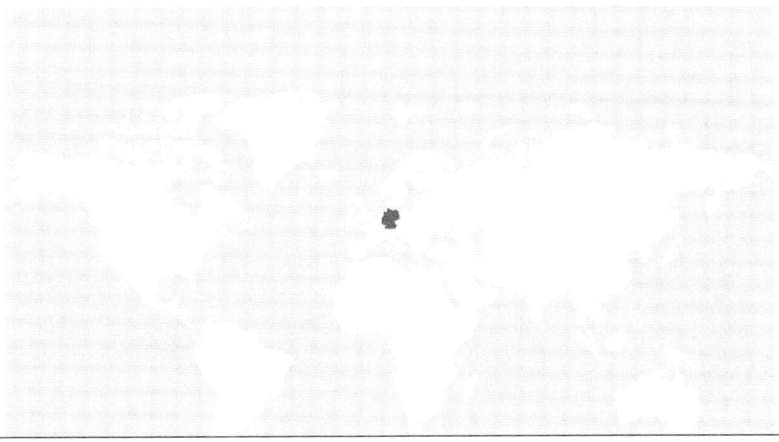

Figure 7.14 Travel Alert Email with Upcoming Travel Details

7.5 Summary

In this chapter, we discussed just a few apps and services from the large number available to Concur customers. These examples should provide an idea of the value you can gain from each individual app and how transformational the experience can be once dozens of third-party integrations increase the level of automation and comfort for your business travelers and back-office teams.

The general activation of integrations is easy, but the workload for setting up and integrating with a particular service can vary greatly. We recommend picking a few integrations for the go-live of your Concur project to show some quick wins for users, then continuously increase the number of apps and services provided thereafter.

Concur was acquired by SAP in December of 2014. Ever since, customers have expected an easy-to-use integration between Concur and SAP's other solutions. Such integrations take time to design and build, but some are available now and cover the scenarios asked for by most customers.

8 Integrating Concur with Other SAP Solutions

Traditionally, SAP customers have always had a high expectation of integration among the various IT solutions supporting their business processes across all functions. Therefore, good integration between Concur and SAP solutions is still an important driver for new Concur customers; users of the on-premise SAP Travel Management solution especially would prefer to switch to Concur and continue to benefit from the same level of integration they enjoyed before.

Since April 2016, the Concur to SAP ERP integration has been available for early adopters (with general availability since September 2016) as a set of four add-ons:

- ▸ CTE_FND, the foundation component for the integration
- ▸ CTE_HCM for SAP ERP Human Capital Management integration
- ▸ CTE_FIN for SAP ERP Financial integration for expense posting
- ▸ CTE_INV for SAP ERP Financial integration for invoices (only relevant for the Concur Invoice product, so we won't discuss this any further in this book)

You will need to download and install these add-ons with the usual tools; see SAP Note 2298170 for download and technical installation guidance. The foundation component needs to be deployed regardless of which of the other three you want to use.

Further guidance can be found on the SAP Service Marketplace, via PRODUCTS • INSTALLATION & UPGRADE GUIDES • CLOUD SOLUTIONS FROM SAP • SAP INTEGRATION WITH CONCUR SOLUTIONS. We recommend you check these documents before embarking on an implementation. Concur partners with a strong background in the respective SAP solutions are often a good source of the latest information.

> **Activating the Integration**
>
> To be able to use the integration, it needs to be activated by Concur. As of February 2017, a reasonable one-off activation fee is being charged for this—no matter how many SAP systems are involved.
>
> Note that although the integration does use Concur's web services, no separate subscription fee or setup fee for web services is being charged. This is often misunderstood, causing customers to overestimate integration costs.

As shown in Figure 8.1, if you have one Concur instance, one HR system from SAP, and several SAP ERP Financials systems, the process runs as follows:

▶ HR master data is sent from your HR system to Concur

▶ Financial master data (cost objects) is sent from all your SAP ERP Financials systems to Concur

▶ Your expense reports are pulled from your Concur system into the respective SAP ERP Financials systems

▶ Posting feedback/confirmation is sent from the respective SAP ERP Financials systems to Concur

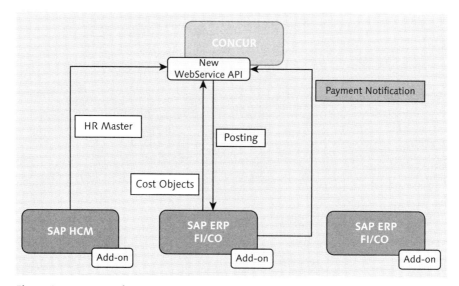

Figure 8.1 Overview of Concur to SAP ERP Integration Architecture

In the following section, we'll discuss the individual integration points in more detail. We'll go over HR master data, financial master data and posting, and payroll, the most important integrations for most customers; we'll also talk a bit about further SAP solutions.

8.1 Integrating with HR Master Data

For most SAP customers, HR master data is still held in SAP ERP HCM, but SAP SuccessFactors Employee Central has become increasingly important, with a quickly growing customer base.

In Chapter 2, we discussed why the user master data in Concur is important and what it is comprised of. If you're using one of SAP's HR solutions, the best way to keep user data in Concur current is to use the standard integration with the leading system for employee data: your HR system.

8.1.1 Integration with SAP ERP HCM

This integration makes use of the CTE_HCM integration add-on. Once the add-on is deployed per the guidelines, it needs to be configured to match your requirements. This configuration is set up in the SAP ERP system, where the add-on is installed using Transaction CTE_SETUP (see Figure 8.2), your central command center for Concur to SAP ERP integration.

Setting Up the Integration with Concur

| ⓘ Documentation | Integration Activities | 🔁 Download Guide |

System ↲	Employee ↲	Cost Center ↲	Network Activity ↲	Financial Posting ↲	Vendor ↲
S...	RFC Destination		D	Employee	Cost Center	Network A...	Financial Po...	Vendor
1	CONCUR		DE	☐	☐	☐	☐	

Figure 8.2 Initial Screen of Transaction CTE_SETUP

In the following subsections, we'll walk through the steps necessary for this integration: creating the secure connection, configuring the HR data, and running the integration. We'll conclude with a short summary of the integration features available.

Creating the Secure Connection

Before you can use any of the integrations, you need to establish the secure connection between your SAP system and your Concur instance. To do so, once in Transaction CTE_SETUP, click on the SYSTEM button and then select CREATE CONNECTION to start the setup wizard for the technical integration (see Figure 8.3).

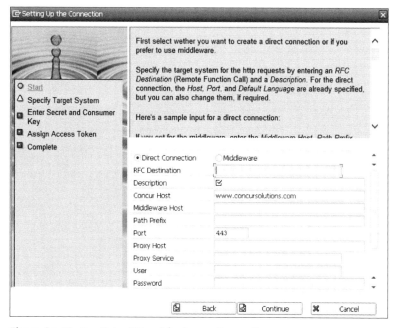

Figure 8.3 Starting Setup Wizard for Secure Connection

Before you can process the wizard for the secure connection, you need to liaise with Concur, your SAP Basis team, and your data security team to ask for technical data such as remote function call (RFC) connection info, encryption keys, and access tokens. For more details, refer to the technical guide, which you can also download from Transaction CTE_SETUP.

Note the following three important points of interest regarding this setup wizard:

1. The wizard asks you to choose between a direct connection and using middleware. Not requiring middleware is a strength of this solution, so you should avoid middleware if you can. However, many organizations have policies requiring middleware. In these cases, SAP Process Integration (SAP PI)/SAP Process Orchestration (SAP PO) or SAP Cloud Platform Integration (formerly

SAP HANA Cloud Integration) are the most likely solutions. A standard integration package for SAP Cloud Platform Integration is available on the SAP Content Hub under the title Concur Integration: Data Replication and FI Posting.

2. The field Concur Host is prepopulated with Concur's US data center. Don't forget to change it to the European data center (eu1.concursolutions.com at the time of writing) if that is where your instance is hosted.

3. The wizard also asks for a Default Language. It's important to understand the implication of this choice:

> ► If the name of a cost object (e.g., a cost center) is not available in the user's language, the default language is picked instead.

> ► All error messages that occur in SAP during posting are sent as a text in the default language to Concur. It's therefore important that you pick a language that all processors in Concur understand. Unfortunately, the error messages can't be translated in Concur, because the actual text (as defined in table GLE_VECS_MSG in SAP), not a code, is transferred from SAP.

HR Data Configuration

To activate user/HR data integration, click on the Integration Activities button in Transaction CRE_SETUP and select Employee. Further configuration is then done via the button Employee. Then, click on Specify Field Mapping to get to the screen shown in Figure 8.4. The field mapping allows you to map fields from the Concur user data to fields from SAP ERP HCM master data by specifying an infotype, subtype, and field name. All HR master infotypes, including custom developments, can be used.

> **Note**
>
> This does not include data from SAP ERP HCM Organizational Management, and your data needs to be unambiguous. Don't use infotypes and subtypes with time constraints other than 1 or 2.

Figure 8.4 also shows the SAP Implementation Code column. This column refers to methods in a BAdI and allows you to apply a more complex logic using custom ABAP coding. Some methods are already deployed in the standard solution, such as EE_RLU_MANAGER_ID, which determines the approver through the line manager relationship.

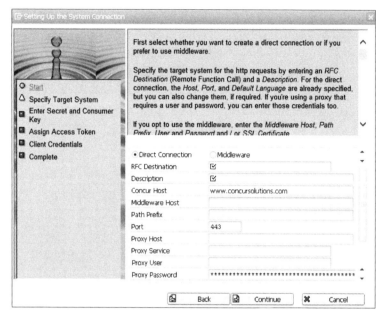

Figure 8.4 Configuring User Data Interface: Field Mapping

There are currently some constraints placed on what you can configure with this integration:

▸ Only the first approver and no second approver can be determined through the integration.

▸ Some Concur user data fields can't be filled through the interface, because the APIs provided by Concur don't include all fields.

▸ Concurrent (multiple) employment can't be processed.

Repeat Setup for All Systems

Note that the add-ons need to be deployed in all systems involved, and configuration needs to be done in each system. That means that the SAP ERP HCM add-on needs to be installed on all SAP ERP HCM systems, the SAP ERP Financials add-on on all finance systems, and the foundation add-on on both groups. This can amount to quite a few days of work if you have several HR and financial SAP systems.

However, the previously mentioned activation fee only needs to be paid once per customer.

Running the HR Data Integration

You can trigger the transfer of HR data to Concur by selecting EMPLOYEE • MANUAL EXPORT. This open the selection screen for the integration tool, as shown in Figure 8.5; here, you can select the employees to be transferred. Please note that the transfer creates live users, never test users. We recommend you use the tool in test mode until you feel confident about the export.

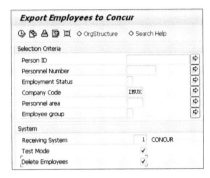

Figure 8.5 Running HR Data Transfer in Test Mode

Once the process is established and stabilized, we recommend you run the transfer as a job. Transaction CTE_MONI serves as a central monitoring tool for all replication jobs, as shown in Figure 8.6.

Communication Monitor

Receiving System   1 CONCUR

Show Run Logs

Export/Import	Replicated	Successfully Created	Deleted	Not Created	Not Updated
Employee	2	0	0	2	0
Cost Center	0	0	0	0	0
Network Activity	0	0	0	0	0

Figure 8.6 Transaction CTE_MONI to Monitor Replication Jobs

Note: Data Security

As you can see from the technical setup of the connection, the data is sent through a secure, encrypted connection. We also should emphasize that the connection is always initiated from the on-premise SAP system. This applies to HR master data replication, financial master data replication, and financial posting. Concur will never initiate the connection with SAP. This is good news for your security team, because they don't have to worry about a rogue system in the cloud accessing your SAP ERP system while pretending to be your Concur instance.

Features for HR Data Integration

Table 8.1 describes the availability of integration features as of February 2017. The features listed are those most frequently inquired after by customers. Many of the features not yet available can be expected in one of the coming updates, but there is no guarantee.

Feature	Availability
Transferring a restricted set of employees	Available, but may need workaround
Handling concurrent employment and global assignments	Not available
Concur employee ID able to be determined via SAP ERP HCM personnel number, central person ID, or employee ID from Infotype 0709	Available
Setting employees as inactive in Concur when they leave the company	Available
Assigning expense approver via interface (*Note:* change of manager in SAP ERP HCM Organizational Management does not trigger a new replication for the employee)	Available
Filling email and login ID in Concur from subtypes in Infotype 0105	Available
Requiring password to be requested by employee at first Concur logon	Available
Deleting employees in Concur	Not available (can only be set inactive)
Creating test users via interface	Not available
Transferring data for travel (frequent traveler data, etc.)	Not available
Transferring data for Concur Expense Pay Global	Not available
Transferring credit card details	Not available
Transferring company car data	Not available
Transferring delegates	Not available
Transferring authorized approvers	Not available
Defining users for Concur Request	Not available
Assigning second approvers	Not available

Table 8.1 Features for User Data Integration

8.1.2   Integration with SAP SuccessFactors

As of February 2017, integration with SAP SuccessFactors has started as part of the early adopter program for a few selected customers. Going by the experience with the SAP ERP integration, we expect this integration to be available for all customers by mid-2017.

The integration for HR data/user data is much simpler in nature than that for financial data, so you can easily bridge the gap by extracting the required data from SAP SuccessFactors Employee Central via file export and uploading it into Concur, as discussed in Chapter 2. Such an export can be created using SAP SuccessFactors ad hoc reporting, accessed via ANALYTICS • REPORTING • AD HOC REPORTS • CREATE NEW REPORT, as shown in Figure 8.7.

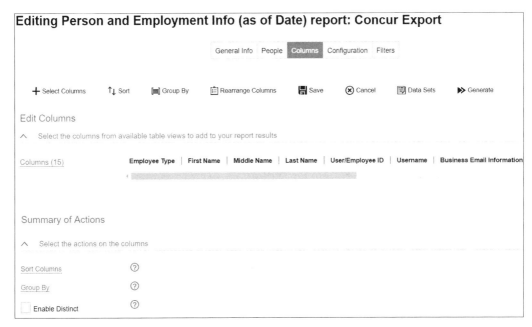

Figure 8.7 Creating Ad Hoc Report for Concur Data in SAP SuccessFactors

You can then run the report online and export it in CSV or Microsoft Excel format (see Figure 8.8) or choose to run it offline or download it right away without showing the data on your screen first.

Employee Type	First Name	Middle Name	Last Name	User/Employee ID	Username	Business Email Address	Email Information	Mobile Formatted Phone Number	Company	Country	Currency	Employee Status	Cost Centre	Supervisor
Salaried	Gabrielle		Pape	102048	gpape	Gabrielle.pape@bestrun.com			2200-BestRun France	France	EUR	Active	2200-4200-France Production	Maigne, Hubert
Salaried	Renee		Laparte	100498	rlaparte	Renee.Laparte@bestrun.com			2200-BestRun France	France	EUR	Active	2200-4200-France Production	Maigne, Hubert
Salaried	Francois		Trombley	1	ftrombley	francis.trombley@bestrun.com			2200-BestRun France	France	EUR	Active	2200-4200-France Production	Maigne, Hubert

Figure 8.8 Export Options after Ad Hoc Report Execution

However, it is quite difficult to fully automate this process without using middleware, because Concur requires user data files in exactly the format specified in its templates. Because the format of an export from SAP SuccessFactors will likely not match the templates exactly, we recommend you follow a semimanual process if you require this integration before the standard solution becomes available.

8.2   Integrating with SAP ERP Financials

Before you integrate with SAP ERP Financials, you must set up the technical connection between SAP and Concur (see the discussion of creating a secure connection in Section 8.1.1). Setting up and running the financial integration with Concur also occurs via Transaction CTE_SETUP and comprises three main elements:

1. Transferring financial master data (cost objects) from SAP ERP to Concur

2. Posting expense reports from Concur to SAP ERP

3. Transferring feedback from SAP ERP back to Concur

We'll explain these elements in the following subsections, and we'll conclude with a section on the features available for financial integration.

8.2.1   Financial Master Data Replication

To allow users in Concur to assign their expenses to cost centers, orders, or projects, these *cost objects* need to be available in Concur. The master data replication between SAP ERP and Concur makes sure that all cost objects required are available; at the same time, cost objects that can no longer be used for posting in SAP are also not available in Concur.

The replication logic in the integration add-on filters out all cost objects that can't be posted to in SAP ERP. We therefore recommend you set up the replication to run at least every 15 minutes to minimize the risk of obsolete cost objects being used.

As of February 2017, the following types of cost objects were available for the integration:

▶ Cost centers

▶ Internal orders

▶ Networks

▶ Network activities

▶ WBS elements

▶ Sales order items

> **Note**
>
> Service organizations will likely notice the current lack of integration for service orders. This functionality is expected to be added, though there is no official timeline set.

To decide which types of cost objects should be replicated, click the INTEGRATION ACTIVITIES button in Transaction CRE_SETUP, then select the respective objects, as shown in Figure 8.9.

For each cost object type selected, a button will show up to access the respective configuration through a wizard. We'll describe this configuration for cost centers only; it is exactly the same for other cost objects.

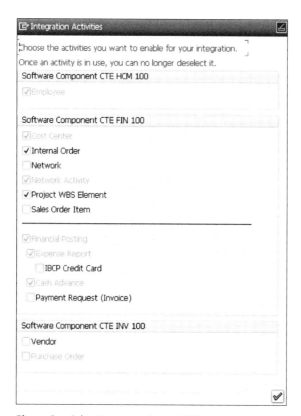

Figure 8.9 Selecting Integration Activities

Start the wizard via COST CENTER • SET UP EXPORT. Figure 8.10 shows the first wizard step, in which you define a hierarchy to organize all your cost objects (this must be the same for all cost object types, not just cost centers). Select your CONCUR LIST (this setup is explained further in Section 8.2.2), then assign SAP hierarchy levels. The bottom entry is always the ID of the actual cost object—in this case, the cost center ID—and we recommend you set the next-to-last level to be the cost object type. For the levels above, choose from among the logical system ID of your SAP system (recommended for the top entry), controlling area, country, company code, or business area.

The second step (Figure 8.11) allows you to set up a phased rollout. Here, you can select groups of cost objects based on filter criteria you pick to represent the rollout phases and decide the date on which replication for each phase should start.

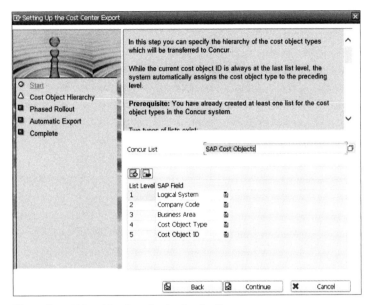

Figure 8.10 Wizard for Cost Center Replication

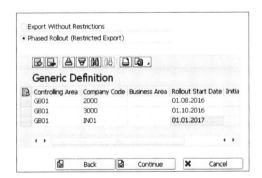

Figure 8.11 Establishing Phased Rollout

The final step of the wizard allows you to choose between manual and automatic export; for automatic export, you can also decide the job schedule. We recommend you start with manual export so that you can monitor whether it works and become familiar with the process. Once the process has stabilized, you should switch to automatic export.

As soon as the setup wizard is complete, you can start replication via COST CENTER • MANUAL EXPORT. The simple selection screen presented allows you to select the cost centers you want to distribute, but for a live environment we'd recommend that you don't restrict the selected cost centers here, unless there's an exception; instead, make that the selection in the setup wizard. Figure 8.12 shows the results of the cost center export, as follows:

▸ A list of successfully transferred objects

▸ Objects that weren't transferred because they can't be used for posting in SAP ERP

▸ Any error messages

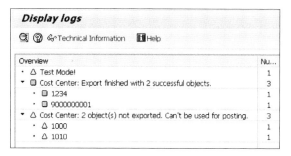

Figure 8.12 Results of Cost Center Replication Run

Once you've gone through the same process for all relevant cost objects, you are ready to capture expenses in Concur and post them into SAP ERP.

8.2.2 Financial Posting

Start the wizard for the posting setup via FINANCIAL POSTING • CREATE IMPORT. The first decision to make is whether you want to post expense reports, cash advances, or both.

The general settings step is more interesting. Here, you decide whether you want to accept postings from test users in Concur. You should allow this only in your SAP test system to avoid test expense reports being turned into real postings in SAP. You also choose between two options for how to interpret account codes in Concur:

1. Account codes in Concur are the same as in SAP.

2. Account codes in Concur are interpreted as symbolic accounts in SAP; you must map these symbolic accounts to actual GL accounts in the SAP configuration.

The second option allows for more flexibility. Most notably, this option allows you to deal with changes to SAP General Ledger (G/L) account codes in SAP without necessarily making any changes in Concur.

The next step in the wizard establishes the expense posting settings, as shown in Figure 8.13. Here, you choose the posting date used for expense postings (e.g., current day or the end date of each expense report) and the document type used for all postings from Concur. You can also set filters based on various fields in Concur to stop some expense reports from being posted. The figure shows a filter by company, which is represented in Concur by the CUSTOM2 field.

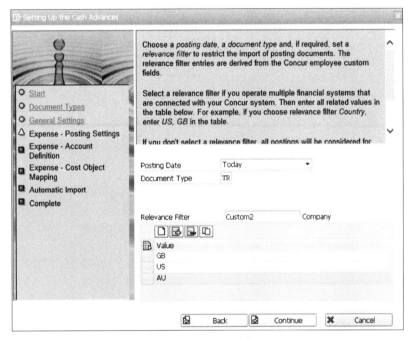

Figure 8.13 Financial Posting Wizard: Posting Settings

Defining Legal Entities for Direct Integration

When Concur activates the direct integration in your Concur instance for you, it can perform the activation per group configuration. Groups are often defined by country or even as regions that include several countries. If you plan to use the integration described in this chapter for only some of your employees, this detail should be considered in the group configuration. We highly recommend you raise and review this option early in the project.

In the CostObjectMapping step (see Figure 8.14), you define the fields in the expense report or expense screens in Concur in which the various cost object IDs and types and the hierarchy levels from SAP ERP are held. Note that not all fields are captured for each expense or each expense report. The SAP system ID would in all but very few exceptional cases be recorded in Concur at the user level and autopopulate a corresponding background field in the expense report. The same would often be true for other fields, like company code or business area, but depending on your policy you may also allow for users to assign expenses to company codes other than their own. This all occurs in Concur Expense configuration (see Chapter 4).

Figure 8.14 Financial Posting Wizard: Cost Object Mapping

Capture Cost Assignments for Integration in Allocations

Assignment to cost centers and other cost objects can be arranged in normal expense screen fields or via the Allocation button in Concur. Note that the standard SAP ERP integration tool expects cost assignment to be performed via allocation, so your Concur system must be set up accordingly.

There is one piece of Concur configuration which is of utmost importance for the standard integration with SAP ERP Financials: the setup of the cost hierarchy, which contains the cost objects to be populated through cost object replication. The objects in this hierarchy are mapped to the fields as discussed in the previous paragraph. This hierarchy is set up as a connected list in Concur via Administration • Expense • List Management. This setup needs to be discussed and tested thoroughly early in the implementation project; changing it late in the project can require a lot of effort and create delay, and a change after go-live can create considerable disruption.

Figure 8.15 shows the minimal possible setup as a connected list with four levels:

- SAP logical system ID
- Company code

- Cost object type
- Cost object ID

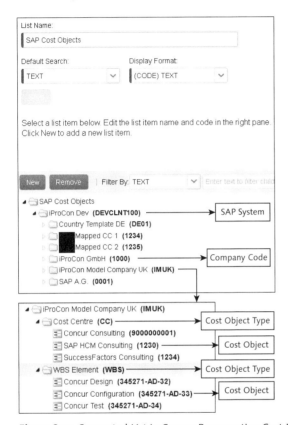

Figure 8.15 Connected List in Concur Representing Cost Hierarchy

The example in Figure 8.15 starts with the logical system DEVCLNT100 as the only SAP system, which has several company codes. The company code IMUK has two cost object types assigned: cost centers and WBS elements. For each of those types, two IDs are assigned, which can then be used in expense allocations and posted to.

Once all this configuration has been set up, you can create and process expense reports. Once the processing step has been finalized, the expense reports are ready for posting through the integration. However, the posting is triggered not out of Concur but from SAP ERP, via Transaction CTE_SETUP (or from an automated job).

To manually post the expense reports waiting in Concur, navigate to FINANCIAL POSTING • CONCUR DOCUMENTS • FEEDBACK LOOP • START AUTOMATICALLY, then select the relevant Concur system (if you have several instances connected) and run the report. Any errors are shown in the log; when you go back, using the green BACK button, you'll see a list of all documents and their respective statuses (see Figure 8.16).

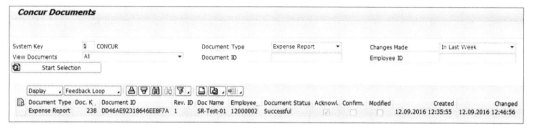

Figure 8.16 Overview of Documents from Concur

For documents successfully posted (see the DOCUMENT STATUS column), you can see the posting document by selecting DISPLAY • FINANCIAL POSTING DOCUMENT, as shown in Figure 8.17.

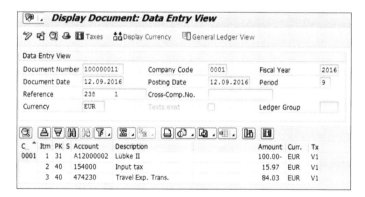

Figure 8.17 Posted Document in SAP Finance

For documents that couldn't be posted, such as those with locked cost objects or missing allocations, you can see the log via DISPLAY • DOCUMENT PROTOCOL. Note that an expense report is always posted entirely or not at all. If only one of several cost objects in a report results in an error, the whole repost is not posted. This makes it easier to manage errors and maintain the integrity of the process.

8.2.3   Feedback Loop

The beauty of this integration is that the result of the posting run in SAP ERP is fed back to Concur, so processors as well as users can see which documents have been posted successfully and which documents require a change. The big difference from other integration methods, which are based on Standard Accounting Extract (SAE) file transfers or other technologies, is that an error in posting an expense report sets the status of that expense report accordingly so that the processor can reopen it for changes. If you use other integration methods, you usually can't change and repost an expense report from Concur; you must make the corrections in the target system or the export file. This leads inevitably to inconsistencies between your Concur data and the data in your financial systems.

Figure 8.18 shows how the status in Concur changes during the process for an expense report going through financial posting in SAP ERP.

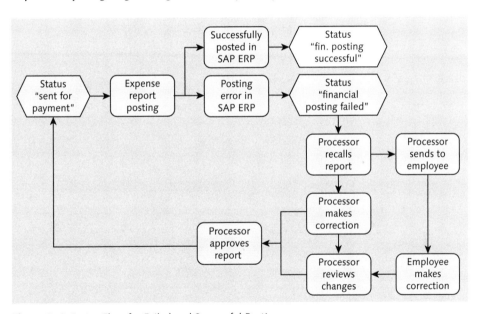

Figure 8.18 Status Flow for Failed and Successful Postings

When an expense report is approved by the processor in Concur and therefore ready for posting, the status is *sent for payment*. Then, it's picked up by the integration when the respective program in SAP ERP is run either manually or as a background job, as described in Section 8.2.2. If the posting is successful, the status in Concur changes accordingly, and the processor and the employee can see the change. If the posting fails, again, the status in Concur changes accordingly; the processor has the option then to recall the expense report, thus opening it for corrections. He or she then can make the correction directly or send it back to the employee to make the corrections.

For example, the problem might be due to a locked cost center; the employee must decide which other cost center should be used. The processor can see the reason for the problem in the expense report's audit trail, accessible through Details • Audit Trail. Once the employee has made his/her change and re-submitted, the report goes through the normal approval workflow, eventually getting to the processor, who sends it to financial posting again. If everything is ok this time round, the posting will go through.

If the posting fails, there is also another option not indicated in Figure 8.18: If the problem is caused by data in SAP ERP rather than Concur, the correction can be made in SAP ERP and the posting run repeated. In this case, there is no need for the processor in Concur to recall the expense report.

8.2.4 Features for Financial Integration

Table 8.2 describes the availability of integration features as of February 2017. The features listed are those most frequently inquired about by customers. Some of the features list as not yet available may be possible to implement using BAdIs or other enhancement options in SAP ERP on-premise.

Feature	Availability
Determining G/L account directly or via symbolic accounts	Available
Determining vendor account based on employee ID or CustomField17 in Concur	Available
Determining vendor account determination based on other fields	Not available
Controlling exported expense reports via authorization profiles in SAP ERP	Not available
Reconciling cash advances via G/L clearing account	Available
Reconciling cash advances via vendor account	Not available
Handling IBIP, CBCP, and IBCP credit cards, as well as cash advances	Available

Table 8.2 Features for Financial Posting Integration

Feature	Availability
Connecting multiple SAP ERP systems with one Concur instance	Available
Using middleware (SAP PI or SAP Cloud Platform Integration)	Available, but not necessary
Transferring receipt images with postings	Not available
Adjusting posting data via BAdIs	Available
Receiving payment notification when vendor payment run has paid expenses	Not available
Defining custom line item text and assignments	Not available
Posting itemized expenses	Available
Handling expense entries with single or multiple cost allocations	Available
Handling employee-paid and company-paid expenses, as well as payment via Concur Expense Pay Global	Available
Handling intercompany postings	Available
Capturing cash advance returns as administrator	Available
Handling fringe benefits tax (Australia)	Available
Handling VAT, including various scenarios for nondeductible VAT and partially deductible VAT	Available
Handling VAT via vendor accounts for Italy and Spain	Not available
Handling tax processing with an external tax engine	Case-by-case decision
Transferring cost object managers (user/person responsible for cost object in SAP ERP)	Not available
Transferring only a selected set of cost objects	Available via phased rollout
Deleting cost objects	Available
Defining flexible keys for sales orders and network activities	Available
Handling customer-specific objects in cost object hierarchy	Not available

Table 8.2 Features for Financial Posting Integration (Cont.)

When to Start Using the Standard Integration

As of February 2017, Concur has officially stopped selling the integration described in this chapter to existing customers; it is now available to new customers only. The official reason given is that existing customers often require a change in their cost object hierarchy in Concur, which is difficult to achieve for live customers.

As such, we strongly recommend to new customers that they go live with the new integration and don't put it off until a later stage, as it may not be possible to activate it then. If that's not possible, customers should make sure that they build a cost object hierarchy matching the requirements of the new integration as discussed in Section 8.2.2 and have confirmed in writing by Concur—ideally as part of the Concur subscription contract—that they can set up the new integration later.

For live Concur customers who would like to use the new integration but aren't allowed to, the best option is to wait and check back occasionally.

8.3 Integrating with Payroll in SAP ERP HCM

Many customers want integration with Payroll in SAP ERP HCM for one or more of three reasons:

1. To pay expenses through Payroll

2. To calculate and retain taxes on taxable expense payments

3. For statutory reporting managed through Payroll

As of February 2017, SAP's standard Concur integration add-on does not yet cover Payroll. SAP indicates that it's on the roadmap and is expected to become available in the second half of 2017.

If paying expenses is the only reason for integrating Concur with Payroll, our advice is to use this opportunity to change your process and switch to payment through SAP ERP Financials Accounts Payable. Paying through Payroll has several drawbacks:

▶ It delays reimbursement unnecessarily, particularly if payroll runs monthly.

▶ Delayed payment leads to a high number of advance requests, which are difficult to handle. Switching from monthly to timely reimbursement, which is easily feasible with Concur and integration with Accounts Payable, has in many cases lead to a drastic reduction of advance payments, thus reducing process cost significantly.

▶ Even if weekly payroll is currently used, tying expense reimbursement to payroll can make it more difficult to switch to monthly payroll (bringing a large reduction in payroll process costs) in the future.

▶ Overpayments of expenses are much easier to handle through Accounts Payable than Payroll. Overpayments can happen due to advance payments being set too high, data-capturing errors, reimbursements of tickets paid for by employees, or cancellation of trips when advances have already been paid.

▶ Reimbursement through Payroll only works for employees. Contractors, candidates, guests, and other travelers requiring expense reimbursements will need to be paid through Accounts Payable anyway, so it makes sense to have one standardized process for all groups.

If there are taxable elements that require processing through Payroll or if statutory reporting through Payroll requires some expense data (e.g., UK P11D forms or the M-flag in German tax reporting), then SAP customers need an interim solution, similar to what they need for third-party payroll solutions.

The required information can be pulled from Concur through custom reports, global standard reports, or bespoke reports available for some countries and, for example, exported into a spreadsheet and then imported into the Payroll system.

Of course, much more sophisticated solutions are possible, most notably when making use of Concur's web services, but developing such solutions can take some time; we recommend to keeping the cost of interim solutions low and aiming to use the standard integration once it's available.

In the following subsections, we'll look at two pragmatic approaches for an interim solution.

8.3.1 Import Data through Infotype 2010

One approach is to use Infotype 2010 (Employee Remuneration Info) in SAP ERP HCM to import expenses. Figure 8.19 shows the full screen of Infotype 2010, although you usually only need to capture wage type, amount, and currency.

The wage types required may already exist in Payroll and may just need to be made eligible for Infotype 2010 using table V_T512Z. If they don't exist yet, you need to liaise with your Payroll experts to have them created. How many you need and how they need to be configured depends on the tax, national insurance, and reporting requirements of the countries affected and on how you want to present and report on these wage types out of Payroll.

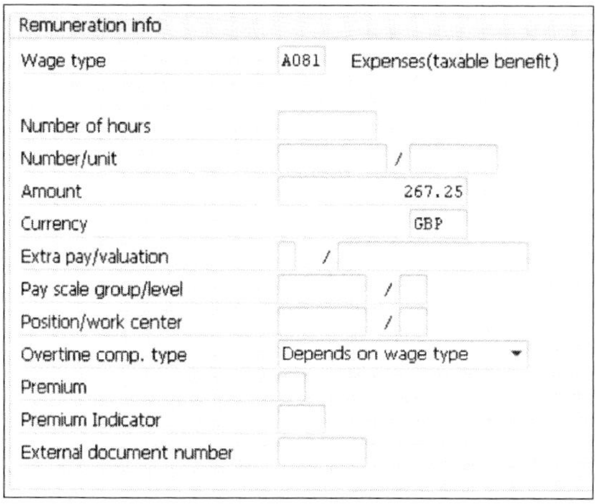

Remuneration info		
Wage type	A081	Expenses(taxable benefit)
Number of hours		
Number/unit		/
Amount		267.25
Currency		GBP
Extra pay/valuation	/	
Pay scale group/level		/
Position/work center		/
Overtime comp. type	Depends on wage type ▾	
Premium		
Premium Indicator		
External document number		

Figure 8.19 Using Infotype 2010 in SAP ERP HCM to Import Expenses

The import can be performed via manual upload or a job set up to run each night. A quick way to build an import tool is to use SAP's Legacy System Migration Workbench (LSMW) or Computer-Aided Test Tool (CATT). You will need to ask the respective technical specialist to build it.

8.3.2 Import Data through SAP Travel Management Database

Another approach is to make use of the SAP Travel Management module, which can be done even if it hasn't been set up or used in the past. The idea is to import the data extracted from Concur into the result tables of SAP Travel Management. Once they're in there, SAP's internal standard interfaces are available with very little configuration. Figure 8.20 illustrates the data flow from the Concur export (the SAE file), into the SAP Travel Management tables; from there, the data can be transferred into Payroll, posted into the Finance module, or even paid directly through the SAP Travel Management's Data Medium Exchange (DME) feature.

This approach based on a simple template has been tried and tested with several clients as a stable and cost-effective solution to bridge the gap until the availability of the required standard integration. It can also be used for a proof of concept or pilot in which Concur runs live for a small population in parallel with the on-premise SAP Travel Management solution.

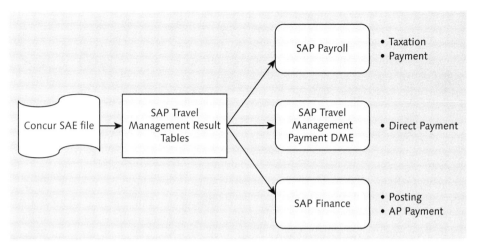

Figure 8.20 Using SAP Travel Management to Import Concur Data

In the long run, we recommend you aim to use the standard integration. Doing so will guarantee you the updates required to stay compliant with changing statutory requirements and keep up with further innovations in the Concur solutions, such as the capability to process retroactive changes.

8.4   Integrating with Further SAP Solutions

SAP and Concur are working on further integrations; we expect several to be added during 2017 and probably 2018. The current statuses for some other important integrations are as follows:

▸ Financial integration with SAP S/4HANA Finance has been available since October 2016. Given the limited number of organizations using this solution at the time of writing, the early version is expected to change quickly.

▸ Integration with SAP S/4HANA Cloud is not yet available, but is expected in the near future, in line with SAP's strategy.

▸ Further integrations customers are expecting include those for SAP Ariba, SAP Fieldglass and SAP Business One (on-premise and cloud). As discussed earlier, the speed of development is quite high, so keep yourself informed in the respective forums and stay in touch with your service partners so that you'll know when the right integration scenario for your organization is supported.

8.5   Summary

SAP and Concur offer direct integration between SAP ERP and Concur Expense covering HR master data, financial master data, and financial posting. Payroll integration is not yet available at the time of writing, but is expected in the future. We highly recommend using the standard integrations whenever possible to ensure a stable, easy-to-manage process and to avoid being cut off from future developments.

The integration is delivered through add-on components that must be installed and configured in each SAP client involved and via a web services interface in your Concur instances.

Integration with further SAP solutions are expected in the future, so we recommend checking not just with your Concur sales contact but also with experts in the community before you make architectural decisions.

When Concur implementations fail to deliver the expected value, it's usu-ally the software that gets the blame. However, a poor scope definition and misunderstandings about managing a Concur project are usually the points of failure. Moreover, many customers get much less out of Concur than they could but don't even realize they're falling short, because Con-cur still beats their old systems.

9 Making Concur Work for You: Tips for Implementation Projects

Although the usual rules for good project management apply for Concur, there are also quite a few points that are easily missed or underestimated when you don't have previous Concur experience. In fact, we've seen several customers not as happy with the result as they should have been not because of the software, but because it had been implemented like an on-premise solution, the distribu-tion of responsibilities between Concur and the customer was misunderstood, or the scope was too small.

In this chapter, we discuss the scope first in Section 9.1 to make you aware of potential pitfalls to watch out for and to get the basis for your schedule and resource plan. Section 9.2 builds on this, introducing the Concur project method-ology, which sometimes leaves unprepared customers feeling a bit overwhelmed. Section 9.3, Section 9.4, and Section 9.5 add some insights about global rollout projects, change management, and pitfalls we've seen a number of customer stumble into.

9.1 Getting Your Scope Right

It looks easy at first sight: You pick the Concur modules you want to implement—say, Concur Expense, Concur Travel, and Concur Intelligence. Then, you pick the countries you want to implement the modules in—say, the United States, Brazil,

Sweden, and Malaysia. There, scope done. However, there is much more to it, and a vague scope or a scope kept too small is among the most common reasons that customers don't get full value out of Concur.

First, we need to differentiate between the solution scope and the project scope. The *solution scope* is focused on the Concur system. In addition, there may be a lot of significant, supporting initiatives in your project that are not directly system related but are required to make the implementation a success: These are part of the *project scope*. Figure 9.1 shows the solution scope for Concur as a subset of the whole project scope.

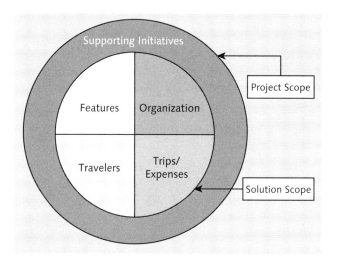

Figure 9.1 Solution Scope and Project Scope

Solution scope and project scope are often underestimated in Concur projects, because legacy system implementations are used to define the scope, and then the implementation time is cut to 50% or less because the SaaS model allows for much faster implementation. This is true, if we compare like with like. However, Concur is much more feature-rich than any legacy system we have ever seen it replace, and a Concur implementation has a much wider impact on an organization, if the business value discussed in Chapter 1 is to be realized.

A Question of Size

We will discuss certain isolated aspects of the size of your scope in the following sections, but here are two overarching points that highlight why a minimal initial scope is usually not ideal (nor is the maximum, by the way):

1. A successful Concur implementation requires buy-in from the workforce and line managers. To achieve this, you need to offer them some advantages right from the start. This is easy if the old process was paper-based only, but if you come from, say, a well-configured SAP ERP solution with a decent self-service setup, you need to make a bit of an effort. For example, it's not crucial to have the Uber e-receipt integration active from day one, but if your employees do use Uber a lot, doing so can make it easy to get a quick win and make them happy.

2. There is a certain scope included in the fixed implementation price from Concur. For example, this will often include configuration for three countries. So, you can decide to only include one country in the first implementation, and depending on your readiness, resources, and complexity, it may still make sense. However, to get the most out of what you pay to Concur for the implementation, you should try to get all three countries configured.

In the following subsections, we'll look at both solution scope and project scope and some of their most important features of each.

9.1.1 Concur Solution Scope

In this section, we'll ask a few questions; the answers will help you determine the scope of your Concur solutions.

Organizational View: Which Countries or Departments Should Use Concur?

The natural subset of the solution scope to start with is the organizational scope. This defines the countries, subsidiaries, or departments you want to use Concur in. For the best return on investment, the objective is usually to include the whole organization. However, countries with few trips and complex rules not covered by Concur's preconfigured solution may be out of scope. In general, it's good practice to start not with all countries, but with a pilot country, followed by a staged rollout.

One aspect to consider when you compare Concur to the scope in your legacy system is the Concur pricing model. Usually, Concur is priced by number of expense reports, which makes it a fair deal if cost and benefit are aligned. If your legacy system had a user-based license or subscription pricing, you may have excluded departments with very few trips per employee, such as manufacturing plants. In that case, you should expand the scope to include those parts of the organization so you have one solution for all.

Another reason for excluding whole departments was availability of PC access. This factor needs to be reviewed. With Concur in place, most if not all transactions for employees and line managers can easily be performed on a mobile device, so establishing a bring your own device (BYOD) policy will probably allow you to cover 90 percent of your workforce, and low-cost shared devices like tablets can close the remaining gap.

People View: Which Individuals Need Concur?

We find that often large groups of people do not get user accounts for T&E systems in corporate or public sector organizations. In some cases, the reason is that these people have very few trips and expenses. Here, the same argument applies that we made earlier about whole departments with low-frequency travel.

A more significant chunk of expenses excluded applies to parts of the workforce without a regular, permanent employment contract. Although apprentices, interns, holiday workers, and other special groups of employees are often excluded from T&E booking systems, we recommend they be included. If different rules and approval processes apply for them, this can be configured accordingly in the system.

However, this question goes beyond just employees; consider the part of the workforce without any employment contract with your organization. Agency staff, contractors, consultants, and even nonexecutive board members all work for you, book travel for this work, and incur expenses, but most organizations don't grant them access to their usual T&E system, asking them to send in invoices instead—and this is a huge missed opportunity. Not only does the contingent workforce grow globally, but these groups often travel even more than your average employee. If consultants charge you expenses to get to various sites, surely it makes sense for you to be in control of managing such expenses through your policy, approval workflows, and reporting. We've seen companies in which consultants and contractors incurred more than half of airfare and hotel spending. If you get this to go through your normal system and process, there are several advantages:

▸ One standardized process is in place for all expenses.

▸ Line managers and project managers have a complete view of all expenses and can also proactively manage them through approvals of bookings, if required. This is particularly interesting if you use the budgeting function for line managers: it would be no use at all if a significant, but unknown, number of expenses were not handled by Concur.

▸ Everything booked through your system can count towards your discounts with hotels, airlines, and other vendors, so adding contingent workforce spending can reduce costs for your permanent workforce, too.

▸ Corporate analytics have access to the full set of data available, all captured in the same structure.

As such, our recommendation is to try and include the contingent workforce into your Concur scope.

There are further groups to consider, like guests and candidates. There certainly is an argument that you don't want to bother these groups with learning your travel booking or expense system, but you have several options to address this issue:

▸ Create user accounts for them, but capture their expenses using the on-behalf features. With the appropriate rights, you can select a user to capture expenses via PROFILE • ACT ON BEHALF OF OTHER USER or PROFILE • ACT AS USER IN ASSIGNED GROUP, then pick a user from the CHOOSE A USER box and click on START SESSION.

▸ Book travel for another user via PROFILE • BOOK TRAVEL FOR ANY USER; pick a user from the SEARCH BY NAME OR ID box and click on START SESSION. You can make use of the arranger features through TRAVEL • ARRANGERS, where you can see the travelers you have been assigned to as arranger and can also view or edit their travel preferences, as shown in Figure 9.2.

▸ Book travel for a guest without an account in your Concur system using the guest booking feature via TRAVEL • ARRANGERS or TRAVEL • TRAVEL and then selecting BOOK FOR A GUEST in the search box. This takes you through the normal booking process, but asks for the guest's traveler details, as shown in Figure 9.3.

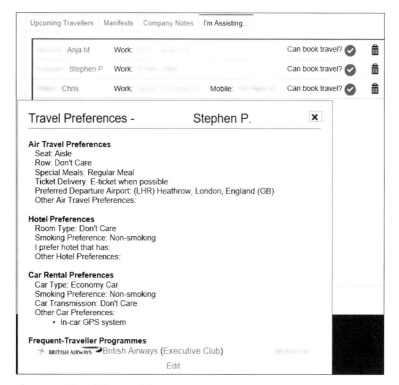

Figure 9.2 Travel Arranger View

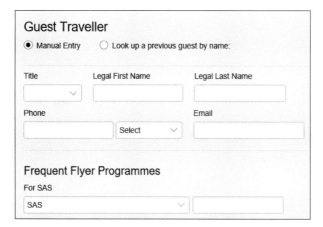

Figure 9.3 Capturing Guest Traveler Data

Object View: Which Trips or Expenses Will Use Concur?

It sounds simple: a T&E system deals with all trips and individual expenses. However, when we do a quick current state analysis with new Concur customers, we find that this is often far from the truth. It may make sense to leave the responsibility for certain types of travel with specialized teams, but it still should all go through the same system. Concur makes it easy to allow de-centralized responsibility while applying global policies and providing global visibility in analytics.

Trips that often are not or are only partially booked and processed through the usual corporate expense system include the following:

▸ Team events, when transport and accommodation are booked for a group of people.

▸ Customer events.

▸ Trade fairs and exhibitions, often managed by the marketing department in their own spreadsheets.

▸ Travel to external or internal trainings or seminars, often managed by the HR/training department.

▸ Personal car mileage, sometimes managed by the payroll team directly, because it can affect tax. (This makes it difficult to see when other modes of transport would have been more efficient. It's much better to route it through the corporate T&E team and integrate the expense software with the payroll system.)

▸ Trips with company cars or carpools.

Other organizations use their expense system for travel-related expenses only. Again, this doesn't usually make sense. A system like Concur is perfectly positioned to deal with all types of expenses that need to be reimbursed by the employee or are processed through a personal corporate credit card or purchasing card. Establishing a separate system for these transactions or passing them through a spreadsheet or paper-based process is rarely efficient.

How to Process Petty Expenses at a Reasonable Cost

Decision makers often shy away from processing small ticket items, such as a newspaper for $2.50 or 10 miles of personal mileage, through Concur, because the subscription fee is based on the number of expense reports. However, it's important to remember that processing such items manually isn't likely to be cheaper. Concur usually does increase overall efficiency, so the subscription fee is compensated for by the gain in efficiency. The price tag on each expense report just makes the processing cost more transparent.

That said, we indeed would not recommend submitting an expense report for each small expense item; this recommendation holds whether the process is completely manual or managed with a spreadsheet, an SAP ERP system, or Concur. The expense policy and user education should suggest collecting small-ticket items in one expense report and only submitting such items once per month.

Feature View: What Functionality Do We Need?

As mentioned in previous sections, picking the modules is one part of the solution scope definition. We call this *feature scope* because it describes the system functionality. However, for successful project planning and delivery, we need to consider more factors for the feature scope, most notably:

- Reports for the corporate T&E teams
- Reports for line managers
- Dashboards
- Financial system integration (e.g., SAP ERP)
- Payroll integration, including the calculation of taxable payments (often not handled in Concur, so the interface or the payroll system needs to be able to split between taxable and tax-free)
- HR systems integration for user data
- Credit card integration (every credit card feed needs some work and comes with a fee to be paid, so you may consider a third-party aggregator service if you have more than 10 feeds in one country)
- E-receipt integration
- Using the Concur mobile app and understanding its constraints
- Concur ExpenseIt professional app
- Concur TripIt app
- Concur TripLink
- Scanning devices or even fax integration
- Other third-party apps for travelers
- Foreign VAT reclaim services

- Messaging service to comply with your duty of care regarding travel risk or just to make travelers' lives easier
- Audit service (from Concur or third-party)
- Billing of expenses to customers
- Other third-party services
- Documentation and guides for users

It is important that this scope is communicated to the implementation manager at the start of the project and confirmed in writing. The usual spreadsheet-based workbook used by Concur as a standard tool for the system configuration (see Section 9.2) fails to cover many of these factors explicitly or comprehensively, so unless you add supporting documents or make extensive use of the comment fields, your project may start with the wrong targets.

9.1.2   Project Scope

The scope defined per the factors discussed in Section 9.1.1 is an important input for the project plan. However, there are several additional activities that can impact the project timeline, as we'll discuss in the following subsections.

The Contract

First, you need to plan for some time to finalize the subscription contract with Concur. If you are already using SAP's solutions, it's usually easy to add another module or more users to an existing contract. You can even start playing with or configuring that module in your development system before having it included in your license, so long as it's not used in production.

Concur has its own pricing model and usually requires a finalized contract before the project can start. You usually need an implementation manager assigned from Concur directly (at least, if it's a new implementation rather than a rollout), so it will take some time even after contract conclusion before resources are available.

We've observed that European customers in particular struggle with the data privacy and data security aspects of the contract. There isn't much experience with the SaaS model yet in many corporate legal departments there, and even customers using other SAP cloud solutions like SAP SuccessFactors often need more time than expected to agree on the proper wording of these aspects with Concur.

In essence, don't wait too long to start the contractual process, and make it part of your project scope. Get your legal team to review Concur's standard contracts as early as possible, and plan for a few weeks more than you would for a traditional on-premise license. It's fair to assume that contract negotiation will become less significant over time as European legal teams become more familiar with SaaS or general cloud contracts and Concur finds the language to be understood faster in European markets.

Change Management and Education

It should go without saying, but if you set up your Concur implementation properly, there will be a lot of change in your policy, processes, user experience and in responsibilities. If not, why would you want to do it in the first place?

We'll elaborate a bit on this in Section 9.4, but if you transition from a spreadsheet-based or on-premise expense system to a cloud-based, mobility-enabled solution with a much bigger scope, you'll have a considerable change management task on your hands. Therefore, communicating changes, convincing the workforce that they're the right things to do, and getting workers to use the new system effectively is also part of your project scope and shouldn't be taken for granted.

Side Projects

It's part of project management 101 that you should try to go step by step rather than attempt wide jumps—so why would anyone try to run side projects with a Concur implementation rather than try to conclude the Concur implementation first and add the other elements later? Well, some changes are just easier to make before you implement the new system, and some do in fact make Concur implementation easier.

Here are some examples of typical initiatives that run in parallel with or immediately before a Concur project and that should be included in the project scope to be managed by the same team:

▶ Transitioning to a single global TMC or at least minimizing the number of TMCs can make implementation of Concur Travel easier. In any case, if you're planning for TMC consolidation, it should definitely happen before Concur Travel go-live.

- Rolling out corporate credit cards to employees or changing/consolidating credit card providers.

- Writing and communicating a new T&E policy that makes use of the possibilities Concur offers and ideally allows for a more decentralized, empowering approach.

- Creating a legal framework to go paper-free.

- Setting up contracts with third-party services you want Concur to integrate with, such as travel vendors, aggregators, audit services, and so on.

9.2   Project Planning and Methodology

If you've got your scope right, you're already off to a good start and can do the following:

- Identify the people within your own organization you need to involve, from finance experts to event organizers.

- Identify third-party resources required, from TMC representatives to Concur Service partner consultants.

- Define a project and resource plan.

- Prepare any interface work required.

- Prepare any legal and contractual tasks.

- Last but not least, ensure you include the right services in your contract with Concur.

In the following subsections, we'll provide a refresher on the differences among the three editions of Concur, walk through the phases of the project plan, and conclude with some tips for project management of your Concur implementation.

9.2.1   Concur Editions

As discussed in Chapter 1, there are three editions of Concur you can subscribe to. In this section, we assume you're working with the professional edition. Project management does look similar for the standard edition, except that it would be on a much smaller scale with fewer configuration choices, fewer integrations, and usually a much smaller population of users. A typical implementation of Concur Expense in the professional edition can be finished in three months when all prerequisites are in place, whereas we've seen the standard edition successfully implemented in three *weeks*. Note that the time can increase depending on circumstances.

The biggest difference between the professional and the premium editions is that you get much more support from Concur in the premium edition. That includes Concur consultants working with you onsite, whereas the standard and professional implementations are usually managed through web conference sessions only. Therefore, although the system has the same features for both editions, the premium implementation allows for a higher level of complexity for custom requirements.

A blend of the Concur professional implementation with third-party expertise can be a good and cost-effective alternative to the premium edition. The following guidelines may help you choose an edition:

▸ If you think you'll require heavy configuration and most of the extra expertise you need will be technical in nature in Concur, then the premium implementation could be the best choice.

▸ If you expect help in business and solution design, change, communication, and third-party integration, you may find that the right third-party consultants (ideally Concur partners) are the best choice.

▸ You may need a blend of both. Customers have been known to buy the premium service to deal with configuration, but still engage a third party to help with decision-making or project management. As always, this third party should understand Concur and its options to allow for effective communication among all parties involved.

Note that with few exceptions, as of the time of writing, neither customers nor service partners are allowed to perform configuration for the initial implementation. Amendments after go-live or rollouts to additional countries can both be configured by customers or third-party consultants, but customers usually need to go through Concur's advanced configuration training first.

The Concur Implementation Team

Problems in a Concur professional implementation often come from a simple misunderstanding about the roles of the Concur implementation team and the customer. Concur provides a purely technical deployment, assuming the customer knows exactly what the future system should look like and that this objective is based on the new possibilities Concur opens rather than on the old system's capabilities. Implementation also requires companies to manage the project, including vendors' resources, plan and implement the business change and communication, test independently, manage third-party integration with minimal guidance, and build its own reposts based on the training video.

It should be noted that this service does not include business design, project management, training, test support, and so on, unlike many other solutions, such as SAP SuccessFactors or SAP Customer Relationship Management (SAP CRM). We recommend that you seek information on the role of the customer, ideally from a discussion with other customers, so that you can decide whether you need extra resources to meet these expectations.

9.2.2 The Project Plan

The project plan applied by Concur in professional implementations is quite rigid. The project is usually driven by weekly web conference sessions between the Concur implementation manager, the customer team, and any third parties involved (e.g., the TMC for Concur Travel or service partner consultants supporting the customer) as and when required. These sessions can be complemented by further conference calls with Concur's technical consultants or other experts. Figure 9.4 shows the basic project methodology applied, without going into any details.

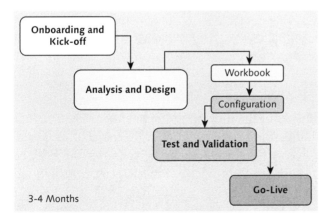

Figure 9.4 Typical Project Plan for Concur Implementations

The following sections will cover the four main phases of the project.

Phase 1: Onboarding and Kickoff

The first step, *onboarding and kickoff*, is just one single session. It may not yet involve the implementation manager, but will be used to understand your high-level requirements, make your team familiar with the tool, discuss the schedule, and eventually decide on your implementation manager. This step is often taken too lightly by customers, leading to unnecessary delays later.

A few points to keep in mind for this step:

▸ Try to have your whole project team on this call so all members can familiarize themselves with the particular language used by Concur, the tools, and the document-sharing environment.

▸ Make sure that the project schedule is discussed and the whole team signs on to it.

▸ Do not assume that what you've discussed with the sales team has been handed over to the implementation team. Clarify your intended scope and constraints in this meeting and verify it has been communicated to your implementation manager when you talk to him or her later.

▸ Come to this session well prepared. You should have your project team in place, have discussed a feasible schedule with them, have a clearly defined scope, and most notably know your integration requirements. Postpone the session if you don't have all these points covered.

▸ This all sounds much the same as you would hear for any software implementation, but we can't emphasize enough that it's even more important for a Concur project because of the rigidity the project plan will be interpreted with and the little contact time you'll have with the Concur implementation team.

Why Is It Critical to Stick to the Timeline?

Once the schedule has been agreed to, it can't be easily extended. You can take a project break, during which the project will be dormant as far as Concur is concerned, and then pick it up again, but this comes with the risk of having a different implementation manager assigned after the break. Other than that, the end date of the project will be fixed, with only a little wiggle room.

That doesn't mean you must start using Concur live, but your system will be set to production readiness, which introduces with a few changes:

▸ The system will be purged; that is, all data will be deleted and data captured from that point will be treated as live.

▸ To test anything from that point, you need to use user accounts marked as test users, which have limited value for testing reports.

▸ There will be a handover from your implementation manager to support. Any changes required after that point will need to be submitted to support.

▸ You'll probably need to pay the agreed upon minimum subscription fee for production at that point.

You can always try to extend the help you get from the implementation team, but as a rule, it will be more difficult when you go past the originally planned go-live date, so try not to—and make sure the schedule is realistic to begin with.

Phase 2: Analysis and Design

The *analysis and design* stage does what it says on the tin. However, there is potential for losing important information due to an overemphasis on filling in the design workbook, a Microsoft Excel document that constitutes the basis for configuration. Customers who aren't doing anything more than answering the questions in this workbook will find that they lost a lot of their requirements, and that those they didn't lose are often misunderstood. Make sure you provide all information required to the implementation manager in a format agreed upon and ask for confirmation of the implementation timeline.

It's telling that the official project plan diagram from Concur doesn't show configuration as one of the main project phases, because Concur doesn't expect the customer to be involved. Therefore, going by the letter of the methodology, the implementation manager will configure what's been defined in the workbook and any supporting documents, then start the test and validation stage right afterwards.

In reality, you can expect some kind of iteration, as is state-of-the-art practice for cloud implementations. However, you should still try to get the design workbook right the first time and discuss the test stage with your implementation manager at the beginning. Try to agree on an iterative approach in which small changes to the design workbook are still possible once you've seen the first results from configuration.

Phase 3: Test and Validation

The *test and validation* stage comes without much handholding or training. A quick run-through of your processes in Concur during a session and a reference to standardized video training material is all your project team will get. For teams with no prior Concur experience, getting in some extra help to provide project team training and support during testing is arguably the one of the points from which you can benefit most from Concur service partner consultants. Untrained users testing without the necessary help will either miss a lot of problems or report many issues that are actually user errors, thus delaying the project.

Phase 4: Go-Live

Apart from the timing, it's important that you are the master of your project plan and know what needs to be in place for go-live. Although the technical consultants from Concur may provide information about integration, single sign-on (SSO), and other technical tasks, the customer needs to drive these details and make sure they are in place for go-live.

The same holds true for documentation, user guides, and communication. Concur may provide some communication templates, but otherwise this is completely the customer's responsibility or that of the customer's third-party consultants.

We recommend that you plan for go-live very early in the project with a list of activities that need to be finished by that time and a cutover plan, including communication. Update this plan as you go through the various project stages.

If your legacy system and integration allow, starting with a small pilot group can be very helpful. That means you can get to production readiness with Concur, but instead of opening it up to all users, you do so for a smaller group of maybe 100 users only to see how processes, user guides, and communication have worked. This approach also helps test those integrations that can't be fully tested without live data, such as credit card feeds.

9.2.3 Tips for Project Management

Here are some tips that proved useful in several projects:

▸ Don't forget about reporting as you go along. Implementation managers tend to and would love you to sign off on the configuration without looking at reports, so make sure the standard reports work as designed. Also, build at least those custom reports that are mandatory for go-live before signing off to see how they work with the configuration.

- If you need to build custom reports, getting third-party help for on-the-job training may be a good idea to make sure it fits into the schedule.

- If you have very little budget for third-party consultants, these are the tasks you'll benefit from the most:

  - Scope definition

  - Project plan review

  - Training—one day of high-level training before kickoff, one to three days before testing, and two days for custom reporting

  - SAP ERP integration

  - Third-party integration

- Make sure the business has signed on to the project vision and scope before kickoff. You'll often find business users pushing back process changes during testing. Having-top level buy-in for a project that's meant to change things will help you to fend off sabotage of the "but this isn't how we do things here" type.

- Your project team shouldn't only include people from finance, procurement, HR, and IT. As discussed in Chapter 1, a Concur implementation should be a transformational project serving the mobile workforce, the members of which spend much of their lives traveling to serve customers. This is difficult to achieve when only representatives of overhead departments are involved in the project. We highly recommend that your project team includes a frequent traveler and/or line manager responsible for a team with a lot of travel. Ideally, you'll also get your head of sales or head of customer service to join the project steering group.

9.3 Global Rollout

The usual principles for international rollout projects apply to Concur implementations as well, so we won't elaborate on this too much. However, there are a few points to be aware of.

As mentioned earlier, your initial implementation scope from Concur is likely to comprise three countries. Although it's efficient to make use of that, it's more important to have a manageable scope so that you implement the countries you do pick for stage one properly. It may therefore be a good strategy to have two countries with small employee populations in addition to your chosen pilot country in stage one. Even if you won't have the resources to set them all live at the same time, you can still benefit from the configuration for the three countries included in your fee. Further rollout stages should include between three and five countries, though that number is sometimes increased for very small populations.

As usual for this kind of rollout, there will be a learning curve, and the time needed to implement new countries will go down. However, pilot implementation will take longer than a single-country implementation usually would because that pilot also builds the template for further rollouts. We recommend that you have a pre-project stage to discuss and build the global template. If you have more than 20 rollout countries, we also recommend taking a bit more time for the first rollout stage—possibly as much as for the pilot country. This is because a rollout is by nature different that an initial implementation, and if you have many more to do, taking a bit of extra time to learn from the first one will pay off.

Figure 9.5 shows a typical Concur Expense global rollout plan for 23 countries across Europe and North America. This is a real-world plan, though anonymized to make sure the organization can't be recognized.

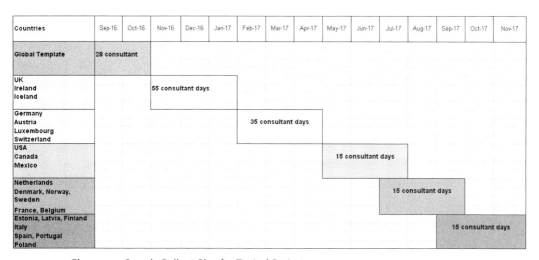

Figure 9.5 Sample Rollout Plan for Typical Project

The size of the rollout batches deviates from five due to size and complexity of the various countries. It features a two-month period to define the global framework and then then months of rollout sprints, which overlap at the later stages when the team has progressed up the learning curve. It also notes the resource plan for external service partner consultants. This plan assumes a high demand at the start, when the customer project team is learning, and a much lower demand after the first rollout stage, when the customer team takes over and the partner acts as a mere coach. The whole project is based on the normal professional implementation service from Concur, so there's no switch to self-implementation in the rollout stages.

When assessing the complexity of a country rollout, it's important to understand how well a country's requirements are covered by Concur. Globally, all countries can be grouped into three tiers: Tier one countries are fully covered, tier two countries have most aspects covered, and tier three countries don't have a pre-configured localization at all.

This doesn't mean that you can't roll out Concur to tier three countries. Concur can still be configured to work in these countries; it just isn't preconfigured. One of the authors was involved in a major Concur rollout to Estonia several years ago, which is tier three even today, and this rollout has worked very well without any major issues. One typical strategy to deal with tier three countries is to copy the configuration from a tier one country with similar requirements. For example, France or Spain is often used as a foundation for Portugal.

The countries listed in Table 9.1 were tier one or two as of February 2017.

Tier 1		Tier 2
► United States	► Italy	► Russia
► Canada	► Austria	► China
► Mexico	► Czech Republic	► India
► United Kingdom	► Poland	► Thailand
► Ireland	► Denmark	► Malaysia
► Spain	► Norway	► Vietnam
► France	► Sweden	► Indonesia
► Netherlands	► Finland	► Philippines
► Belgium	► Australia	► South Korea
► Germany		► Japan
► Switzerland		► New Zealand

Table 9.1 Tier 1 and Tier 2 Countries

It needs to be noted that legal compliance doesn't necessarily mean that everything an organization can do in its expense policy is easy to implement. For instance, if travel allowances are used, the local law usually only limits how much can be paid tax-free, whereas employers can pay less (easy to implement) or more with a tax impact (not always easy). Here are two examples:

▶ German legislation allows a certain tax-free allowance per day depending on hours traveled and destination. Most organizations pay exactly that amount to make it tax-efficient and easy. However, if the tax-free limit for a particular day is €20, an employer could still choose to pay €50, with €20 tax-free, €20 paid by the employer with an attractive default tax rate applied, and €10 to be taxed against the employee through payroll. Standard legal tax-free rates are available by default in Concur and lower rates can be configured easily, but the two tiers of taxable amounts require quite a bit of work in configuration and interfaces.

▶ In the United Kingdom, meals are usually reimbursed based on the amount paid according to the receipt. However, employers can also agree with HMRC to pay certain daily allowances. This is unusual but does happen. In this case, a bit of extra configuration would be required in Concur.

Do not assume that there is nothing to do for a country, even if Concur does fully comply with its regulations. Legislation usually leaves a lot of leeway for employers, and depending on how they use that leeway, you may have some extra work to do. On the other hand, even countries not covered by the default configuration may be easy to implement if the rules are simple and like those for a country already implemented.

9.4   Change Management and Communication

We've mentioned change management and the importance of communication throughout the book, so here we want to note a few useful points on the topic:

▶ Concur is quite intuitive to use in most cases, but you still need to provide some guidance for users. Tools that have proved to create the best effects include the following:

  ▸ *Quick guides*: Small pieces of laminated paper with the most important tips to always have at hand. You can also create electronic versions of these guides to be quickly accessed by clicking on a link on a desktop computer or tapping on a smartphone icon.

▸ *Small "bite-sized" videos*: No longer than two to three minutes, demonstrating individual tasks (e.g., itemization or allocation). All end user videos need to be customized to your process and system. Using Concur's standard videos will confuse users, because they may see different fields or labels that are not in line with your process.

▸ In most cases, it is more difficult to teach process and policy than to use the system. Therefore, *training and user documentation* should never be completely outsourced. You need your internal business and policy expertise to feed into the training material.

▸ Identify employees who are *multipliers* and make sure they are properly trained and buy into the system. The most important group usually are assistants or team secretaries, who will often be asked for help if employees struggle with their expenses.

▸ Don't overestimate the tolerance for *foreign languages*. Although an English-only system and documentation may work in countries with high English proficiency, like the Netherlands or Denmark, it is much more difficult to use in countries with low levels of proficiency, like France or Japan.

▸ As discussed in Section 9.1, the scope for a Concur project is often surprisingly large. Together with the transformational nature the project should have, this also brings several important *stakeholders* to engage beyond the departments usually involved in the project anyway, like finance, HR, and IT (see Figure 9.6).

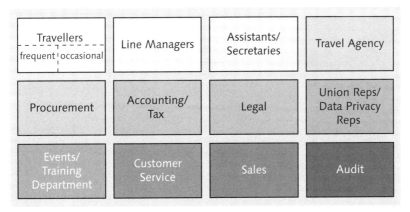

Figure 9.6 Typical Stakeholders for Concur Project

9.5   Typical Pitfalls

We've mentioned most of the notorious pitfalls along the way, so there are only two left we want to mention.

First, because of Concur's huge market share in the United States, many global organizations with headquarters outside of the United States will find that their US subsidiary has already implemented Concur when they decide they want to implement it globally. We've heard of a few cases in which this implementation has been managed as a rollout based on the US implementation, and none of these cases went to the customer's satisfaction.

The United States is quite different from many other countries. Concur was originally built for the United States, and with that still being by far its most important market, it's still influenced heavily by US customers. Therefore, and because of the lack of many other countries' special requirements, US implementation can be comparatively simple. If you try to replicate what you did in the United States in other countries, you can easily hit a brick wall—particularly when your US subsidiary is quite small compared to some of the other countries to implement. If you're in this situation, perform a thorough evaluation of what has been implemented for the United States and figure out how different it would need to be for other countries.

The last heads-up we want to give you concerns the test instance. If you're used to large system implementations such as SAP ERP HCM or SAP SuccessFactors, you're used to having at least one system or instance to develop and test in that is separate from the production system or instance. Only changes successfully tested are then moved to production, usually automatically or semiautomatically. You may even have more systems or instances for QA, sandbox, or training.

The normal Concur professional implementation doesn't come with a test instance at all, and if you get one in the premium implementation model, it's usually available for a limited time only. We've seen some customers react in shock when they found out—usually only at the start of the testing stage, sometimes even later. Due to Concur's concept of test users and using test policies, you can indeed handle an implementation and ongoing support in this one-system setup, but it certainly can't be recommended for any but the smallest organizations. We therefore recommend addressing this problem with Concur in the contract stage and subscribing to a permanent test instance for an extra cost.

9.6   Summary

Whereas Chapters 1 through 8 should have made you keen to implement Concur, this chapter will help you at various stages throughout the project to get the best value out of your investment. To achieve this, it's paramount that you take the time to make sure you get the scope right, plan the project schedule accordingly, and agree on it with your Concur implementation manager.

Even experienced project managers will run into problems if they don't consider the bespoke nature of a Concur project, most notably the roles of the Concur team and the customer team in the various Concur editions, the rigidly enforced project methodology, stakeholder engagement, and the lack of a test instance in some of the deployment models.

Taking all these points into consideration and having the right resources in place will make sure your project is successful and deliver a transformational experience for your T&E process. Maybe you'll hear what we heard from a frequent traveler recently after a Concur Expense go-live: "Wow! Doing expenses is fun now!"

A   Further Reading

This appendix will provide you with some additional resources regarding Concur and your T&E processes.

The following information is available for current, logged-in users of Concur:

▶ The HELP menu in the top right corner of Concur screen provides links to user help for all modules as well as a TRAINING link for video demos and FAQ documents.

▶ Detailed information about the content of monthly release updates can be found here: HELP • CONTACT SUPPORT • RESOURCES • RELEASE/TECH INFO.

▶ The Concur Knowledge Base with a collection of articles across all modules can be found here: HELP • CONTACT SUPPORT • RESOURCES • KNOWLEDGE BASE.

▶ The Concur Community, where you can engage with other customers and suggest improvements can be found here: HELP • CONTACT SUPPORT • COMMUNITY INFO.

Additional official information from SAP and Concur is available as follows:

▶ You can find release notes and error fixes for SAP to Concur integration by opening the SAP Support Portal on *https://www.support.sap.com* and searching for "Concur".

▶ The open LinkedIn group (managed by Concur) can be found here: *https://www.linkedin.com/groups/149969*.

▶ The customer-only Linkedin group (managed by Concur) can be found here: *https://www.linkedin.com/groups/3760755*.

▶ The Concur video channel with training, as well as sales, videos can be found here: *https://www.youtube.com/user/ConcurTechnologies*.

▶ Get 30 days access to a free trial version here: *https://www.concur.com/en-us/free-trial*.

▶ Current information regarding integration between Concur and other SAP solutions (for partners only) can be found in the SAP Jam Group "SAP Integration with Concur Solutions – Partner Information".

Some additional useful, though non-official, information can be found on the following sites:

▸ You can find blogs in the SAP Community using *https://blogs.sap.com/* where you should type "Concur" into the FILTER BLOGS BY TITLE field.

▸ Comparisons of Concur vs SAP Fiori-based expense management are found on the following site: *http://www.bluefinsolutions.com/blogs/tiago-almeida/july-2016/concur-or-fiori-for-travel-expense-management-unde*.

▸ A blog on Concur with articles on technical topics as well as project management and strategy can be found here: *https://www.iprocon.de/category/concur-travel-and-expense/?lang=en*.

B   The Authors

Sven Ringling is a consultant and the UK director of iPro-Con (*www.iprocon.com*), an SAP SuccessFactors, SAP ERP HCM, and Concur consulting partner. He works with large and medium-sized organizations to drive people-led digital transformation and to optimize HCM, payroll, and T&E processes. He is the author of two editions of *Mastering HR Management with SAP ERP HCM* and a SAP Mentor.

Hannah Smith is an experienced SAP ERP HCM, Concur Travel, and Concur Expense consultant, helping customers to implement, manage, and improve their Concur implementations. Hannah has worked on a range of SAP products, focusing on SAP ERP HCM and Payroll for the last five years. She was the Concur SME for iProCon in the UK, specializing in Concur for the UK and across Europe.

Andy Wittmann is a senior consultant and the director of Global Services at Lyndon Group. His responsibilities include all aspects of global services and implementations and helping organizations improve their overall travel and expense programs on an international scale. He brings extensive experience to all his clients, having deployed Concur Travel, Concur Expense, and Concur Invoice for clients in North America, Asia, Europe, and the Middle East. He has more than 15 years of experience in consulting, technology, and project management. He leverages his technical, process development, and Concur expertise to create optimal solutions for clients.

B.1   Contributors

Anja Marxsen, senior consultant at iProCon in Germany, is a seasoned consultant with more than 15 years of experience with Concur Travel and Concur Expense as well as SAP ERP Financial Travel Management (FI-TV).

Mick Lavers (Director) and **Rebecca Cheung** (Senior Consultant) from Nesoi Solutions Australia, New Zealand and the APAC region have supported more than 100 Concur clients in the Australia, New Zealand, and APAC region. Mick has led many Concur user group events across Australia.

Index

A

Account codes, 128, 274
Actionable analytics, 238
Agency proposals, 201
Airline tickets, 60
Alerts, 217
Analysis, 214
    licences, 216
Approval process, 194
Approval workflows, 132
    approval routing with authorization limits,
        132
    basic approval routing, 132
    manager's manager, 133
    second approver, 133
Approvals, 198
Approved senders, 157
Approvers, 266
Approving manager, 50, 120
Asia Pacific, 190
Attendee forms, 128
Attendee types, 148
Audit group, 51
Audit rules, 148
    create new, 150
    custom rules, 149
    exception, 148
    hard-stop rule, 149
    random rules, 149
    validation rules, 149
Australia and New Zealand, 183
    employee name change, 189
    e-receipts, 190
    flex faring, 190
    fringe benefits tax, 185
    goods and services tax, 183
    mixed supplies, 184
    personal car mileage, 188
    travel allowance, 188
    travel diary, 188
    Uber, 185

Australian Taxation Office (ATO), 188
Authorized approver, 158

B

Benefits in kind (BIK), 33
BI managers, 234
BIK report, 182
Booking process, 70, 73, 202
Booking switch, 203
    approval, 203
    criteria, 204
    parameters, 204
Bring your own device (BYOD) policy, 290
Budget approvers, 205
Budget Insight, 205
Budget manager, 238
Budget threshold percentage, 239
Bursting reports, 214, 234
    configuration, 235
Business travel account (BTA) card, 100

C

Canada, 170
    car mileage reimbursement, 172
    enter expenses, 171
    extraction factor, 170
    taxes, 170
    VAT, 170
Canceling trips, 87
Car mileage, 293
Car rental, 81, 110
    agencies, 82
    search results, 82
Card feed import logs, 141
Cash advance, 193
CES standard report workflow, 158
CFDi XML files, 157
Change management, 296, 306
Changing trips, 87

Chart types, 232
Cognos, 35, 213, 217, 222, 233
Company card settings, 136
Compliance and regulations, 115
Compliance controls, 134
Compliance rules, 135
    settings, 135
Computer-Aided Test Tool (CATT), 284
Concur, 17
    activating the integration, 262
    Asia Pacific, 190
    Australia and New Zealand, 183
    available languages, 28
    benefits, 38
    business case, 37, 40
    Canada, 170
    card feeds, 140
    choosing an edition, 298
    configuration, 36
    direct cost reductions, 38
    direct integration activation, 275
    editions, 297
    Germany, 177
    host, 265
    implementation team, 298
    integration, 241
    market-specific requirements, 169
    mobile app, 246
    overview, 27
    premium edition, 28, 298
    price limits, 105
    pricing model, 290
    process efficiencies, 39
    professional edition, 27, 298
    reporting, 35
    SAP integration, 261
    self-registration, 56
    standard edition, 27, 297
    standard edition limitations, 28
    standard integration, 281
    third-party integration, 241
    United Kingdom, 172
    United States, 169
    web services, 244
Concur Analysis, 35
Concur App Center, 31, 89, 243, 246, 247

Concur Connection homepage, 220
Concur Expense, 33, 50, 94, 113, 170, 195,
    210, 217, 235, 252, 276, 298
    advanced configuration, 141
    business principles, 113
    configuration, 125
    creating a claim, 116
    policy configuration, 141
Concur Expense Pay Global, 30, 124, 139, 159
    configuration, 161
    creating payment batches, 163
    employee group, 167
    expense reports, 160
    funding accounts, 161
    payment delays, 167
    processes, 159
    settlement, 160
Concur ExpenseIt, 29, 249
    autopopulation, 250
    process overview, 251
    settings, 250
    subscription fee, 252
Concur Intelligence, 28, 35, 101, 214, 215
    licences, 216
    tools, 216
Concur Invoice, 29
Concur Messaging, 30, 88, 204, 207
Concur mobile app, 118
Concur profile, 238
Concur Receipt Audit, 30
Concur receipt store, 118
Concur Request, 34, 193
    approvals, 200
    business principles, 194
    car rental, 195
    configuration, 200
    deployment, 208
    flights, 195
    hotel reservation, 197
    integration, 210
    project implementation schedule, 209
    reviewing requests, 199
    segments, 194
Concur Travel, 31, 48, 59, 88, 217, 247
    address and contact information, 63
    advanced configuration, 108

Concur Travel (Cont.)
  booking process, 70
  business principles, 59
  business trips, 62
  configuration, 90
  credit card, 67
  custom text, 95
  direct, 61
  frequent traveler program, 65
  indirect, 61
  languages, 96
  name fields, 63
  out of policy, 72
  predefined rules, 94
  profile, 63
  reason code, 102
  reporting, 101
  search results, 69
  travel alternatives, 99
  travel management company, 32
  travel preferences, 65
  upcoming trips, 87
Concur TripIt, 30, 88, 89, 242
  integration, 90
Concur TripLink, 30, 61, 88
Concurrent employment, 266
Connected list, 152
Contact data, 50
Corporate (nonbillable) travel, 92
Corporate cards, 139, 297
Cost assignments, 276
Cost center export, 274
Cost centers, 271, 277
Cost hierarchy, 276, 277
Cost object, 271
  approver, 158
  configuration, 271
  locked, 278
  mapping, 276
Country groups, 206
Country rollout, 305
Credit card BIN restrictions, 101
Credit card receipts, 247
Credit cards, 48
Crosstab report, 225
Crosstab-explicit reports, 235
CTE_HCM integration add-on, 263

Currency administration, 155
Custom reports, 303

D

Dashboards, 238
Data content query, 235
Data Medium Exchange (DME), 284
Data quality, 22
Data security, 267
Data warehouse package, 224
Deactivating user apps, 245
Default reports, 214
Design workbook, 301
Digital transformation, 21
Dimensional reports, 230
Document type, 275
Duty of care, 60

E

Electronic data interchange (EDI), 241
Email notifications, 120
Employee data creation, 55
Employee forms, 51
  Concur Expense, 52
  configuration, 51
  customization, 53
Employee groups, 55, 146
Employee maintenance task, 54
Employee master record fields, 44
Employee record, 43
Employee reimbursement, 139
Enterprise apps, 246
E-receipt, 22, 32, 50, 97, 289
  country restrictions, 23
  integration, 247
Event requests, 207
Exception notifications, 217
Exchange rate framework, 155
Exchange rate variance, 135
Expense claim, 116
  adding expenses, 118
  approval options, 122
  attaching receipts, 118

Expense claim (Cont.)
  checks, 124
  creating expenses, 118
  example, 133
  payment, 124
  recalling, 134
  status, 120
  submission, 120
Expense Configuration API, 255
Expense data, 253
Expense entry, 118
Expense forms, 128, 151
  customization, 129
Expense groups, 146
Expense limits, 137, 146
Expense policy, 114, 148
  country assignment, 137
  create new, 143
Expense process, 113
Expense processor, 122
Expense report, 132, 279, 294
  sent for payment, 279
Expense Report API, 255
Expense role, 54
Expense types, 118, 126, 127, 129, 145, 197
  configuration, 127, 145

F

Feature hierarchy, 152
  areas, 152
Feature scope, 294
Financial posting, 274
Flex faring, 190
Flights, 70, 108
  classes, 104
  direct connects, 109
  multisegment, 109
  options, 70
  purchase ticket, 76
  reserved, 74
  specific airlines, 71
Foreign languages, 307
Forms, 128
Frequent traveler program, 65
Fringe benefit tax, 143

G

Germany, 177
  BIK Report, 182
  deducations, 180
  M-report, 182
  new expense claim, 178
  overnight allowance, 179
  three-month rule, 183
  travel allowances, 178
Ghost card, 100
Global distribution system (GDS), 60
Global rollout
  country tiers, 305
  plan, 304
Goods and services tax (GST), 170
Google Maps, 138
Group configurations, 146
GSA rates, 169
Guest booking, 291

H

Hierarchy levels, 272
Hotels, 76, 109
  map, 77
  rates, 77
  reservation, 80

I

Implementation project, 287
  common pitfalls, 308
  global rollout, 303
Infotype 2010, 283
Internal orders, 271
International Travel Roaming Alerts (ITRA), 258
Internet of Things (IoT), 26
IRS rules, 169
Itemizing expenses, 252

K

Key performance indicator (KPI), 35, 217

L

Leakage, 88
Legacy system, 290
Legacy System Migration Workbench
  (LSMW), 284
Line manager, 265
List management, 121
List report, 225
Localization, 153
Lowest logical fare (LLF), 103

M

Management reporting, 257
Mapping concept fields, 155
Master data
  financial, 270
  human resources, 263
  replication, 271
  SAP ERP HCM, 265
Mileage calculator, 138
Mileage expenses, 135
Mileage reimbursement, 137
Mixed supply purchase, 184
My Travel Network service, 89

N

Network activities, 271
Network economy, 241
Networks, 271

O

OANDA rates, 155, 254
Optical character recognition (OCR) technology, 257

P

Paper receipts, 22, 251
Paper-free, 297
Partner application, 255
Payment batches, 163
Payment Manager, 168
Payment methods, 114
Payment types, 148
Payroll in SAP ERP HCM, 51, 182, 282
  import data, 283
Penny test, 163
Permissions, 53
  role assignment, 53
  tips, 55
Personal credit cards, 47
Personal information, 45
  addresses and contact data, 46
  email address, 46
  full name, 45
  organizational assignment, 46
  phone numbers, 46
Pivot Payables, 252
Pivot Prime, 252
  billing statements, 253
  currencies, 254
  integration, 252
  report, 252, 254
Planned vs actual spending, 194
Policy group, 126
  assignment, 126
Preferred vendors, 106, 107
Pretrip approval, 34
Project management tips, 302
Project plan, 299
  analysis and design, 301
  go-live, 302
  onboarding and kickoff, 300
  test and validation, 301
Project planning, 297
Project schedule, 300
Project scope, 288, 295
  change management, 296
  contract, 295
  side projects, 296
Project timeline, 300

Provincial sales taxes (PSTs), 170
Purchasing cards (P-cards), 100

Q

Queries, 230
Query Studio, 215, 224
   calculations, 228
   column header, 227
   filters, 228
   manipulation data, 227
   report creation, 225
   saving reports, 227
   suppressing cells, 228
Quick guides, 306

R

Receipt handling, 136, 156, 157
Receipt imaging, 157
Receipt limits, 156
Receipt type, 124
Receipts, 251
Reclaim code, 131
Reclaim condition, 131
Reclaim rate, 130
Regional hotel rates, 98
Relational reports, 230
Remote function call (RFC), 264
Replication, 273
   manual and automatic export, 273
   phased rollout, 272
Replication logic, 271
Report layout, 230
Report pages, 231
Report prompt pages, 231
Report Studio, 215, 228
   chart options, 232
   charts, 232
   homepage, 231
   report conversion, 237
   report creation, 231
   report objects, 232
   report types, 230
   schedule manager, 234
   schedule selection screen, 233

Report Studio (Cont.)
   scheduling reports, 232
Report view, 223
Reporting, 213
   configuration, 141
   dashboards, 216
   email delivery, 234
   frequency, 233
   recurring job, 222
   run with options, 218
Reporting preferences, 217
   general preferences, 218
   personal preferences, 219
   portal tab preferences, 220
   preference settings, 218
Request approver, 210
Risk management, 207
Rule classes, 50, 91
   uses, 92

S

Sales order items, 271
SAP Ariba, 285
SAP Business One, 285
SAP Cloud Platform Integration, 264
SAP Customer Relationship Management (SAP CRM), 299
SAP ERP Financials, 270
   Accounts Payable, 282
   cost hierarchy, 276
   integration features, 280
   multiple systems, 262
SAP ERP Financials Travel Management (FI-TV), 39
SAP ERP HCM, 43, 263
   data integration, 267
   direct connection, 264
   HR data integration, 265
   integration, 263
   integration features, 268
   middleware, 264
   Organizational Management, 265
   secure connection, 264
SAP Fieldglass, 285
SAP General Ledger (G/L), 275

SAP Process Integration (PI), 264
SAP Process Orchestration (PO), 264
SAP S/4HANA Cloud, 285
SAP S/4HANA Finance, 285
SAP SuccessFactors, 299
 file export, 269
 integration, 269
 report, 269
SAP SuccessFactors Employee Central, 263, 269
SAP system ID, 276
SAP Travel Management, 43, 284
Scope, 287, 300, 303
 fixed implementation price, 289
 sizing, 289
SeatID, 242
Segment type, 204, 207
Selections criteria, 224
Self-booking, 205
Self-registration, 56
Settling expenses, 115
Single sign-on (SSO), 302
Small-ticket items, 294
Software-as-a-service (SaaS), 27
Solution scope, 288, 289
 contingent workforce, 290
 contractors/consultants, 290
 countries/departments, 289
 employees, 290
 guests/candidates, 291
 special events, 293
Stakeholders, 307
Standard Accounting Extract (SAE), 124, 279
Standard operating procedures (SOPs), 194
Standard reports, 217
 running, 220
System settings, 44
 accessibility mode, 44
 notification preferences, 44

T

T&E policies, 67, 95, 103, 209, 297
T&E problems, 17
 ineffective management, 19

T&E problems (Cont.)
 inefficiency, 18
 user experience, 20
T&E process goals, 21
 automated, 24
 connected, 25
 ease of use, 26
 mobile, 24
 paper-free, 22
T&E vision statement, 26
Target group, 54
Tax authority, 130
Tax condition, 130
Tax groups, 130
Tax information, 123
Tax rate, 130
Tax reclaims, 123
Taxes, 130, 306
Test instance, 308
Third-party apps, 241
 configuration, 242
 connecting, 243
 connecting to user account, 248
 deactivation, 245
 multiple accounts, 247
Third-party services, 242
 benefits, 242
 configuration, 242
Train bookings, 69
Training and user documentation, 307
Transaction CRE_SETUP, 265, 271
Transaction CTE_MONI, 267
Transaction CTE_SETUP, 263, 270, 277
Travel alerts, 258
Travel management, 101
Travel management company (TMC), 20, 47, 61, 203
Travel preferences, 46
Travel Rule Builder, 94
Travel rules, 92
Travel vendor exclusions, 98
Travel Wizard, 55, 67, 76, 203
Travelfusion, 62
Trip itinerary, 258
Trip mapping, 130

U

Uber, 243
United Kingdom, 172
  fuel for mileage, 173
  gifts, 175
  incidentals, 175
  P11D reporting, 175
  receipts, 172
  taxi fares, 177
  VAT invoices, 176
  vehicle hire, 177
United States, 169
Update Expense Reports Imaging API, 255
User account, 43
User administration, 48
  account termination, 49
  general settings, 49
User creation, 57
  automated file transfer, 57
  templates, 57
User experience (UX), 17

V

Value-added tax (VAT), 19, 123
  refund, 247
VAT IT, 255
  dashboard, 257
  integration, 255
  reclaim amounts and claims, 256
  user record, 255
Visage Mobile, 258
  integration, 258

W

WBS elements, 271, 277
Web services, 29
  permissions, 245

► Learn how SAP S/4HANA enables
digital transformation

► Explore innovative financials and
logistics functionality

► Understand the technical foundation
underlying SAP S/4HANA advances

Baumgartl, Chaadaev, Choi, Dudgeon, Lahiri, Meijerink, Worsley-Tonks

SAP S/4HANA

An Introduction

Looking to make the jump to SAP S/4HANA? Learn what SAP S/4HANA
offers, from the Universal Journal in SAP S/4HANA Finance to supply chain
management in SAP S/4HANA Materials Management and Operations.
Understand your deployment options—on-premise, cloud, and hybrid—and
explore SAP Activate's implementation approach. Get an overview of how
SAP HANA architecture supports digital transformation, and see what tools
can help extend your SAP S/4HANA functionality!

449 pages, pub. 11/2016
E-Book: $59.99 | **Print:** $69.95 | **Bundle:** $79.99

www.sap-press.com/4153

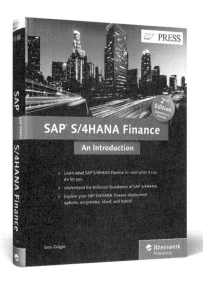

▶ Learn what SAP S/4HANA Finance is—and what it can do for you

▶ Understand the technical foundation of SAP S/4HANA

▶ Explore your SAP S/4HANA Finance deployment options: on-premise, cloud, and hybrid

Jens Krüger

SAP S/4HANA Finance

An Introduction

It's time you got to know SAP S/4HANA Finance. Learn what SAP S/4HANA Finance can do, what it offers your organization, and how it fits into the SAP S/4HANA landscape. Explore critical SAP S/4HANA Finance functionality, from cash management to profitability analysis, and consider your deployment options. Now's your chance to lay the groundwork for your SAP S/4HANA Finance future.

411 pages, 2nd edition, pub. 02/2016
E-Book: $59.99 | **Print:** $69.95 | **Bundle:** $79.99

www.sap-press.com/4122

- ▶ SuccessFactors: what it is, how it works, and what it can do for you

- ▶ Explore the SuccessFactors suite for your entire HR workflow

- ▶ Simplify business processes in Employee Central and other SuccessFactors modules

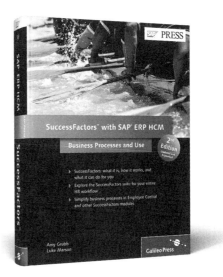

Amy Grubb, Luke Marson

SuccessFactors with SAP ERP HCM

Business Processes and Use

Looking to better your HR workflow? Discover the potential of SuccessFactors, SAP's HR cloud solution, with this introductory guide. Updated and revised, this edition covers new integration packages, additional SAP HANA Cloud Platform information, details on the Metadata Framework, and a look into the new Job Profile Builder. Discover what SuccessFactors is, how it works, and what it can do for you.

644 pages, 2nd edition, pub. 11/2014
E-Book: $59.99 | **Print:** $69.95 | **Bundle:** $79.99

www.sap-press.com/3702

▶ Configure Employee Central to your core HR requirements

▶ Manage employee data using Employee Central features

▶ Learn how to maintain the system after go-live for best results

Marson, Mazhavanchery, Murray

SAP SuccessFactors Employee Central

The Comprehensive Guide

With this guide, move to SAP's next-generation HR information system! Cement your foundation in key concepts and configuration. Then enhance your implementation with functionalities for position and workforce management, employee data, reporting, and more. Finally, discover how to integrate with external systems. In a cloud-based world, this new HRIS has it all.

590 pages, pub. 12/2015
E-Book: $69.99 | **Print:** $79.95 | **Bundle:** $89.99

www.sap-press.com/3834

- ▶ Understand business processes, functions, and configuration options for an FI implementation
- ▶ Apply real-world examples and step-by-step instructions
- ▶ Get details on financial closing, General Ledger, SAP Fiori, and more

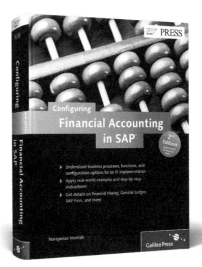

Narayanan Veeriah

Configuring Financial Accounting in SAP

Are you FI savvy? From intricate system configuration to far-reaching mobile apps, even the simplest Financial Accounting implementations are complex. Master the processes, subcomponents, and tools you need to align your FI system with unique business requirements. Get the tips and tricks to handle global settings configuration, SAP ERP integration, and General Ledger use with ease!

907 pages, 2nd edition, pub. 11/2014
E-Book: $69.99 | Print: $79.95 | Bundle: $89.99

www.sap-press.com/3665

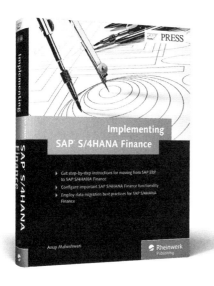

► Get step-by-step instructions for moving from SAP ERP to SAP S/4HANA Finance

► Configure important SAP S/4HANA Finance functionality

► Employ data migration best practices for SAP S/4HANA Finance

Anup Maheshwari

Implementing SAP S/4HANA Finance

Get into the nitty-gritty with this guide to your on-premise SAP S/4HANA Finance implementation project. Migrate your data from SAP ERP Financials to SAP S/4HANA Finance, and then customize its key functionality: SAP General Ledger, Asset Accounting, Controlling, and SAP Cash Management. Consult expert tips, learn transaction codes, and join the brave new world of SAP S/4HANA Finance.

535 pages, pub. 08/2016
E-Book: $69.99 | **Print:** $79.95 | **Bundle:** $89.99

www.sap-press.com/4045

Interested in reading more?

Please visit our website for all new
book and e-book releases from SAP PRESS.

www.sap-press.com